THE EMERGENCE OF
ENTREPRENEURIAL ECONOMICS

RESEARCH ON TECHNOLOGICAL INNOVATION, MANAGEMENT AND POLICY

RESEARCH ON TECHNOLOGICAL INNOVATION,
MANAGEMENT AND POLICY   VOLUME 9

THE EMERGENCE OF ENTREPRENEURIAL ECONOMICS

EDITED BY

G. T. VINIG

*Department of Business Studies, University of Amsterdam,
Amsterdam, The Netherlands*

R. C. W. VAN DER VOORT

*Department of General Economics, University of Amsterdam,
Amsterdam, The Netherlands*

2005

ELSEVIER
JAI

Amsterdam – Boston – Heidelberg – London – New York – Oxford
Paris – San Diego – San Francisco – Singapore – Sydney – Tokyo

ELSEVIER B.V.
Radarweg 29
P.O. Box 211
1000 AE Amsterdam,
The Netherlands

ELSEVIER Inc.
525 B Street, Suite 1900
San Diego
CA 92101-4495
USA

**ELSEVIER Ltd
The Boulevard, Langford
Lane, Kidlington
Oxford OX5 1GB
UK**

ELSEVIER Ltd
84 Theobalds Road
London
WC1X 8RR
UK

First edition 2005

British Library Cataloguing in Publication Data
A catalogue record is available from the British Library.

ISBN: 0-7623-1241-6
ISSN: 0737-1071 (Series)

∞ The paper used in this publication meets the requirements of ANSI/NISO Z39.48-1992 (Permanence of Paper).
Printed in The Netherlands.

CONTENTS

PART II

Contents

LIST OF CONTRIBUTORS

David B. Audretsch	Indiana University, USA and Max Planck Institute of Economics, Germany
Wiliam J. Baumol	New York University, Faculty of Economics, USA
Amar V. Bhide	Columbia University, USA
Mikael Ehrsten	Department of Business Studies, Åbo Akademi University, Turku, Finland
Michael Fritsch	Technical University of Freiberg, Germany
Arnold Heertje	Faculty of Economics, University of Amsterdam, The Netherlands
Tatiana Iakovleva	Bode Graduate School of Business, Bode Regional University, Norway
Anders Kjellman	Department of Business Studies, Åbo Akademi University, Turku, Finland
Frank Lasch	Groupe Sup de Co Montpellier, France
Miri Lerner	Tel Aviv University, Israel
John McMillan	Graduate School of Business, Stanford University, USA
Pamela Mueller	Technical University of Freiberg, Germany
Frédéric Le Roy	University of Montpellier 1 and Groupe Sup de Co Montpellier, France
Thomas Schibbye	Auckland University of Technology, New Zealand
Tom G. Strothotte	University of St Gallen, Switzerland
Martie-Louise Verreynne	Auckland University of Technology, New Zealand

Rolf Wüstenhagen	University of St Gallen, Switzerland
Saïd Yami	University of Montpellier 1 and Groupe Sup de Co Montpellier, France
Orly Yeheskel	The Interdisciplinary Center, Israel

FOREWORD: THE EMERGENCE OF ENTREPRENEURIAL ECONOMICS

"If entrepreneurship remains as important to the economy as ever, then the continuing failure of mainstream economics to adequately account for entrepreneurship indicates that fundamental principles require re-evaluation" (Shook, 2003).

In his 1968 article "Entrepreneurship in economic theory" in the *American Economic Review* (Baumol, 1968), Baumol urged the economists to start paying attention to the role of entrepreneurship in economic development. In the four decades since the article was published, there has been empirical evidence on the importance of entrepreneurship for economic development. Still, there has been little attention for entrepreneurship mainstream economic theory. A review of economic textbooks (Kent & Francis, 1999) shows that only a very marginal part of the content (2.35 pages or about 0.3% on the average) covers entrepreneurship.

There are many possible explanations for the neglect of entrepreneurship by mainstream economic theory. Some scholars attribute this to the fact that entrepreneurship has been perceived as a chaotic, unpredictable economic process, which cannot be modelled by analytical methods used in mainstream economic theory. Other researchers point out to the approaches that tend to treat entrepreneurship as autonomous from ongoing economic systems.

It seems no longer possible to expect that only theoretical refinements and extending known principles can provide for a theory of entrepreneurship. In recent years, attempts have been made to include entrepreneurship into mainstream economic theory, in particular into growth models.

The term 'Entrepreneurial Economics' appears in recent years in academic research on entrepreneurship. Entrepreneurial Economics, or the Economics of Entrepreneurship, can be associated with the scholars who introduced entrepreneurship into economic literature starting with Cantillon and Schumpeter, through Baumol and Kirzner who contributed to the introduction of the Economics of Entrepreneurship notably from economic growth perspective. It has, however, not been defined as a discipline as part of economics research or entrepreneurship research as such.

What is the justification, right of existence for Entrepreneurial Economics as a discipline? Mainstream economics does not include entrepreneurship not because there is no theory or analytical framework for entrepreneurship. Entrepreneurship does not belong in mainstream theory; in fact, mainstream theory makes the entrepreneur an invisible man. The reason for that is that the construct of equilibrium models, which is central to mainstream economics, is exactly what by definition excludes entrepreneurship. As Schumpeter and Kirzner have argued in their writings that entrepreneur does not tolerate equilibrium. Mainstream theory is not 'wrong' by excluding entrepreneurship, it is irrelevant there. Therefore, we need to develop a theory of entrepreneurship within a relevant domain which Entrepreneurial Economics is. Baumol's article in this book provides an interesting insight on this issue.

What are the areas of interest for Entrepreneurial Economics? An interesting aspect of Entrepreneurial Economics is the import/export of knowledge at regional, national and international level. When a large corporation in the U.S., for example, takes over a start-up in other country what happens is an import of knowledge from that country to the U.S. The opposite happens when a large U.S. corporation establishes a research and development centre in a country outside the U.S. Knowledge is being exported. Is such import/export included in the economic models used today? This requires other, new models and techniques for quantifying the economy. In both cases, in addition to the import and export of knowledge, new knowledge is being created and exploited in the process. In both cases, the knowledge is not linked to the physical place, it is placeless and can serve as a basis for entrepreneurial ventures. Audtretsch's article on this subject provides an interesting insight into the role of entrepreneurship and the missing link in growth theory based on his knowledge spillover theory of entrepreneurship.

In Entrepreneurial Economics entrepreneurship can be seen as an intelligent mode of production. The production of knowledge-based ventures, services, technologies and products that create economic value in which innovation is the tool used. Can a new production function that incorporates entrepreneurship and innovation be defined?

Should Entrepreneurial Economics emerge as a discipline, a field of economics, what are its characteristics? Will it indeed be based on the re-evaluation of the fundamental principles of mainstream theory? Will the study of seemingly chaotic, complex, unpredictable processes in the economy contribute to novel insights and better understanding of the knowledge-based economy in which growth is driven mainly by technological progress (and not increase in capital)? Heertje's article in this book provides an interesting historical review of this topic. We may not be able to develop a formal comprehensive model of such a process, but we can try to identify patterns of such processes that can help understand and explain such processes. Entrepreneurship is an example of such an economic process, but not the only example. The stock market, and stock prices development is another example.

Coase surveys the field of economics and believes it has become a 'theory-driven' subject that has moved into a paradigm in which conclusions take precedence over problems. "If you look at a page of a scientific journal like Nature," he said, "every few weeks you have statements such as, 'We'll have to think it out again. These results aren't going the way we thought they would.' Well, in economics, the results always go the way we thought they would because we approach the problems in the same way, only asking certain questions."

Therefore insight, theories, tools and techniques form natural sciences and can also be considered as a source of inspiration and a basis for formalizing a theory of entrepreneurship (e.g. Guardiola et al., 2002; Jenkins, 2005). Using concepts from theoretical physics, chaos theory, and complex systems, we may be able to adopt new approaches to the study of entrepreneurship. Entrepreneurship, the process of starting new venture, can be considered a process of emergence – come into being, with the entrepreneur – the strange attractor (unpredictable yet pattered) at the centre of the process, the one who triggers and drives this process. This is a different approach than the theory that the firm takes.

OVERVIEW OF THE CONTRIBUTIONS

There are two types of contribution in the book. In Part I, we have asked invited articles from recognized scholars in the field of entrepreneurship research. In Part II, we have included selected articles from the 2005 European Entrepreneurship Research Conference held in Amsterdam between 2 and 4 February 2005. The two groups of articles in the book provide interesting new insights that can serve as a stimulus and a step towards the development of the Entrepreneurial Economics discipline.

In the first article, Arnold Heertje provides a review of economic aspects of technology change in the economic literature from the writings of Cantillon through Shumpeter. Economic theory, according to Heertje cannot explain technology change. He goes on with presenting, in chronological order, the history of a few economic theories through the discussion of entrepreneurship with and without technical change. He concludes with describing the entrepreneur as the embodiment of change in general, and technical change in particular, this in real life not only disturb equilibrium but also poses a serious problem for theoretical analysis.

Baumol, in his article, argues that mainstream economic theory does not include entrepreneurship not because a theory of entrepreneurship does not exist, but because its main constructs are generally equilibrium models, which is the very attribute that excludes the entrepreneur by definition. According to Baumol there exists a usable theory of entrepreneurship, which provides for a start of formalized analysis. The basis to the theory according to Baumol is considering innovation as a form of investment and apply the theory of investment with its formal model to entrepreneurship.

Audretsch in his article presents a knowledge spillover theory of entrepreneurship and economic growth. In the papers he argues that entrepreneurship is the missing link in the process of economic growth because it facilitates the spillover of knowledge from universities and firms resulting in commercialization of ideas that otherwise might remain unexploited. Entrepreneurship, according to Audretsch analysis, is an endogenous response to opportunities generated by investment in new knowledge. He than goes on with linking entrepreneurship to growth.

The article of Bhide continues with the discussion of entrepreneurship and economic growth. The discussion in Bhide's article is on entrepreneurship's contribution to economic growth in the 20th century and whether it will continue to make this contribution in the 21st century. Though Bhide focuses on the entrepreneurial system of the U.S., he argues that his general analysis applies to other wealthy countries.

Part II starts with an article by Fritsch and Muller on new business formation. Fritsch and Muller studied the differences in the level of new business formation. In their study they conclude that the level of new business formation is path-dependence and that entrepreneurship and innovation determine the level of regional start-ups. The findings of the study are supported by empirical evidence from West Germany.

In her article Tatiana Iakovleva discusses her study of entrepreneurial orientation of Russian SME. In her study she looks at entrepreneurial orientation and SME performance in the turbulent Russian economy. The findings based on empirical evidence suggest that entrepreneurial orientation enhances the positive relationship between availability of capital and SME performance.

In their article Lasch, Le Roy and Yami present a study of survival and growth of start-ups from the French ICT sector. The study was aimed at

understanding why some ventures fail while others survive, and to try identify the determinants of survival and growth of new ventures. Based on
empirical analysis, they discuss a group of four determinants – Human
capital and working experience of the entrepreneur, pre-funding activities,
initial organization characteristics and inter-firm cooperation. The comparison between survivors and failed ventures is used to design an initial profile
of the successful entrepreneur.

The paper by Strothotte and Wüstenhagen is in the domain of social
entrepreneurship, which has in recent years been emerging as a stream of
research within entrepreneurship. They studied the sustainability of social
entrepreneurship ventures and their financing. They conclude that sustainable mission is a pre-requisite for the sustainability of the social entrepreneurship venture. They argue that though social entrepreneurship venture
aim at creating social value, they do also create economic value.

Schibbye and Verreynne study one of the core questions of entrepreneurship – where and how opportunities are found. Their empirical study
is based on New Zealand firms. Based on their study, they present a
framework they call the 'Opportunity-Sources' framework that can increase entrepreneurial firms' chances of discovering new business opportunities.

Yeheskel and Lerner present a study of the effect of managerial variables
– formalization, centralization, management/leadership style and team solidarity on the performance of technology start-ups. They conclude that the
variables studied contribute to the explanation of performance of technology start-ups even when firm size, age and industry type are controlled.

McMillan's paper, "Quantifying creative destruction: Entrepreneurship
and productivity in New Zealand," provides a framework for quantifying
economy's flexibility based on a review of New Zealand's firms' birth,
growth and death. He concludes that for SME firms labour and financial
markets are doing their job.

In the last article Kjellman and Ehrsten present a holistic, socio-cultural
model of entrepreneurship behaviour. Their model draws on the work of
Kurt Lewin with the addition of system theories. Entrepreneurship is seen as
an emerging behaviour in a complex system. The central construct in their
model is the psychological life span of the individual. This life span, they
argue, can be influenced in order to enhance entrepreneurship.

We do hope that this book contributes to the emergence of the field
of Entrepreneurial Economics – the study of patterns in the complex,
seemingly chaotic and unpredictable process of entrepreneurship and its role
in the economy. If more scholars will.

REFERENCES

Baumol, W. J. (1968). Entrepreneurship in economic theory. *American Economic Review*, *58*, 64–71.

Guardiola, X., Diaz-Guilera, A., Perez, C. J., Arenas, A., & Llas, M. (2002). Modelling diffusion of innovation in a social network. *Physical Review* E, *66*, 1–4.

Jenkins, A. D. (2005). Thermodynamics and economics. *Journal of Ecological Economics*, *1*, 1–23.

Kent, C. A., & Francis, W. R. (1999). Coverage of entrepreneurship in principles of economic textbooks: An update. *Journal of Economic Education*, (Spring), 184–187.

Shook, J. R. (2003). Entrepreneurship and values in a democratic and pragmatic economics: Commentary on A transactional view of entrepreneurship. *Journal of Economic Methodology*, *10*(2), 181.

Tsvi Vinig
Roel van der Voort
Editors

PART I

TECHNICAL CHANGE AND ENTREPRENEURSHIP: AN OVERVIEW FROM CANTILLON TO SCHUMPETER

Arnold Heertje

INTRODUCTION: ECONOMICS, AND TECHNICAL CHANGE

This chapter deals with aspects of technical change and entrepreneurship which have dominated the economics literature. Since we shall confine our attention to the economic aspects of technical change, our approach is one-sided. This is reinforced by the fact that we discuss only a part of the very large body of literature. The tension between wants and the means to satisfy these is directly influenced by technical change, both from a qualitative and a quantitative point of view. This relationship between scarcity and technical change has been studied in detail since the 1970s, although elements have always been part of economic debate (Heertje, 1977).

The way economists treat this subject is constantly changing, and this explains the considerable difference of opinion on several points, such as the causes and effects of technical change and the role that the latter plays, and ought to play, in everyday life. Optimists point out that better and better durable consumer goods are available to most people, while pessimists point

The Emergence of Entrepreneurial Economics
Research on Technological Innovation, Management and Policy, Volume 9, 3–25
Copyright © 2005 by Elsevier Ltd.
All rights of reproduction in any form reserved
ISSN: 0737-1071/doi:10.1016/S0737-1071(05)09001-3

out that new technology can lead to unemployment and more or less enforced leisure on a large scale. Again, some authors stress the prosperity that technical change brings, while others stress its horrors, some point to the greatly increased food production made possible by new and better techniques, while others point to the terrifying wars that modern sophisticated weapons permit. In addition, there have recently been signs of a more widespread public apprehension about technical change. From the point of view of economic policy making, technical change is regarded by some as an inevitable and uncontrollable process, and by others as a process that can to a certain extent be influenced from above.

Some of the Main Problems

With the advent of the Classical economists, ideas about the significance for production of the factors of production came to the forefront of economic debate, and economists gradually developed the notion of a quantitative connection between the level of production and the quantities of the factors of production. This work has culminated in a sophisticated mathematical and economic analysis of the production function and in the econometric verification of this relationship, but the study of the evolution of this concept from its beginning is still worthwhile. The Classical economists' ideas about the effect of diminishing returns on economic growth gave a more precise form to initially vague observations about social phenomena, and these ideas are still valuable today.

The production function relates the level of output to the level of input of the factors of production at a given state of technical knowledge. An increase in technical knowledge causes a shift in the production function, so that technical change is often identified with a shift in this function. Since the range of technical possibilities can increase even without an increase in the stock of technical knowledge: for example, by education, better organization, institutional change and the diffusion of existing technical knowledge, we must make a clear distinction between technical change in the broad sense – meaning the development of technical possibilities – and technical change in the narrow sense – meaning additions to the stock of technical knowledge. If the production function is viewed as an expression of the technical possibilities, then technical change in the broad sense corresponds to a shift in the production function, and – conversely – such a shift indicates technical change in the broad sense.

The application of new technical possibilities is often included in the description of technical development. This interpretation is dominant in everyday language. There is a connection between the application of techniques and the creation of new technical possibilities, if the application leads to new technical knowledge. But the application of new techniques as such does not imply technical change. Often, however, it still is an aspect that receives as much attention as the increase in the range of technical possibilities.

The process of technical change is a phenomenon which is difficult to unravel. For the present purpose four components can be distinguished at a theoretical level. The development of new technical possibilities, the application of new methods of production and of new products, the diffusion of technical knowledge, and the diffusion of applications.

Can the development of new technical possibilities be explained? The answer depends upon the type of explanation sought. If the explanation is satisfactory that a new method of production is, ultimately, the result of creativity combined with the use of scarce resources, the answer would be positive. But the ability to explain this development would be less certain if what were sought were the causes of creativity, the role it plays, and its relation to the allocation of scarce resources. Further, if the criterion for a successful explanation were that predictions are possible on the basis of causes indicated, the answer would be negative – even if the predictions were not necessarily true. The specification of new methods of production and of new products that will become available in the future cannot be predicted. What can be predicted is that the stock of technical knowledge of a certain kind will be higher in the future, if it is decided to allocate resources in that direction with the aim of producing new technical knowledge. Casting the problem in terms of cause and effect, it may be possible to give a description of the relevant causes, but not to establish the relationship between these and the exact nature of new technology. On the other hand, it is possible to establish a relationship between new technology in general and the allocation of resources on both the theoretical and practical levels. Even a nation's technology policy is based on global explanation in this sense, it being aimed at welfare in the broad sense of the satisfaction of wants.

Whether we can explain the application of new technical possibilities is less problematic because it is known what will be applied. Of course, it is still uncertain whether the new production methods and products will be successful, but at least their technical appearance is known. The problem is to explain which new methods and products will, in fact, be applied. This is still a complicated problem, as not only economic, but also social, psychological, sociological, and cultural factors play a role. However, economic theory is capable of explaining why certain technologies are applied, while others are not.

The same kind of reasoning may be applied to the problem of the diffusion process; again, it is not an easy job to explain the exact pattern of diffusion, of new insights, and of the applications, but there are no insurmountable obstacles.

On balance, I conclude that economic theory cannot explain technical change. As the unforeseen cannot be explained, it would be surprising if any science could do the job. We will never be able to predict the exact nature of technical change.

However, it does not follow that nothing can be said about technical change. Technical knowledge, being the product of a production process in which scarce resources are allocated, can be produced. We do not know exactly what will be produced, but we are certain that we will know more after an unknown period. The new technical possibilities can be partly explained in terms of the allocation of scarce resources. In this sense, technical change seems to be a composite of endogenous and exogenous components. In particular, the diffusion process and the choice out of the set of technical possibilities may be explained in economic terms. Still, the interaction between technical change and other social and economic developments demands much of our innovative activity as economists.

There have been sharp exchanges in the history of economic thought between economists about whether the application of new techniques ousts labour from the production process: some say 'no', for the people who lose their jobs find new ones, while others say 'yes', for the capital stock does not increase fast enough to create new jobs for all those who have become redundant through the introduction of labour-saving technology. Technological unemployment is a recurrent theme in the economics literature.

When examining the way technical change alters the relative power of the producers and the owners of the factors of production, one inevitably thinks of Karl Marx. Disentangling the interactions between changes in technology and changes in the type of market competition, the significance of the firm and the role of the entrepreneur is another important issue. This point is not only of theoretical importance, it is also characterized by political considerations, owing to the irreversibility of the social changes involved. Care is needed here to differentiate between statements that involve a value judgment and analytical statements.

The role of technical change in economic growth should be mentioned separately. This separate mention is justified, partly because great stress is placed on the dynamic interpretation of the production function in growth theory, and partly because the literature deals with the contribution of technical change to economic growth.

ENTREPRENEURSHIP WITH AND WITHOUT TECHNICAL CHANGE

Richard Cantillon (1680–1734) was the first to pay attention to the entrepreneur, without looking at technical change. He introduced the concept of 'entrepreneur'. He acknowledged that there exists an entrepreneurial function within the economic system. In Cantillon's book *Essai sur la nature du commerce en général* of 1755, entrepreneurs contribute to welfare at large (Cantillon, 1755; Murphy, 1986; Brewer, 1992).

In his system, Cantillon recognizes, landowners, entrepreneurs, and wage workers. His perception of the market is that of a network of reciprocal exchange between firms or individuals that functions without the intervention of the state. The market leads to equilibrium prices. The entrepreneur has a major role, because he is responsible for all trade in the economy. The class of entrepreneurs brings about a general equilibrium of supply and demand.

The entrepreneurial class engages in pure arbitrage. The motivating factor is the potential profit linked to buying at a certain price. Cantillon recognizes that arbitrage involves uncertainty. Future prices are never known in advance; they depend on future demand and future supply. And these are influenced by changing circumstances.

Cantillon's entrepreneurs also engage in professional activities other than arbitrage, like farming and banking. The distinguishing feature of the entrepreneurial task, as compared with other types of agents, is its risk-bearing nature, which yields uncertain and non-contractually arranged incomes. Income of landowners and wage workers is fixed by contract.

As the entrepreneur's task consists of arbitrage, he has to be alert and forward-looking, but need not be innovative. He adjusts supply to existing demand. And the entrepreneur has to bear the inherent risk. An entrepreneur does not necessarily start his venture backed by his own capital. Capital can be borrowed on the capital market by paying interest to the banker, another entrepreneurial profession.

The laws of demand and supply also determine the number of entrepreneurs in each occupation. If there are too many wine merchants, a number of them will go bankrupt until the surplus disappears. This adjustment process does not take place at random but according to the 'survival of the fittest' principle: the worst-equipped merchants will go bankrupt. On the other hand, if there are too few entrepreneurs, new-comers will be attracted by the prospects of enterprise.

In short, Cantillon was the first economist to grasp the economic meaning of the 'entrepreneur'. The entrepreneur is described as an arbitrageur. By engaging in arbitrage and bearing risk, the entrepreneurial class plays an equilibrating role within the economic system. Without uncertainty, there is no entrepreneur according to Cantillon. The entrepreneur does not create new demand through new products, but he makes sure that he meets the preferences of consumers by providing the proper goods just in time and at the right place. He is a forward-looking supply provider in a world of uncertainty, who satisfies given needs with given means. In this sense, Cantillon is a forerunner of Say (Praag van, 1996, pp. 11–13).

It was not Quesnay, but his followers who developed a more advanced theory of entrepreneurship. The first of these Physiocrats was Abbé Nicolas Baudeau (1730–1792). Baudeau placed the agricultural entrepreneur on an equal footing as Cantillon's risk bearer. But he takes one step further (Baudeau, 1910).

Baudeau's entrepreneur is triggered by profits. He is a decision maker who bears risk, but he is also an innovator in order to reduce costs and to raise his profit. This feature of entrepreneurship represents an advance over Cantillon. Baudeau went beyond Cantillon in emphasizing the significance of the entrepreneur's ability, with respect to the need for knowledge and information. Because the agricultural entrepreneur carries on production at his own risk, he must have the capacity to make use of knowledge and information. The entrepreneur is an innovator, and Baudeau was fully aware of the increase in welfare that invention makes possible.

Physiocratic writings include proposals to improve agricultural techniques, many of which were based on the upgrading of human capital or the diffusion of better information (Hebert & Link, 1982, pp. 23–29).

As was pointed out by Hoselitz in 1960, there was confidence that, with the proper knowledge, these innovations would be adopted by alert entrepreneurs, spurred to action by the opportunity for profit. Along these lines the entrepreneur appeared as innovator in the economics literature (Hoselitz, 1960).

It is useful to compare Cantillon and Turgot (1727–1781) on the subject of the entrepreneur. Turgot may have learned from Cantillon's work but the nature of Cantillon's influence on Turgot remains obscure. Both looked at the entrepreneur as the core of the market system. Capital, in the monetary sense, did not show up in Cantillon's picture of the entrepreneur. Turgot saw the entrepreneur as a wealthy man who employed labour in a productive process either in agriculture or in manufacturing. The essence of Turgot's theory was the motive force of "advances" by the entrepreneur in the productive process. Turgot did not distinguish between a "capitalist" and an "entrepreneur". The same individual, viz. the capitalist–entrepreneur who supplied the capital and employed the labourers, made production possible and played the essential role in his economics.

Turgot presented a clear picture of an economy in which capitalism embraces all spheres of production. The "industrious" classes are divided into entrepreneurs and wage workers, free competition is the rule and monopoly the exception. Landownership appears as another form of investment of capital, and a general glut of goods is impossible because savings are transformed immediately into investment, clearly foreshadowing "Say's Law". What is missing, is technical change in Turgot's analysis, any hint that the entrepreneur is an innovator or more than a capitalist (Turgot, 1769).

It is instructive to compare Turgot's vision of the entrepreneur with that of Baudeau. Baudeau remained close to Quesnay, insofar as his entrepreneur is a farm operator who plans, organizes and takes risks and is a wealthy man. Turgot's entrepreneur is a rich merchant or industrialist who advances capital and plans productive activity in order to accumulate wealth. It is remarkable that Baudeau includes innovation in his description of the entrepreneur and Turgot did not.

In Jean-Baptiste Say's (1767–1832) work, the entrepreneur plays a coordinating role in production and distribution (Say, 1803). Also within the firm, he is the coordinator and, moreover, the leader and manager. Say is the first economist who stresses the managerial role of the entrepreneur. Compared with other classical economists, Say attached a very prominent position to the entrepreneur in the entire system of production and consumption. He extends the entrepreneurial function as defined by Cantillon (Praag van, 1996, pp. 13–15).

In Say's theory of the firm and the entrepreneur, production attaches to materials a utility they did not possess before. A creation of utility for welfare which Say calls the production of wealth. There are three types of industry that create value, the agricultural, the manufacturing and the commercial industry. A particular product is a joint product of the three industries. The contribution of each of these industries consists of three distinct operations that are not embodied in one person, development of knowledge, the application of knowledge and execution.

The application of knowledge to the creation of a consumption good is the entrepreneur's activity. This kind of labour is necessary to set industries in motion and attain welfare within a country. Knowledge, important as it is, easily diffuses from one nation to another, since this diffusion is in the interest of intelligent people.

The entrepreneur has a key position within his own enterprise. He is a coordinator, leader and manager. However, the entrepreneur performs tasks specific to his commercial environment as well, and he supplies his own capital. Furthermore, part of the entrepreneur's job is conducting experiments to find out whether a specific application does indeed satisfy human needs. These experiments, necessary to ensure progress, involve a great deal of risk. There is always the possibility of failure pertaining to any entrepreneurial activity. The entrepreneur may then lose his fortune and even his regard in society. According to Say, a successful entrepreneur has many qualities. Judgment, perseverance, and knowledge of the world as well as of business. A successful entrepreneur must have experience with, and knowledge of the entrepreneurial activity and be able to provide capital. Hoselitz pointed out that Say's view on entrepreneurship came from his practical experience as an industrial entrepreneur, rather than from his knowledge of the theoretical work of other French economists (Hoselitz, 1960). As a consequence of these characteristics, talent and capacity, the number of competitors in the entrepreneurial market is limited. The limited supply maintains the price of successful entrepreneurial labour at a high level, since in Say's classical economy all prices are determined by supply and demand (Palmer, 1997, p. 72).

At the level of the firm, the entrepreneur's renumeration is determined as a residual payment. If this residual is higher than the costs of management and some risk premium, implying positive profits, then the supply of entrepreneurs increases. If profits are negative, then firms go bankrupt until equilibrium prevails.

THE BRITISH CLASSICAL ECONOMISTS

While Say developed a systematic picture of the entrepreneur, the other British Classical economists avoided this topic. They only made some observations on technical change. James Steuart's book, published in 1767, has been overshadowed by Adam Smith's *The Wealth of Nations*. But Steuart, in fact, gives a clearer treatment of the recurrent question of whether the introduction of machines is "prejudicial to the Interest of a State, or hurtful to

Population". His answer is broadly similar to that of the Classical School, the exponents of which put their trust in rapid return to equilibrium after a disturbance in the system. In the case of sudden mechanization, however, Steuart suggests that the government should take corrective measures; thus, although there are some disadvantages of mechanization, these are only temporary. According to him, experience shows that, on the whole, the acquisition of more machines brings about improvements. The introduction of machines does lead to temporary unemployment, but their manufacture offers long-term employment and leads to price reductions (Steuart, 1767).

Adam Smith dealt with the introduction of new machines as part of the wider problem of the division of labour. His contention is that the increase in the productivity of labour is mainly due to the division of labour, and that productivity rises faster in industry than in agriculture, because the division of labour can be taken further in industry. One of the factors that raise per capita production is "the invention of a great number of machines which facilitate and abridge labour and enable one man to do the work of many", and the invention of machines "seems to have been originally owing to the division of labour". The more one succeeds in concentrating on a certain part of the production process, the more likely one is to discover a way of simplifying this process. He added that, for this reason, many machines are developed by "common workmen", whereas numerous other improvements in machines are brought about, not by their users, but by the "ingenuity of the makers of the machines" (Smith, 1776, pp. 5–12).

Discussing mercantilism, Smith challenged the prohibition on exporting machines and argued in favour of the free exchange of capital goods. Smith did not make a sharp distinction between technical change, on the one hand, and internal and external economies of scale, on the other. Nor did he distinguish between the generation of new knowledge and the actual application of new techniques. On the other hand, he shows remarkable insight by recognizing both labour- and capital-saving technical change.

Steuart compares favourably with Smith in that he dealt with the effect of new machinery on economic life more systematically. However, they both discussed problems that are still of interest today, such as the more extensive use of machines, the conditions under which inventions are made, the role of the makers and users of machines, unemployment, the effect on productivity, and the increase in production.

A pamphlet on the investment of capital in agriculture was published anonymously in 1815 by Edward West, a lawyer. This essay deals with the principle that "in the progress of the improvements of cultivation the raising of crude produce becomes progressively more expensive". West thus paved the way for the formulation of the law of increasing and diminishing returns – one of the most important technical relationships in economics (West, 1815).

In connection with Smith's statement that new machines and the division of labour raise productivity in agriculture less than they do in industry, West said that these factors are responsible for only a small part of the difference between the two sectors, because "the effects of the subdivision of labour and the application of machinery are considerable even in agriculture", and that the really important point, overlooked by Smith, is that "each equal additional quantity of work bestowed on agriculture yields an actually diminished return". The concept of diminishing returns was thus introduced into the argument, although it is not clear whether West was thinking here of average or marginal returns.

West distinguishes between an intensive and an extensive variant of this law. In the first case, the returns diminish because of the increasingly intensive cultivation of the same land, while, in the second case, they diminish as land which is less and less fertile is cultivated with the same amount of labour and capital as is used on fertile land. As the population grows, people are compelled to cultivate the less fertile land, because the returns on the more fertile land have diminished.

West did not see any further consequences arising from this recognition of the two reasons for diminishing returns. Today, we would say that West did not distinguish between a movement along the graph of the production function and a shift of the graph itself. But West's treatment is not so abstract, for he wanted to analyse the physical conditions of production in view of the Corn Laws, then being debated at Westminster. In the meantime, however, Malthus and Ricardo were writing their own pamphlets on this subject.

According to Malthus, land is a set of machines, which is steadily improved, but whose productivity falls behind that of industry as the latter is mechanized, since these 'machines' are merely 'gifts of nature'. The stress Malthus puts on this productivity differential suggests that he assumed different rates of technical development for agriculture and industry. He points out that it is possible to produce enough capital- and labour-saving machines in industry, so that the price of goods is "reduced to the price of production from the best machinery", whereas even the most fertile land cannot keep up with the "effective demand of an increasing population". And so, while industrial products become cheaper, the price of agricultural produce rises "till it becomes sufficiently high to pay the cost of raising it with inferior machines and by a more expensive process". The expression "inferior machines" is used here in place of "less fertile land" (Malthus, 1815, p. 11).

Ricardo had a vague notion about diminishing returns even before 1815, and he must have had some idea of their effect on profits and rent, for it took him only a few days to write his *Essay*. Ricardo's *Essay* contains, besides a description of the extensive variant of diminishing returns, some other passages on mechanization that are of interest though they have not been widely discussed. Ricardo puts the invention of machines on a par with the expansion of international trade and the division of labour, on the grounds that all three increase the amount of goods and "contribute very much to the ease and happiness of mankind". His concern for the common good is again evident in his argument against Malthus's opinion to restrict of grain imports, because of possible losses of investment in agriculture, when he says that, by the same token, it would be wrong to introduce the steam-engine and improve Arkwright's spinning frame, on the grounds that "the value of old clumsy machinery would be lost to us". He also thought that in 1815 employees would only benefit from improved machinery, which, "it is no longer questioned, has a decided tendency to raise the real wages of labour". He concluded that impeding the import of cheap grain was like resisting technical improvements. "To be consistent then, let us by the same act arrest improvement, and prohibit importation" (Ricardo, 1815).

Ricardo published his **Principles of Political Economy, and Taxation** in 1817 (Sraffa, 1973).

Diminishing returns are discussed in the chapter on rent, where they are said to arise mostly from land which is less fertile being brought under cultivation. However, Ricardo was also aware of the intensive variant of the law of diminishing returns when he said that "capital can be employed more *productively* on those lands which are already in cultivation" (Ricardo, 1817).

As for the economic significance of mechanization Ricardo was mostly concerned with the price-reducing effect of labour-saving machines, which he found compatible with rising wages, the introduction of machines being the consequence of more expensive labour. The longer the useful life of the machine, the lower the prices would drop. As is well known, in the third edition of his *Principles,* Ricardo added a chapter on machinery, in which he sketched the negative effect of the introduction of machinery on the labourers. His famous statement: "Machinery and labour are in constant competition", paved the way for Karl Marx (Ricardo, 1821, p. 395).

We have seen that Adam Smith viewed mechanization both as the cause and as the effect of the division of labour. Marx looked on Adam Smith as the "political economist *par excellence* of the period of Manufacture", the hallmark of whose work was the importance he attributed to the division of labour. Marx disagrees with Smith's contention that the invention of machines also results from the division of labour, and says that, while workers were involved in the differentiation of tools in the era of Manufacture, the invention of machines came from "learned men, handicraftsmen, and even peasants".

When discussing the emergence of workshops or "manufactories", Marx repeatedly stresses the influence which other changes in the structure of production exerted on the division of labour. The minimum number of workers that the capitalist has to employ in his manufactory is determined by the division of labour, but the advantages of a further division are "obtainable only by adding to the number of workmen". When the manufactory reaches a certain size, it turns into the typical form of capitalistic production but, at the same time, its own narrow technical basis conflicts with the "requirements of production that were created by manufacture itself". The manufactory gives rise to the place where mechanical equipment is designed and made. "This workshop, the product of the division of labour in manufacture, produces in its turn – machines". This brings to an end a society based on the methods of craftsmen and artisans.

The death of the manufactory marks the birth of large-scale, factory-based industry, the beginning of mechanization and the first step in the advance of capital. In order to trace the overall evolution back to minor revolutionary changes, Marx is much more concerned with the physical characteristics of mechanical equipment than any of his predecessors. His description encompasses tools and machinery systems, and he concludes that large-scale industry has the necessary technical foundation only when machines are produced with the aid of machines. Unlike the manufactories, the output of the instruments of labour no longer depends on personal human work. A new division of labour, based on the nature of the machines, arises in large-scale industry and the machines dispose of the old division of labour. In the manufactory, the worker uses tools, while in the factory he serves machines. The emphasis shifts from equipping the men to manning the equipment.

As the accumulation progresses, more and more capital is concentrated in the hands of individual capitalists, and the scale of production is enlarged so that the productivity of labour can be increased further. This type of concentration is limited by the growth of the rate of "social wealth" and is characterized by a uniform distribution of the capital between a large number of capitalists who compete with one another. The next, fundamentally different, stage of accumulation is characterized by the "concentration of capitals already formed, destruction of their individual independence, expropriation of capitalist by capitalist, transformation of many small into few large capitals". This concentration, called "centralization" in Volume I of the third edition of *Das Kapital*, is not limited by the absolute growth of production and accumulation. Competition eliminates the manufacturers who fail to introduce new methods quickly enough. This competition is carried on through the lowering of prices which is made possible by the higher productivity of labour, and this, in turn, derives partly from the larger scale of production. "Therefore, the larger capitals beat the smaller". This marks another revolutionary change in the relationships that characterize production, since centralization ushers in the period in which vast projects, such as a railway network, can be accomplished. Centralization in this sense is complementary to accumulation, because production can be carried out on a very large scale with the utilization of new inventions and discoveries. This utilization of new inventions, inherent in centralization, increases the power of capital, and, at the same time, confers social power.

Marx endorses Ricardo's famous statement that "machinery and labour are in constant competition", but attaches a more general meaning to it than Ricardo. He distinguishes between gradual and sudden mechanization, but adds that the workers lose out in the long run in both cases. Marx does not share the optimism of the compensation theory, in any of its various forms. If workers who have been made redundant in one sector do find jobs in another, this is not because the existing variable capital is transformed into machines, but because of new investments. This weak position of the workers arises partly from the need to retrain them for the new job. Only capital formation can create new jobs (Marx, 1867, pp. 313–387).

While the Classical economists saw the introduction of new machines as an external disturbance to which the system would adapt itself, and whose influence depended on how gradually technical change took place, Marx emphasized the effect of mechanization on production and the factors of production in a wider sense, and so paid more attention to the endogenous aspects of technical change. Marx was the first economist to fully realize the significance of technical change for economics and society. In particular, he realized the significance of the invention and application of new machines for the division of labour, large-scale production, the creation of new products, and the phenomena of concentration and centralization. Although, just like the English Classical economists, he did not follow up on the analysis of the entrepreneurial function by the French economists, Marx looked at the capitalist as an entrepreneur.

THE BEGINNINGS OF PRODUCTION THEORY

Soon after the publication of Volume I of *Das Kapital*, economics began to concentrate on the subjective theory of value. Although the theory of consumer behaviour was rigorously developed, the analysis of production did not by any means stagnate. In fact, the period 1870–1920 saw the foundation of the neo-classical theory of production and the frequent use of the Cobb–Douglas production function. Following in the footsteps of the Classical economists, authors like Wicksell and Wicksteed gave a great deal of thought to production and the capitalist system of production came under the scrutiny of the Austrian school, and in particular Böhm-Bawerk. While the theory of value and price received a sudden impetus in 1870, the development of economic thought on technology was a more gradual process.

Cournot (1801–1877) was a French mathematician and philosopher, who realized that economics could become a more exact science. His main contribution to economics lies in the introduction of the demand function. In retrospect, the determination of market equilibrium in case of monopoly and duopoly seems an incredible achievement, but for Cournot it was simply the application of the hypothesis that "everybody tries to derive the greatest benefit from his work and possessions". Cournot concentrated mainly on the demand side of the economic process and did not formulate a production function, although in his book, published in 1838, he introduced a total cost function, and recognized the importance of the marginal cost function for the "solution of the main problems of economic science". The absence of a production function was one of the reasons why technical change had no place in Cournot's mathematical analysis (Cournot, 1838, pp. 46, 65).

But technical change is discussed in the non-mathematical works of Cournot which were published in 1863 and 1877. In the 1863 edition he deals with general aspects of 'progress', and in the 1877 edition, published shortly before his death, he analyses the industrial production process by a comparison of machines and factories. He then discusses the social effects of 'industrial progress' on the labour market, concluding that there is no problem as long as technical change raises the quality and quantity of goods and lowers price without causing a decrease in the demand for labour. But when it does cause a permanent drop in this demand, we are forced to make a value judgment about the ultimate aim of economic activity. He believes that there are no objective criteria for deciding the direction of economic trends, "since we would have to measure and compare items that are neither measurable nor comparable". The choice of money as a yardstick for economic progress cannot be maintained in the face of "objective criticism".

Cournot clearly understood the difficulty of the welfare evaluation of technical change, but his analysis of the latter does not come up to the level of his contribution to the theory of prices (Cournot, 1863, 1877, pp. 66, 296, 310).

The Scotsman John Rae (1796–1872) published his book *Statement of Some New Principles on the Subject of Political Economy* in 1834. He introduced the concepts of time preference, roundabout production method and liquidity preference, and analysed the connections between them. One can hardly overestimate Rae's importance as a forerunner of both Böhm-Bawerk's and Fisher's theories of capital and interest, but Rae contributed even more to the economic theory of technical change.

Unlike Adam Smith, who thought the interests of the individual coincided with those of society, Rae thought the promotion of individual welfare could not be identified with the interests of society as a whole, this lack of coincidence being closely connected with the creative nature of technical change. Technical development is a major means of increasing the riches of society, because this process is "a creation, not an acquisition", while it plays no part in increasing the riches of the individual because this "may be simply an acquisition not a creation". The objectives of society are different from those of the individual, the former pursuing innovations, the latter possessions. Their means of achieving these are also different. Work and saving raise the assets of the individual, while only the "inventive faculty" can raise the assets of society. Unlike Adam Smith, Rae therefore believes that it is an important function of government to promote scientific and technical development and encourage inventions and improvements in existing techniques.

Anticipating the recent discussions on the subject of technical change embodied in capital goods, Rae says "before capital can increase, there must be something in which it may be embodied". Only technical development brings profit to capital formation and provides the population with sufficient goods, so that it has "most title to be ranked as the true generator of states and people". Rae, in effect, adds the application and diffusion of new technology to the accumulation of capital and the division of labour, as the main factors contributing to the prosperity of society.

Rae devotes a complete chapter to technical change and its consequences. He first considers the psychology of the inventor and concludes that he is motivated by the same urge to create as the artist or the mathematician. They are all people who do not imitate but create new things, whether in the spiritual, mental or material field. The handing-down of existing knowledge is still important, but those who do nothing else "neither oppose, nor direct the current". However, technical development depends not only on inventors but also on natural resources and the discovery of the laws of nature.

Rae, a somewhat neglected figure, but whose importance is now being recognized, was not only a pioneer of the theory of capital but also made a significant contribution to the theory of technical change (Rae, 1834, pp. 15, 31, 118–120, 213, 240, 264).

There is an understandable tendency to regard 1870 as a turning point in the development of economic theory, because the publications of Menger, Jevons and Walras appeared around that time. Although there was a new emphasis on the behaviour of the individual consumer, as a reaction to the neglect of Classical theory, the marginal utility school did not completely ignore the objective aspects of production. All of them paid some attention to technology and technical change, and Böhm-Bawerk and Wicksell, in particular, produced an important analysis of the effect of capital formation on economic development.

Menger (1840–1921), the founder of the Austrian school, did not give much thought to technology and, when he did deal with it, he concentrated on the process of the creation of new products and the improvement of old ones. In his system, the structure of production is determined mainly by the subjective value that the consumers put on "goods of the first order" and not by the underlying economic framework. Menger does not mention technical development among the causes of increasing prosperity.

But, although the Austrian economists are regarded as exponents of a theory of static equilibrium, they did not ignore technical development altogether. In an account of capital formation, Menger says "human life is a process", and establishes a connection between the productivity of capital and the systematic underestimation of future needs. His terms of reference are utility, benefit and satisfaction of needs, but, by treating capital as a factor of production, he introduces an element which is to a great extent determined by the technology used in the production process. Technical development – as far as one can perceive it in Mengers work – is the acquisition of knowledge about new products (Menger, 1871, pp. 26ff).

Jevons (1835–1882) paid considerable attention to capital formation. He thought that capital can open up roundabout routes of production. He anticipated Böhm-Bawerk and Wicksell, especially since he viewed production time as a variable (Jevons, 1871, p. 22).

In Volume II of his *Eléments d'économie politique pure*, published in 1877, Walras (1834–1910) devotes a chapter to capital. The demand for, and the supply of, capital are treated in monetary terms and are incorporated in the general equilibrium system. But the formal approach vanishes when Walras discusses the idea of progress in an economic system of perfect competition. He makes an important distinction between economic progress and technical progress. In the former, the technical coefficients are changed quantitatively by the use of more capital and less land, while, in the latter, there is qualitative change in the technical coefficients, for some of them disappear and are replaced by new ones (Walras, 1877). As has been pointed out by D. Walker, Walras paid attention to the entrepreneurial function in his writings (Walker, 1986, pp. 1–24). The entrepreneur plays an essential role in the dynamics of the market system (Walker, 2001).

Schumpeter called Böhm-Bawerk (1851–1914) the "bourgeois Marx", because of his detailed analysis of the capitalistic system (Schumpeter, 1954, p. 846). Böhm-Bawerk makes it clear that both increased productivity and technical progress are possible without an extension of roundabout production methods, for an invention often leads to a less roundabout production method. There is no consistent relationship involved, although Böhm-Bawerk believes that inventions associated with a more roundabout production method form the majority. Inventions which shorten this route quickly oust existing methods, whereas the realization of the opposite type of invention depends on the relatively slow growth of the subsistence fund. Since the anticipated profit determines whether a roundabout production method is applied or not, both recent and older inventions will be in use at any given moment. More technical knowledge exists than can be put to use, due to scarcity of capital.

Böhm-Bawerk distinguishes between a lengthening of the roundabout route of production at a given level of technical knowledge and the influence of inventions on the length of this route. The introduction of the concept of the production period follows from Böhm-Bawerk's starting point, which is that only the original factors of production – labour and scarce natural resources – are important for characterizing capitalistic production. Of the two types of capital, only the circulating type is involved. The concept of the roundabout production method and the related concept of a production period only adequately fit into a model in which circulating capital is the only type taken into account: when fixed capital is introduced as a factor of production, these two concepts can no longer be used as analytical tools, because the length of the production period cannot then be accurately defined. These concepts may have limited validity, but Böhm-Bawerk's basic idea was important, and intertemporal production functions are discussed in modern microeconomic production theory (Böhm-Bawerk, 1921, pp. 111–113).

It is rather surprising that Böhm-Bawerk did not formulate a production function in view of his explicit references to Von Thünen (1783–1850).

In the second edition of his work, Von Thünen describes the intensive variant of diminishing returns and considers production the result of two factors of production; labour and capital. He explicitly formulates the concept of the marginal products of labour and capital and he equates the wage rate with the value of the marginal products. But the most remarkable thing is that he added a mathematical formulation to his description of the concept of the production function and worked out several numerical examples, using empirical data from his estate. His general production function is of the following form:

$$p = h(g + k)^n \tag{1}$$

where h, g and n are constants, p is per-capita production and k the ratio between capital and labour (Von Thünen, 1863).

In a remarkable study, *An Essay on the Coordination of the Laws of Distribution* published in 1894, Wicksteed (1844–1927) further developed Jevons' vague notion of a production function. Admittedly, Edgeworth introduced a production function in 1893 in a footnote to a discussion of Von Wieser's book (Von Wieser, 1893), but Wicksteed was the first to develop this concept in clear and precise terms.

Wicksteed introduced the production function in the context of the theory of marginal productivity. It is interesting that Wicksteed first proposed a general-welfare function, where the "total satisfaction (S) of a community is a function (F) of the commodities, services, etc. ($A, B, C, \ldots$)". If the amount of a good is denoted by K, then dS/dK gives the "marginal efficiency or significance of K as the producer of satisfaction". The exchange value of the whole stock is then

$$\frac{dS}{dK} K$$

After giving this general definition, Wicksteed proceeds to treat social welfare as a product, and the goods and services as factors of this product. Simultaneously, with the introduction of the production function. Wicksteed laid the foundation of the theory of marginal productivity (Wicksteed, 1894, p. 189).

Meanwhile Marshall's *Principles of Economics* had appeared in 1890. Marshall concludes his discussion of the effect of mechanization on the division of labour by saying that "any manufacturing operation that can be reduced to uniformity...is sure to be taken over sooner or later by machinery". Like Marx, Marshall displays a wide knowledge of technology, which enabled him to identify and project future developments. Thus, he mentions the elimination of human control work by the introduction of "an automatic movement which brings the machine to a stop the instant anything goes wrong". He believes that an improvement in machinery goes hand in hand with an increase in the division of labour, though the connection between them is not as close as many economists imagine. He also stresses that machines can work with greater precision than the human hand, and realizes that this encourages a system of replaceable or interchangeable parts made by machines. He draws general conclusions from his observations of the textile industry and discusses how machines make work lighter.

Marshall points out the importance of new and cheaper means of communications and stresses the significance of the application and export of new inventions: "English mechanics have taught people in almost every part of the world how to use English machinery". Discussing the effect of mechanization on the ratio between agricultural and industrial activity, Marshall uses numerical data to show that not all those who have become redundant in agriculture can find employment in industry because of the "wonderful increase in recent years of the power of machinery", which permits a great increase in production to be achieved without a proportional increase in the labour force, so that the redundant labour drifts into sectors where "the improvements of machinery help us but little". It can be safely assumed that Marshall is thinking here of service industries.

Starting with Babbage's preoccupations, Marshall discusses in detail the advantages of large-scale production, notably the use of specialized machines, the greater chance of inventing things, the financial resources for making mechanical equipment, more favourable purchasing conditions and better utilization of scientific and technical knowledge.

In connection with increases in scale, Marshall distinguishes between "external economies", derived from the general development of a whole sector, and "internal economies", derived from increased production within the enterprise. As well as the law of diminishing returns for agriculture, he believes in a law of increasing returns for industry, which is mainly due to better organization, in its turn due to larger inputs of labour and capital. He mentions, in passing, that one external diseconomy is "the growing difficulty of finding solitude and quiet and even fresh air" (Marshall, 1890; 1961, pp. 255–332).

In general, the neoclassical model with a production function, optimizing behaviour and perfect information does not include the dynamic role of an active entrepreneur. However, Marshall's theory attached a prominent role to the entrepreneur. His view is considered to be the dominant neoclassical view of entrepreneurship. In a Marshallian economy, the entrepreneur's task is the supply of commodities and, at the same time, the concern for innovations and progress.

Businesses which benefit the economy are not necessarily the firms which survive within the competitive Marshallian environment. The reward of every business undertaker is proportionate to the private, rather than to the social benefits he renders to society.

Within the firm, the entrepreneur is responsible and exercises all control. He directs production, undertakes business risks, coordinates capital and labour, and is both the manager and employer. The alert entrepreneur continuously seeks opportunities to minimize costs in view of a given benefit.

Consequently, successful entrepreneurship obviously requires skills and capacities. General knowledge, flexibility and social intelligence are required to enable one to attain great success in any pursuit and especially in business.

This general ability depends on family background, education and innate ability. Successful entrepreneurship also requires specialized abilities such as knowledge of the trade and power of forecasting, of seeing where there is an opportunity and of undertaking risks. To perform his role as an employer, the entrepreneur should be a "natural leader of men".

Not only are these abilities required to make a successful entrepreneur; good fortune as well as business opportunities are necessary requirements too. The opportunity of acquiring the capital required to allow ability to be effectively utilized differs among persons. Entrepreneurs working with borrowed capital have a disadvantage over those who have capital themselves. If the business-man working on borrowed capital is less successful, lenders easily draw back their loans. Consequently, one misfortune may rapidly lead to another. Sons of entrepreneurs have additional advantages over others when starting a business. And these advantages are not restricted to their fathers' business. The son of an entrepreneur has more business opportunities than an average individual.

Entrepreneurial supply is constrained by the abilities required for it. The entrepreneurial supply price, as determined by the equilibrating forces of supply and demand, is high. And as long as entrepreneurial profits are higher than the earnings in other occupations, and as long as there are still people with the required abilities and enough opportunity, fresh businessmen enter into the economy. If there are too many businessmen in command of capital to sustain the high price, the "survival of the fittest" principle, referred to by Marshall as the "substitution principle", determines who remains in business and who must close the shop.

In brief, the Marshallian market economy centres on the class of entrepreneurs. Entrepreneurs drive the production and distribution process. They coordinate supply and demand on the market, and capital and labour within the firm. They undertake all the risks that are associated with production. They lead and manage their firms. They are cost minimizers and are also innovators and at the basis of progress. Many abilities are required and combinations of them are scarce in the economy. Consequently, the supply price for entrepreneurship will generally be high (Praag van, 1996).

In conclusion, we have seen a clearer expression of the relationship between production and the factors of production, but at the price of some of the caution, qualifications and richness of the older literature. Wicksteed's analysis of the production function is distinctly more elegant and incisive than Marshall's, but Marshall had a wider knowledge of actual production techniques.

As the importance of the production function increased, so the question of technical change receded into the background. Those who produced the most advanced mathematical treatment of the production function tended to ignore the changes caused by technology. In contrast, those with a less mathematical bent gave more emphasis to the role played by technical change. If the production function expresses a dynamic relationship that includes technical change, economists needed to have a clear idea about the various types of technical change before economic theory could incorporate this phenomenon into the production function.

EPILOGUE

It is needless to add that I have presented only a very brief and sketchy impression of a rich and large literature. The entrepreneur as the embodiment of change in general, and technical change in particular, does not only disturb the status quo in real life but also poses a serious problem for theoretical analysis. As is well known, in his writings Schumpeter dealt with this role of the entrepreneur as innovator in the process of creative destruction. Nowadays, the mathematical approach is also being developed, in order to analyse these phenomena in a rigorous manner.

It is interesting to note that in the aftermath of the Schumpeter revival, since the eighties of last century, our field observes the emergence of entrepreneurial economics. Several threads come together. Economic theory substituted the paradigm of perfect knowledge for imperfect information, developed a more refined analysis of risk and uncertainty in economic life and the theory of games provided the framework for the analysis of strategic behaviour in general. The theory of industrial organisation entered a higher level of sophistication and chaos theory as part of economic dynamics helped to transform verbal Schumpeterian ideas and intuitions into a refined mathematical structure. Also the application of insights from theoretical physics, like thermodynamics and entropy are very promising. These developments have brought the modern entrepreneur of flesh and blood, being embedded in a global world of enduring technical change, uncertain challenges, threats and opportunities in the forefront of advanced economic analysis.

REFERENCES

Baudeau, N. (1910). *Première introduction à la philosophie économique* (1st ed., Paris 1767). Paris: Libraizie Paul Geuthner.

Böhm Bawerk, E. von (1921). *Geschichte und Kritik der Kapitalzins Theorien*. Jena: Gustar Fischer.

Brewer, A. (1992). *Richard Cantillon pioneer of economic theory*. London: Routledge.

Cantillon, R. (1755). *Essai sur la nature du commerce en général*. London: Fletcher.

Cournot, A. A. (1838). *Recherches sur les principes mathématiques de la théorie des richesses*. Paris: Libraizie Hachette.

Cournot, A. A. (1863). *Principes de la théorie des richesses*. Paris: Libraizie Hachette.

Cournot, A. A. (1877). *Revue somaires des doctrines économiques*. Paris: Libraizie Hachette.

Hebert, R. F., & Link, A. N. (1982). *The entrepreneur*. New York: Praeger.

Heertje, A. (1987). *Economics and technical change*. London: Weidenfeld and Nicholson.

Hoselitz, B. F. (1960). The early history of entrepreneurial theory. In: J. J. Spengler & W. R. Allen (Eds), *Essays in economic thought: Aristotle to Marshall*. Chicago: Free Press.

Jevons, W. S. (1871). *Theory of political economy*. London: Macmillan.

Malthus, T. R. (1815). *An inquiry into the nature and progress of rent*. London: John Murray.

Marshall, A. (1890). *Principles of economics* (Vol. 1, Guillebaud edition). London: Macmillan (London, 1961).

Marx, K. (1867). *Das Kapital, Hamburg*. London: Otto Meissner (Capital, London, 1974).

Menger, C. (1871). *Grundsätze der Volkswirtschaftlehre*. Vienna: Wilhelm Braummüller.

Murphy, A. E. (1986). *Richard Cantillon, entrepreneur and economist*. Oxford: Clarendon Press.

Palmer, R. R. (Ed.) (1997). *J. B. Say, An economist in troubled times*. Princeton: Princeton University Press.

Praag, C. M. van (1996). *Determinants of successful entrepreneurship*. Amsterdam: Thesis.

Rae, J. (1834). *Statement of some new principles on the subject of political economy*. Boston: Hilliazd, Gray and Co.

Ricardo, D. (1815). *An essay on the influence of a low price of corn on the profits of stock*. London: John Murray.

Ricardo, D. (1817). *On the principles of political economy, and taxation* (3rd ed.). London: John Murray (London, 1821).

Say, J. B. (1803). *Traité d'économie politique*. Paris: Chez Deterville.

Schumpeter, J. A. (1954). *History of economic analysis*. London: Geozge Allen and Unwin.

Smith, A. (1976). *An inquiry into the nature and causes of the wealth of nations, I and II*. London: W. Strahan and T. Cadell.

Sraffa, P. (1973). *The works of David Ricardo,* (I − X). Cambridge 1951, XI Index, Cambridge: Cambridge University Press.

Steuart, J. (1767). *An inquiry into the principles of political economy*. London: A. Millar and T. Cadell.

Turgot, A. R. J. (1769). Réflexions sur la formation et la distribution des richesses. Ephémérides des Citoyen (XI, XII, 1770, I). Libraize Lacombe.

Von Thünen, J. H. (1863). *Der isolierte Staat in Beziehung auf Landwirtschaft und Nationalökonomie*. Hamburg 1826; 2nd ed. I, 1842, II, part 1, 1850 and part 2. Rostock.

Walker, D. (2001). Walras's theory of the entrepreneur. De Economist, 1986, in Walker, D. (ed.), *The legacy of Léon Walras*, I. Cheltenham: Edward Elgar.

Walras, L. (1877). *Eléments d'économie politique pure*. Lausanne: Guillaumin.

West, E. (1815). *Essay on the application of capital to land*. London: John Murray.

Wicksteed, P. H. (1994). *An essay on the coordination of the laws of distribution*. London: Macmillan.

MICROTHEORY OF ENTREPRENEURSHIP: MORE EXISTS THAN IS RECOGNIZED

William J. Baumol

INTRODUCTION

To amend a standard *bon mot*, entrepreneurship is known to play a critical role in reality, leaving economists concerned whether it fits into the theory. The answer, I will argue here, is that it not only fits prospectively, but that the theory already exists and does much of what is done for the other inputs of the production process via the theory of distribution and the theory of production.

There do remain substantial obstacles to full parity in these bodies of analysis. But the misunderstanding that the entrepreneur is altogether absent from current theory stems primarily from two sources. The first is that he is virtually never mentioned in neoclassical writings and beyond, either in production/distribution theory, or in the theory of the firm. The second source of misunderstanding is that we tend to expect the theory of entrepreneurship to deal with topics that we do not demand of the theory of labor or land, for example.

But in the theory of, say, labor, what is described is the nature of its demand, the determinants of its supply, the mechanism by which it is allocated among alternative uses, and the determinants of its earnings and the

The Emergence of Entrepreneurial Economics
Research on Technological Innovation, Management and Policy, Volume 9, 27–35
Copyright © 2005 by Elsevier Ltd.
ISSN: 0737-1071/doi:10.1016/S0737-1071(05)09002-5

prices of its products. I maintain that the literature already provides coherent analyses of all these matters for entrepreneurship, as it does for labor, albeit more qualitative and less formal.

ABSENCE OF THE ENTREPRENEUR FROM STATIC THEORY OF THE FIRM AND PRODUCTION

There is a very good reason why the entrepreneur is virtually never mentioned in modern theory of the firm and distribution, a reason that does not imply that there exists no relevant theory. The explanation is that in mainstream economics the constructs are generally equilibrium models in which, structurally, nothing is changing. But, this very attribute excludes the entrepreneur by definition. She is absent from such a model because she does not belong there. This has been definitively argued by Schumpeter (1911) and Kirzner (1979), who have demonstrated that sustained equilibrium is something that the entrepreneur does not tolerate, any more than he tolerates sustained disequilibrium. Here, Schumpeter's key insight is that the entrepreneur's occupation is focused upon the search for profitable opportunities to upset any equilibrium. That is exactly what any innovation, in the broadest sense, entails. But the rest of the story is told by Kirzner who recounts that the entrepreneur, with his critical ability: alertness, recognizes in any disequilibrium a profitable arbitrage opportunity, and by taking advantage of that opportunity he provides the pressures that move the economy back toward an equilibrium condition. This is the mechanism underlying continuous industrial evolution and revolution, and it is surely not the stuff of which stationary models are built. Thus, it should hardly be surprising that a stationary Walrasian model, even in a more sophisticated variant, makes of the entrepreneur an invisible man.

This is particularly evident of the standard theory of the firm, which analyses the repetitious decisions of an enterprise that is already present and fully grown. In such a scenario the entrepreneur has already completed his job and left for places elsewhere that his firm creation activities can again be used.

We conclude that the neoclassical theory is not wrong in excluding the entrepreneur, because it is dealing with subjects for which he is irrelevant. But that does not mean that no theory of entrepreneurial is needed, or that such a theory is lacking. Evidently, it is needed, and I will argue that much of such a theory exists.

WHAT WE SHOULD NOT EXPECT OF THE THEORY

Much of the early literature that deals with the entrepreneur, in writings by Cantillon (1755), Say (1803) and others, provides descriptive material on the activities of this input. We are told that he assembles the necessary funds and the labor force needed to operate a newly created firm, that the entrepreneur assumes risks greater than those affecting other inputs, etc. But this is not what we expect of a theory of labor, where we do not single out the plumber's tasks of installing sink faucets and drains, and separate out the use of wrenches from the employment of drills. As already indicated, in the theory of labor we focus on the attributes and determinants of demand, supply, allocation among alternative uses, product prices and wage payments. But, to a substantial degree, the modern theory of entrepreneurship already does all that.

SCHUMPETER: SUPPLY AND EARNINGS OF ENTREPRENEURIAL ACTIVITY

Much of this is accomplished by the Schumpeterian model that focuses upon the entrepreneur as innovator and not just the creator of replicative firms. As we all know, the earlier Schumpeterian model (1911) tells us that the effort of the successful innovative entrepreneur is rewarded by temporary monopoly profits that, if substantial, attract rivals who seek to acquire some of those profits via imitation, and in the process erode those super-competitive earnings. Thus, the entrepreneur who is determined to prevent termination of these rewards is driven never to desist from seeking further innovations and is precluded from resting on his laurels.

This scenario, it should be noted, tells us about at least three of the topics, listed above, with which I asserted the theory should deal. The model tells us about the supply behavior of this input into the economy's productive processes; it tells us about the prices of its final products and about the earnings of the input supplier. We are evidently well on our way.

ALLOCATION BETWEEN PRODUCTIVE AND UNPRODUCTIVE ENTREPRENEURSHIP

I trust I will be excused for reintroducing at this point some work of my own (Baumol, 2002, Chapter 14). My excuse is that, if valid, it will tell us much of

the rest of the story about the supply and allocation of productive entrepreneurship and the comparative-dynamic role in this process of changes in
the relative earnings offered by different activities as the result of evolving of
institutions.

In the nonmathematical growth literature it has often been asserted that
the appearance of an abundant supply of entrepreneurs effectively stimulates growth, while shrinkage in the economy's cadre of entrepreneurs becomes a significant impediment to growth. But those apparently vital
phenomena, the appearance and disappearance of the entrepreneurs, are left
as a great mystery, with hints that they hang on cultural developments in the
economy and changes in other psychological and sociological influences,
more or less vague in character. It is almost as though we have returned to
ancient conjectures about the appearance of species such as a plague of
insects by a process entailing "spontaneous generation".

But review of the historical evidence suggests an alternative explanation,
less magical or science-fictional in character. The alternative scenario holds
that the entrepreneurs do not suddenly appear from nowhere or just as
mysteriously begin to vanish. Rather, in this account, the entrepreneurs are
always with us, but as the structure of the rewards offered in the economy
changes, they switch the locus of their activity, moving into the arenas where
the payoff prospects have become the more attractive. And in doing so, they
move in and out of the activities that are most generally recognized as
entrepreneurial, exchanging them with other activities that also require
considerable enterprising talent but are often quite distant from the production of goods and services. The Roman generals, the Mandarins of Tang,
Sung or Ming Chinese empires, the captains of late medieval private and
mercenary armies, the rent-seeking contemporary lawyer, and the Mafia
don are all evidently enterprising and often successful. And when institutions have changed so as to modify profoundly the relative payoffs offered
by the different enterprising activities, the supply of entrepreneurs has
shifted accordingly, from the now less rewarding to the more rewarding
activities. Just as technological change led workers and engineers to reallocate themselves from canal building to railroad construction and then on
to still more modern enterprises, so too, the entrepreneurs have repositioned
themselves in response to similar changes in the structure of payoffs.

Elsewhere, in discussing this reallocation process, I have found it helpful
to distinguish between two categories of entrepreneurs, the "productive entrepreneurs" and the "unproductive entrepreneurs", with the latter, in turn,
divided into subgroups such as rent-seeking entrepreneurs and destructive
entrepreneurs such as the organizers of private armies or criminal groups.

While general use ascribes entrepreneurship only to those that fall into the productive category, this is misleading because it camouflages the process via which the body of entrepreneurs appears to expand and contract. Thus, once we recognize that entrepreneurial talent can be driven to reallocate itself from one category to another, it becomes clear that, when there is a pertinent change in the institutions that govern the relative rewards, the entrepreneurs will be induced to shift their activities among the affected fields of endeavor and so the set of productive entrepreneurs will appear to expand or contract autonomously.

Thus, when institutions change to prohibit private armies and to create a national military force capable of making this prohibition effective, the rewards offered by innovative operation of private military forces are reduced, and entrepreneurs will be led to look elsewhere to realize their financial ambitions. If, simultaneously, rules against confiscation of private property and for patent protection of inventions are adopted, this will lead those with entrepreneurial talent to shift their efforts into productive and, indeed, innovative directions.

PROFITS, PRICES, SUPPLY BEHAVIOR, AND ALLOCATION

We are now well under way toward demonstrating what I have contended. It is true that we have not used any mathematics to derive any formal theorems, and our results are informal and qualitative, with no pretence at quantification or rigor. I will turn presently to the reasons for which, I believe, this should have been expected.

But at the same time we have gone a considerable distance toward provision of what it was asserted above, the mainstream theory of distribution and production tells us about the other factors of production – those that are evidently not absent from the theory. For, as stated, this body of theory tells us about the supply, the demand, and the earnings of such inputs, their role in the pricing of their products, and the role of the price mechanism in determining their allocation among alternative activities and uses. The Schumpeterian model tells us about the determination of the entrepreneur's profits and the prices of his final products, as well as their influence on the supply of his activity. The model of productive and unproductive entrepreneurship tells us more about supply as well as about the allocation of this resource.

But of the five central topics, we have omitted any substantial discussion of only one: the *demand* for entrepreneurship. And the reason, for this omission, already mentioned, is clear. Normally, the services of the entrepreneur are not demanded by others. Rather, it is the individual himself who elects to undertake that role.[1] One can perhaps think of the demand structure consisting of the workings of the market as a whole, when it dangles before the prospective entrepreneur the opportunity to earn profit and perhaps power and status. It is not clear, however, how this observation can be carried beyond vague observations such as "entrepreneurial activity is encouraged by absence of restrictive governmental rules, low taxes, and a prosperous economy".

But, other than that, what has been reviewed above shows that much of the theory of entrepreneurship is already under way. This is not to say that everything that is pertinent has already been discovered, and that no more research on the subject is needed. Fortunately, we who are engaged in research on the theory of entrepreneurship need not feel that we are about to be out of a job. But surely, that is also true of the theory of land, labor, and capital.

Let me review briefly what has been shown on the four remaining topics with which we can expect the theory to deal.

On supply we have seen from the Schumpeterian model how the happenstance of an invention elicits entrepreneurial effort, how this in turn, enhances the supply of imitative entrepreneurship and how the success of these imitators forces the initiating entrepreneur to continue or to attempt to continue the supply of further innovation.

We have also seen how institutional change affects the supply of productive entrepreneurship, leading to its reallocation from unproductive or destructive but nevertheless entrepreneurial activities. This, then, is the supply story, but it is also the resource allocation scenario, describing, in considerable detail if this is desired, how such institutional changes modify the directions in which entrepreneurial effort is moved.

At the same time, profits and prices are fully integrated into these scenarios. In Schumpeter's account, the early period after introduction of an innovation brings with it supercompetitive profits and prices significantly above the pertinent costs. And in the model of allocation between productive and unproductive activities the relation between variation of relative profits and the movement of entrepreneurial activity follows an obvious pattern.

In sum, the analysis does deal, albeit in a very informal manner with all of the elements that we recognize to emerge from the theory of any other factor of production.

INNOVATIVE ACTIVITY AS FORM OF INVESTMENT: A STEP TOWARD FORMALIZATION

We can go a bit further and observe that in terms of the properties that underlie the formal analyses there is a great resemblance between the innovation and investment processes. This is important for our discussion if it indicates, as I believe it to do, that with little modification, some of the sophisticated formal models of the theory of investment can be applied directly to the innovative activities of the entrepreneur.

The defining attributes of capital are, of course, durability and reusability. But the life of an invention that is promoted by an entrepreneur normally also extends over a multiplicity of periods. And all of the accompanying features are present in both – the extension over time of their outlays and revenues, the unpredictability of their returns and, consequently, their special risks and uncertainties (Knight, 1921).

Here we should pause to take note of the argument that since the entrepreneur can and often does operate with other people's money, it is the latter, the capitalists, who assume the risks of the entrepreneur's activities. But even if the entrepreneur invests no funds of his own, he surely invests considerable time and effort in his undertaking, and their opportunity cost is rarely negligible. The sad tales of failed entrepreneurs surely make that clear. And when successful, the inter-temporal trajectory of the rewards from an innovation he has brought to fruition can vary considerably. They can continue high for a substantial period, and then suddenly collapse like the one-horse shay when a good substitute appears on the market, or their profits may decline gradually, just like the usefulness of an item of capital equipment.

Other parallels can no doubt be found, but this is enough to make my point. There does exist a rich body of theory on investment and capital, much of it formalized. Moreover, those models are operational and yield helpful conclusions, many of them not obvious to the intuition, at least not in advance. And a good deal of this material should, with little modification be applicable to entrepreneurship as a ready-to-wear body of theory.

LIMITATIONS AND SPECIAL OBSTACLES

This, then, is most of my story. There does exist, or almost exists, a usable theory of entrepreneurship, with even an entree to formalized analysis. Yet, it seems likely that even a reader who is convinced that there is something to my argument, will still feel some disquiet. Somehow, we are all apt to feel that this is not all, that the story has left out something that should not have been omitted. In conclusion, I will first return to my argument, that there are some things often expected of a theory of entrepreneurship that should not really be demanded of it. Second, I will submit, in contrast, that there are other pertinent elements that do elude our grasp, and may well continue to do so. Finally, I will discuss the special attributes of the entrepreneur's inputs that impede and may prevent us from filling these gaps.

What should not be expected of the theory? Particularly because those of us who write about entrepreneurship are likely also to be engaged in the teaching of prospective entrepreneurs, we can expect to be led to focus upon details of their activities. What we can teach them relates to legal prerequisites affecting the creation of the firm, bookkeeping and accounting, taxation, marketing techniques, etc. In other words, the prospective entrepreneur can most readily be taught details that make up her day to day activities. But surely that is not the content of the theory of this input, any more than it is the stuff of the theory of land, labor or capital. Indeed, much of it is arguably not primarily about entrepreneurship but about management – not about the creation of firms and the introduction of innovations, but rather the ho-hum specifics of daily oversight of the on-going enterprise. Though there are gaps enough in the theory, these are not those.

Yet, there are two handicaps that do beset further development of a theory of entrepreneurship and, particularly, its formalization. First, there is the heterogeneity of the product. By definition, an innovation is the ultimate in unstandardized products, for if along with the product in question there exists even a single other product that is essentially the same in construction and utilization, the former is evidently not an invention. But we know that great product heterogeneity is a primary source of difficulty for theory construction.

Second, the activity of the entrepreneur entails relationships beset with uncertainty and discontinuity and that therefore apparently cannot be described in neat and simple mathematical forms. A major consequence is that it has little room for formal optimization analysis. This is surely an arena in which satisficing rather than maximization is all that can be done. What is it that the entrepreneur can maximize and how can he do it? But if there are no defensible answers, the usual foundation for formal theory construction is undermined.

NOTES

1. It is true that some large firms have sought to launch quasi-independent sub-sidiaries and to assign the task of their direction to employees deemed to have an entrepreneurial orientation. But, then, the relevant theoretical construct is surely the modification of marginal productivity theory as adapted to highly lumpy inputs. Here, evidently, theory already does exist.

REFERENCES

Baumol, W. J. (2002). *The free-market innovation machine: Analyzing the growth miracle of capitalism.* Princeton: Princeton University Press.

Cantillon, R. (1755). *Essai sur la nature de commerce en général.* London: Macmillan & Co. Ltd., 1931 [English translation].

Kirzner, I. M. (1979). *Perception, opportunity and profit.* Chicago: University of Chicago Press.

Knight, F. H. (1921). *Risk, uncertainty and profit.* Boston and New York: Houghton Mifflin Co.

Say, J.-B. (1803). *Traité d'économie politique.* Paris: l'Imprimerie de Crapelet.

Schumpeter, J. A. (1911). *The theory of economic development.* Cambridge, MA: Harvard University Press. [English translation published in 1936.]

THE KNOWLEDGE SPILLOVER THEORY OF ENTREPRENEURSHIP AND ECONOMIC GROWTH

David B. Audretsch

INTRODUCTION

Why should entrepreneurship matter for economic growth, employment creation and international competitiveness? The entrepreneurship literature has traditionally suggested that entrepreneurship matters to individuals and firms, but rarely for economic growth.

This chapter presents the knowledge spillover theory of entrepreneurship, which suggests that entrepreneurship is the missing link in the process of economic growth because it facilitates the spillover of knowledge from universities and private firms, resulting in commercialization of ideas that otherwise might remain uncommercialized.

The knowledge spillover theory of entrepreneurship inverts the traditional approach to entrepreneurship. Traditional theories of entrepreneurship have held the context within which the individual finds oneself and probed why certain individuals will make the decision to start a new firm. This typically leads to a focus on variations in characteristics, attributes and inclinations across individuals.

By contrast, the knowledge spillover theory of entrepreneurship instead assumes the individual characteristics to be constant and then analyzes how

The Emergence of Entrepreneurial Economics
Research on Technological Innovation, Management and Policy, Volume 9, 37–54
Copyright © 2005 by Elsevier Ltd.
ISSN: 0737-1071/doi:10.1016/S0737-1071(05)09003-7

the cognitive process inducing the entrepreneurial decision is influenced by placing that same individual in different contexts. In particular, high knowledge contexts are compared with impoverished knowledge contexts. A strikingly different view of entrepreneurship emerges. Instead of being a phenomenon that is exogenously determined by preconditioned personal attributes and family history, entrepreneurship instead becomes seen as an endogenous response to opportunities generated by investments in new knowledge made by incumbent firms and organizations, combined with their inability to completely exhaust the ensuing opportunities to commercialize that knowledge. Thus, the knowledge spillover theory of entrepreneurship shows how entrepreneurship can be an endogenous response to investments in new knowledge where commercialization of that knowledge is constrained by the existence of a formidable knowledge filter.

The next section explains how entrepreneurship combines the cognitive process of recognizing opportunities with pursuing those opportunities by starting a new firm. The third section introduces the knowledge spillover theory of entrepreneurship, which suggests that entrepreneurship is an endogenous response to investments in knowledge that are not fully appropriated by incumbent firms. The fourth section links endogenous entrepreneurship based on knowledge spillovers to economic growth. Finally, the summary and conclusions are provided in the last section. In particular, we suggest that entrepreneurship education and the transfer of technology from universities for commercialization make a key contribution to the societal values of economic growth, employment creation and competitiveness in globally linked markets by reducing the knowledge filter and facilitating the missing link to economic growth – entrepreneurship.

ENTREPRENEURIAL OPPORTUNITY: EXOGENOUS VERSUS ENDOGENOUS

Entrepreneurship involves the recognition of opportunities and the commercialization of those opportunities (Venkataraman, 1997). This has resulted in a focus on the cognitive process by which individuals reach the decision to start a new firm. As Krueger (2003, p. 105) explains, "The heart of entrepreneurship is an orientation toward seeing opportunities". Thus, the literature on entrepreneurship has been concerned with, "What is the nature of entrepreneurial thinking and What cognitive phenomena are associated with seeing and acting on opportunities?" (Krueger, 2003, p. 105).

According to Sarasvathy, Dew, Velamuri, and Venkataraman (2003, p. 142), "An entrepreneurial opportunity consists of a set of ideas, beliefs and actions that enable the creation of future goods and services in the absence of current markets for them".

The methodological approach in the literature on entrepreneurship has been to hold the context constant and then to analyze how the cognitive process inherent in the entrepreneurial decision varies across different individual characteristics and attributes (Shaver, 2003; McClelland, 1961). As Shane and Eckhardt (2003, p. 187) summarize the entrepreneurship literature, the focus is on "the process of opportunity discovery and why some actors are more likely to discover a given opportunity than others".

Some of these differences involve the willingness to incur risk, others involve the preference for autonomy and self-direction, while still others involve differential access to scarce and expensive resources, such as financial capital, human capital, social capital and experiential capital. This approach, focusing on individual cognition in the entrepreneurial process, has generated a number of important and valuable insights, such as the contribution made by social networks, education and training, and familial influence. The literature certainly leaves the impression that entrepreneurship is a personal matter largely determined by DNA, familial status and access to crucial resources.

While entrepreneurship theory revolves around opportunities, in fact such entrepreneurial opportunities are taken as being exogenous to the individual. By contrast, a very different literature suggests that opportunities are endogenous. In the model of the knowledge production function, introduced by Griliches (1984), innovation is the result of purposeful firm-specific investments in knowledge inputs. The unit of analysis in this literature is the firm. Innovative opportunities are generated through investing resources in R&D and other types of knowledge, such as human capital.

Thus, the firm is exogenous while the opportunity is created endogenously. An important implication is that the opportunity recognition and exploitation take place within the same organizational unit creating those opportunities – the firm. Just as the firm serves as the organizational unit generating the opportunities, that same firm appropriates the returns to those purposeful knowledge investments through innovative activity.

The empirical evidence from systematic empirical testing of the model of the knowledge production function contradicted the assumption of singularity between the organization creating the opportunities and the organization exploiting the opportunities. In particular, the empirical evidence pointed to a much more vigorous contribution to small and new-firm innovative activity than would have been warranted from their rather limited investments in new knowledge, as measured by R&D and human capital (Audretsch, 1995).

THE KNOWLEDGE SPILLOVER THEORY OF ENTREPRENEURSHIP

The discrepancy in organizational context between the organization creating opportunities and those exploiting the opportunities that seemingly contradicted Griliches' model of the firm knowledge production function was resolved by Audretsch (1995), who introduced the Knowledge Spillover Theory of Entrepreneurship, "The findings challenge an assumption implicit to the knowledge production function – that firms exist exogenously and then endogenously seek out and apply knowledge inputs to generate innovative output. It is the knowledge in the possession of economic agents that is exogenous, and in an effort to appropriate the returns from that knowledge, the spillover of knowledge from its producing entity involves endogenously creating a new firm" (pp. 179–180).

The knowledge spillover theory of entrepreneurship suggests that knowledge spillovers serve as the source of knowledge creating the entrepreneurial opportunities for small and new firms. "How are these small and frequently new firms able to generate innovative output when undertaken a generally negligible amount of investment into knowledge-generating inputs, such as R&D? One answer is apparently through exploiting knowledge created by expenditures on research in universities and on R&D in large corporations" (p. 179).

The empirical evidence supporting the knowledge spillover theory of entrepreneurship was provided from analyzing variations in startup rates across different industries reflecting different underlying knowledge contexts. In particular, those industries with a greater investment in new knowledge also exhibited higher startup rates while those industries with less investment in new knowledge exhibited lower startup rates, which was interpreted as a conduit, transmitting knowledge spillovers (Audretsch, 1995; Caves, 1998).

Thus, compelling evidence was provided suggesting that entrepreneurship is an endogenous response to opportunities created but not exploited by the incumbent firms. This involved an organizational dimension involving the mechanism transmitting knowledge spillovers – the startup of a new firm.

In addition, Jaffe (1989), Audretsch and Feldman (1996) and Audretsch and Stephan (1996) provided evidence concerning the spatial dimension of knowledge spillovers. In particular, their findings suggested that knowledge spillovers are geographically bounded and localized within spatial proximity to the knowledge source. None of these studies, however, identified the actual mechanisms which actually transmit the knowledge spillover; rather, the spillovers were implicitly assumed to automatically exist (or fall like manna from heaven), but only within a geographically bounded spatial area.

As the second section emphasized, while much has been made about the key role played by the recognition of opportunities in the cognitive process underlying the decision to become an entrepreneur, relatively little has been written about the actual source of such entrepreneurial opportunities. The knowledge spillover theory of entrepreneurship identifies one source of entrepreneurial opportunities – new knowledge and ideas. In particular, the knowledge spillover theory of entrepreneurship posits that it is new knowledge and ideas created in one context, but left uncommercialized or not vigorously pursued by the source actually creating those ideas, such as a research laboratory in a large corporation or research undertaken by a university, that serves as the source of knowledge generating entrepreneurial opportunities. Thus, in this view, one mechanism for recognizing new opportunities and actually implementing them by starting a new firm involves the spillover of knowledge. The organization creating the opportunities is not the same organization that exploits the opportunities. If the exploitation of those opportunities by the entrepreneur does not involve full payment to the firm for producing those opportunities, such as a license or royalty, then the entrepreneurial act of starting a new firm serves as a mechanism for knowledge spillovers.

LINKING ENTREPRENEURSHIP TO GROWTH

In the Romer (1986) model of endogenous growth, new technological knowledge is assumed to automatically spillover. Investment in new technological knowledge is automatically accessed by third-party firms and economic agents, resulting in the automatic spillover of knowledge. The assumption that knowledge automatically spills over is, of course, consistent with the important insight by Arrow (1962) that knowledge differs from the traditional factors of production – physical capital and (unskilled) labor – in that it is non-excludable and non-exhaustive. When the firm or economic agent uses the knowledge, it is neither exhausted nor can it be, in the absence of legal protection, precluded from use by third-party firms or other economic agents. Thus, in the spirit of the Romer model, drawing on the earlier insights about knowledge from Arrow, a large and vigorous literature has emerged obsessed with the links between intellectual property protection and the incentives for firms to invest in the creation of new knowledge through R&D and investments in human capital.

However, the preoccupation with the non-excludability and non-exhaustibility of knowledge first identified by Arrow and later carried forward and assumed in the Romer model, neglects another key insight in the original Arrow (1962) article. Arrow also identified another dimension by which knowledge differs from the traditional factors of production. This other dimension involves the greater degree of uncertainty, higher extent of asymmetries and greater cost of transacting new ideas. The expected value of any new idea is highly uncertain, and as Arrow pointed out, has a much greater variance than would be associated with the deployment of traditional factors of production. After all, there is relative certainty about what a standard piece of capital equipment can do, or what an (unskilled) worker can contribute to a mass-production assembly line. By contrast, Arrow emphasized that when it comes to innovation, there is uncertainty about whether the new product can be produced, how it can be produced, and whether sufficient demand for that visualized new product might actually materialize.

In addition, new ideas are typically associated with considerable asymmetries. In order to evaluate a proposed new idea concerning a new biotechnology product, the decision-maker might not only need to have a Ph.D. in biotechnology, but also a specialization in the exact scientific area. Such divergences in education, background and experience can result in a divergence in the expected value of a new project or the variance in outcomes anticipated from pursuing that new idea, both of which can lead to divergences in the recognition and evaluation of opportunities across economic agents and decision-making hierarchies. Such divergences in the valuation of new ideas will become greater if the new idea is not consistent with the core competence and technological trajectory of the incumbent firm.

Thus, because of the conditions inherent in knowledge – high uncertainty, asymmetries and transactions cost – decision-making hierarchies can reach the decision not to pursue and try to commercialize new ideas that individual economic agents, or groups or teams of economic agents think are potentially valuable and should be pursued. The basic conditions characterizing new knowledge, combined with a broad spectrum of institutions, rules and regulations impose what could be termed as the knowledge filter. The knowledge filter is the gap between new knowledge and what Arrow (1962) referred to as economic knowledge or commercialized knowledge. The greater is the knowledge filter, the more pronounced is this gap between new knowledge and new economic, or commercialized, knowledge.

The knowledge filter is a consequence of the basic conditions inherent in new knowledge. Similarly, it is the knowledge filter that creates the opportunity for entrepreneurship in the knowledge spillover theory of entrepreneurship. According to this theory, opportunities for entrepreneurship are the duality of the knowledge filter. The higher is the knowledge filter, the greater are the divergences in the valuation of new ideas across economic agents and the decision-making hierarchies of incumbent firms. Entrepreneurial opportunities are generated not just by investments in new knowledge and ideas, but in the propensity for only a distinct subset of those opportunities to be fully pursued by incumbent firms.

Thus, the knowledge spillover theory of entrepreneurship shifts the fundamental decision-making unit of observation in the model of the knowledge production function away from exogenously assumed firms to individuals, such as scientists, engineers or other knowledge workers – agents with endowments of new economic knowledge. As Audretsch (1995) pointed out, when the lens is shifted away from the firm to the individual as the relevant unit of observation, the appropriability issue remains, but the question becomes: how can economic agents with a given endowment of new knowledge best appropriate the returns from that knowledge? If the scientist or engineer can pursue the new idea within the organizational structure of the firm developing the knowledge and appropriate roughly the expected value of that knowledge, one has no reason to leave the firm. On the other hand, if one places a greater value on his ideas than do the decision-making bureaucracy of the incumbent firm, one may choose to start a new firm to appropriate the value of his knowledge.

In the knowledge spillover theory of entrepreneurship the knowledge production function is actually reversed. The knowledge is exogenous and embodied in a worker. The firm is created endogenously in the worker's effort to appropriate the value of his knowledge through innovative activity. Typically, an employee from an established large corporation, often a scientist or engineer working in a research laboratory, will have an idea for an invention and ultimately for an innovation. Accompanying this potential innovation is an expected net return from the new product. The inventor would expect to be compensated for his/her potential innovation accordingly. If the company has a different, presumably lower, valuation of the potential innovation, it may decide either not to pursue its development, or that it merits a lower level of compensation than that expected by the employee.

As investments in new knowledge increase, entrepreneurial opportunities will also increase. Contexts where new knowledge plays an important role are associated with a greater degree of uncertainty and asymmetries across economic agents evaluating the potential value of new ideas. Thus, a context involving more new knowledge will also impose a greater divergence in the evaluation of that knowledge across economic agents, resulting in a greater variance in the outcome expected from commercializing those ideas. It is this gap in the valuation of new ideas across economic agents, or between economic agents and decision-making hierarchies of incumbent enterprises, that creates the entrepreneurial opportunity.

The knowledge spillover theory of entrepreneurship posits that, ceteris paribus, entrepreneurial activity will tend to be greater in contexts where investments in new knowledge are relatively high. In a high-knowledge context, new ideas will generate entrepreneurial opportunities by exploiting (potential) spillovers of that knowledge. By contrast, a paucity of new ideas in an impoverished knowledge context will generate only limited entrepreneurial opportunities. Thus, the knowledge spillover theory of entrepreneurship provides a clear link, or prediction that entrepreneurial activity will result from investments in new knowledge and that entrepreneurial activity will be spatially localized within close geographic proximity to the knowledge source.

In their 2005 book, Audretsch, Keilbach, and Lehmann derive a series of hypotheses emanating from the Knowledge Spillover Theory of Entrepreneurship. The first hypothesis is the Endogenous Entrepreneurship Hypothesis, which suggests that entrepreneurship will be greater in the presence of higher investments in new knowledge, ceteris paribus. Entrepreneurial activity is an endogenous response to higher investments in new knowledge, reflecting greater entrepreneurial opportunities generated by knowledge investments.

Systematic empirical evidence supporting the endogenous entrepreneurship hypothesis has been provided by Audretsch, Keilbach, and Lehmann (2005) and Acs et al. (2004). Both studies find that where investments in new knowledge are higher, the propensity for economic agents to start a new firms also tends to be higher. In particular, Audretsch et al. (2005) find that even after controlling for other sources of entrepreneurial opportunities access to entrepreneurial resources, those regions with a greater investment in new knowledge induce a greater degree of entrepreneurial start-ups, particularly in high-technology and other knowledge-based industries.

Jaffe (1989) and Audretsch and Feldman (1996) provided systematic empirical evidence that spatial proximity is a prerequisite to accessing such knowledge spillovers. However, they provided no insight about the actual mechanism transmitting such knowledge spillovers. As for the Romer, Lucas and Jones models, investment in new knowledge automatically generates knowledge spillovers. The only additional insight involves the spatial dimension – knowledge spills over but the spillovers are spatially bounded. Thus, the second hypothesis emerging from the knowledge spillover theory of entrepreneurship is the locational hypothesis, which posits that Empirical evidence of the locational hypothesis has been provided by Audretsch et al. (2005) and Audretsch and Lehmann (2005), who analyze a database consisting of technology and knowledge-based start-ups making an initial public offering (IPO). Their results suggest that those with a higher knowledge capacity and greater knowledge output also generate a higher number of knowledge and technology start-ups, suggesting that university spillovers are geographically bounded.

The knowledge spillover theory of entrepreneurship, which focuses on how new knowledge can influence the cognitive decision-making process inherent in the entrepreneurial decision links entrepreneurship and economic growth, is consistent with theories of industry evolution (Jovanovic, 1982; Ericson & Pakes, 1995; Audretsch, 1995; Hopenhayn, 1992; Klepper, 1996). A distinguishing feature of these evolutionary theories is the focus on change as a central phenomenon. Innovative activity, one of the central manifestations of change, is at the heart of much of this work. Entry, growth, survival and the way firms and entire industries change over time are linked to innovation. The dynamic performance of regions and even entire economies, that is the Standort, or location, is linked to the efficacy of transforming investments in new knowledge into innovative activity.

For example, Audretsch (1995) analyzes the factors that influence the rate of new firm start-ups. He finds that such start-ups are more likely in industries in which small firms account for a greater percentage of the industry's innovations. This suggests that firms are started to capitalize on distinctive knowledge about innovation that originates from sources outside of an industry's leaders. This initial condition of not just uncertainty, but greater degree of uncertainty vis-à-vis incumbent enterprises in the industry is captured in the theory of firm selection and industry evolution proposed by Jovanovic (1982). Jovanovic presents a model in which the new firms, which he terms entrepreneurs, face costs that are not only random but also differ across firms. A central feature of the model is that a new firm does not know what its cost function is, that is its relative efficiency, but rather discovers this through the process of learning from its actual post-entry performance. In particular, Jovanovic (1982) assumes that entrepreneurs are unsure about their ability to manage a new-firm startup and therefore their prospects for success. Although entrepreneurs may launch a new firm based on a vague sense of expected post-entry performance, they only discover their true ability – in terms of managerial competence and of having based the firm on an idea that is viable on the market – once their business is established. Those entrepreneurs who discover that their ability exceeds their expectations expand the scale of their business, whereas those discovering that their post-entry performance is less than commensurate with their expectations will contact the scale of output and possibly exit from the industry. Thus, Jovanovic's model is a theory of noisy selection, where efficient firms grow and survive and inefficient firms decline and fail. The links between entrepreneurship on the one hand and growth and survival on the other have been found across a number of social science disciplines, including economics, sociology and regional studies.

One of the important findings of Glaeser et al. (1992) and Feldman and Audretsch (1999) is that economic performance is promoted by knowledge spillovers. However, their findings, as well as the corroborative results from a plethora of studies, focused on a spatial unit of observation, such as cities, regions and states. For example, Glaeser et al. (1992) found compelling empirical evidence suggesting that a greater degree of knowledge spillover leads to higher growth rates of cities. If the existence of higher knowledge spillovers bestow higher growth rates for cities, this relationship should also hold for the unit of observation of the (knowledge) firm. The performance of entrepreneurial firms accessing knowledge spillovers should exhibit a superior performance. Thus, the Competitive Advantage Hypothesis states that the performance of knowledge-based start-ups should be superior when they are able to access knowledge spillovers through geographic proximity to knowledge sources, such as universities, when compared to their counterparts without a close geographic proximity to a knowledge source.

Evidence supporting the Competitive Advantage Hypothesis at the firm level has been provided by Audretsch et al. (2005), Audretsch and Lehmann (2005) and Gilbert et al. (2004), all of whom find that the competitive advantage of new-firm start-ups within close geographic proximity to knowledge sources, such as universities. In particular, Audretsch, Keilbach and Lehmann (2005) and Audretsch and Lehmann (2005) show the exact relationship between location and the competitive advantage of entrepreneurial start-ups is complex. Whether or not geographic proximity to a knowledge source, such as a university, bestows competitive benefits to an entrepreneurial firm depends on a number of factors. In particular, the impact of geographic proximity on competitive advantage is shaped by the amount and type of knowledge produced at a particular university. If the research output of a university is meager, close geographic proximity to a university will not bestow a superior competitive advantage. However, close geographic proximity to a university with a strong research output and spillover mechanisms enhances the competitive advantage of entrepreneurial start-ups. Similarly, Audretsch and Lehman (2005) and Audretsch et al. (2006) show that the benefits of geographic proximity in enhancing competitive advantage are not homogeneous but apparently vary across academic fields and disciplines.

However, the Competitive Advantage Hypothesis and supporting empirical evidence not be interpreted as attributing the entire impact of entrepreneurship on growth to be restricted to the growth of entrepreneurial firms themselves. Such an extreme assumption of no external impacts is implicit in the analyses of new and small enterprises found in the path-breaking Birch (1979) study, as well as the more recent Davis et al. (1996a, b) update. While there is severe methodological disagreement between the Davis and Birch approaches to measuring the impact of small firms on economic performance, both implicitly agree in an absence of external impact. Thus, in a type of statistical apartheid or segregation, in the Birch and Davis studies, the impact of small and new firms is measured only within that set of firms.

By contrast, the impact of entrepreneurship on economic growth is not constrained to be limited to manifest itself solely in those entrepreneurial firms, but rather has an external impact of far greater significance. The link between entrepreneurship and economic growth should also exist at the more aggregated level of economic activity. A location, or Standort endowed with a higher degree of what is Audretsch et al. (2005) and Audretsch and Keilbach (2004) term as Entrepreneurship Capital, will facilitate knowledge spillovers and the commercialization of knowledge, thereby generating greater economic growth. The Growth Hypothesis states, "Given a level of knowledge investment and severity of the knowledge filter, higher levels of economic growth should result from greater entrepreneurial activity, since entrepreneurship serves as a mechanism facilitating the spillover and commercialization of knowledge".

In introducing the model of the production function, Solow (1956) argued that economic growth is determined explicitly by the stocks of capital and labor. Technical change entered the production function exogenously as a shift factor. More recently, Romer (1986), Lucas (1993) and others extended the neoclassical model of growth by suggesting that not only is knowledge an important factor generating growth, but because it spills over for use by third-party firms, it is actually the most potent factor.

The knowledge spillover theory of entrepreneurship explained in the previous section suggests that this assessment of the role of knowledge overlooks some of the most fundamental mechanisms driving the process of economic growth. The spillover process that Romer and the endogenous growth theory assumes to be automatic is not at all automatic. Rather, it is a process that is actively driven by economic agents. According to Audretsch et al. (2005), Entrepreneurship Capital serves as a mechanism facilitating the spillover of knowledge.

While Romer and Lucas added the factor of knowledge capital to the traditional factors of physical capital and labor, Audretsch et al. (2005) do not dispute the importance of the traditional factors, but suggest an additional factor as well – the degree of entrepreneurship capital specific to a Standort, or location. By entrepreneurship capital Audretsch et al. (2005) mean the capacity for the Standort, that is the geographically relevant spatial units of observation, to generate the start-up of new enterprises.

While the neoclassical tradition identified investment in physical capital as the driving factor of economic performance (Solow, 1956), the endogenous growth theory (Romer, 1986, 1990; Lucas, 1988) put the emphasis on the process of the accumulation of knowledge, and hence the creation of knowledge capital. The concept of social capital (Putnam, 1993; Coleman, 1988) could be considered as a further extension because it added a social component to those factors shaping economic growth and prosperity. According to Putnam (2000, p. 19), "Whereas physical capital refers to physical objects and human capital refers to the properties of individuals, social capital refers to connections among individuals – social networks and the norms of reciprocity and trustworthiness that arise from them. In that sense social capital is closely related to what some have called 'civic virtue'. The difference is that 'social capital' calls attention to the fact that civic virtue is most powerful when embedded in a sense network of reciprocal social relations. A society of many virtues but isolated individuals is not necessarily rich in social capital".

Putnam also challenged the standard neoclassical growth model by arguing that social capital was also important in generating economic growth, "By analogy with notions of physical capital and human capital – tools and training that enhance individual productivity – social capital refers to features of social organization, such as networks, norms and trust, that facilitate coordination and cooperation for mutual benefits".

A large and robust literature has emerged trying to link social capital to entrepreneurship (Aldrich & Martinez, 2003; Thorton & Flynne, 2003). However, while it was clear that Putnam was providing a link between social capital and economic welfare, this link did not directly involve entrepreneurship. The components of social capital Putnam emphasized the most included associational membership and public trust. While these may be essential for social and economic well being, it was not obvious that they involved entrepreneurship, per se.

Social capital and entrepreneurship capital are distinctive concepts that should not be confused. According to Putnam (2000, p. 19), "Social capital refers to connections among individuals – social networks and the norms of reciprocity and trustworthiness that arise from them. In that sense social capital is closely related to what some have called 'civic virtue'. (…) Social capital calls attention to the fact that civic virtue is most powerful when embedded in a sense network of reciprocal social relations. (…) Social capital refers to features of social organization, such as networks, norms and trust, that facilitate coordination and cooperation for mutual benefits".

Audretsch et al. (2005) and Audretsch and Keilbach (2004) argue that what has been called social capital in the entrepreneurship literature may actually be a more specific sub-component, which we introduce as entrepreneurship capital. Entrepreneurship has typically been defined as an action, process or activity. Entrepreneurship involves the start-up and growth of new enterprises. Entrepreneurship capital involves a milieu of agents and institutions that is conducive to the creation of new firms. This involves a number of aspects such as social acceptance of entrepreneurial behavior but of course also individuals who are willing to deal with the risk of creating new firms[1] and the activity of bankers and venture capital agents that are willing to share risks and benefits involved. Hence, entrepreneurship capital reflects a number of different legal, institutional and social factors and forces. Taken together, these factors and forces constitute the entrepreneurship capital of an economy, which creates a capacity for entrepreneurial activity (Hofstede, Noorderhaven, Thurik, Wennekers, & Uhlaner, Wildeman, 2002).

It should be emphasized that entrepreneurship capital should not be confused with social capital. The major distinction is that, in our view, not all social capital may be conducive to economic performance, let alone entrepreneurial activity. Some types of social capital may be more focused on preserving the status quo and not necessarily directed at creating challenges to the status quo. By contrast, entrepreneurship capital could be considered to constitute one particular sub-set of social capital. While social capital may have various impacts on entrepreneurship, depending on the specific orientation, entrepreneurship capital, by its very definition, will have a positive impact on entrepreneurial activity.

Audretsch et al. (2005) and Audretsch and Keilbach (2004) include a measure of entrepreneurship capital, along with the traditional factors of production of labor, physical capital and knowledge capital, in a production function model to estimate economic growth. Their evidence suggests that entrepreneurship capital exerts indeed a positive impact on economic growth. This finding holds for difference measured of entrepreneurship capital, ranging from the more general to the more risk oriented.

While the findings by Audretsch et al. (2005) and Audretsch and Keilbach (2004) certainly do not contradict the conclusions of earlier studies linking growth to factors such as labor, capital and knowledge, their evidence points to an additional factor, entrepreneurship capital, that also plays an important role in generating economic growth.

The results from including measures of entrepreneurship capital in the context of estimating economic growth in a production function model are consistent with other studies also finding a positive relationship between various measures of entrepreneurship and economic growth. For example, Acs, Audretsch, Braunerhjelm, and Carlsson (2004) find a positive relationship between entrepreneurship and growth at the country level. Carree et al. (2000) provided empirical evidence from a 1984–1994 cross-sectional study of the 23 countries that are part of the Organization for Economic Co-operation and Development (OECD), that increased entrepreneurship, as measured by business ownership rates, was associated with higher rates of employment growth at the country level. Similarly, Audretsch et al. (2002) and Carree et al. (2000) find that OECD countries exhibiting higher increases in entrepreneurship also have experienced greater rates of growth and lower levels of unemployment.

In a study for the OECD, Audretsch and Thurik (2002) undertook two separate empirical analyses to identify the impact of changes of entrepreneurship on growth. Each one uses a different measure of entrepreneurship, sample of countries and specification. This provides some sense of robustness across different measures of entrepreneurship, data sets, time periods and specifications. The first analysis uses a database that measures entrepreneurship in terms of the relative share of economic activity accounted for by small firms. It links changes in entrepreneurship to growth rates for a panel of 18 OECD countries spanning five years to test the hypothesis that higher rates of entrepreneurship lead to greater subsequent growth rates. The second analysis uses a measure of self-employment as an index of entrepreneurship and links changes in entrepreneurship to unemployment at the country level between 1974 and 1998. The different samples including OECD countries over different time periods reach consistent results – increases in entrepreneurial activity tends to result in higher subsequent growth rates and a reduction of unemployment.

CONCLUSIONS

The prevalent and traditional theories of entrepreneurship have typically held the context constant and then examined how characteristics specific to the individual impact the cognitive process inherent in the model of entrepreneurial choice. This often leads to the view that, given a distribution of personality characteristics, proclivities, preferences and tastes, entrepreneurship is exogenous. One of the great conventional wisdoms in entrepreneurship is "Entrepreneurs are born not made". Either you have it or you don't. This leaves virtually no room for policy or for altering what nature has created.

The knowledge spillover theory of entrepreneurship suggests an alternative view. In the knowledge spillover theory, the individual attributes constant and instead focus on variations in the context. In particular, we consider how the knowledge context will impact the cognitive process underlying the entrepreneurial choice model. The result is a theory of endogenous entrepreneurship, where (knowledge) workers respond to opportunities generated by new knowledge by starting a new firm. In this view, entrepreneurship is a rationale choice made by economic agents to appropriate the expected value of their endowment of knowledge. Thus, the creation of a new firm is the endogenous response to investments in knowledge that have not been entirely or exhaustively appropriated by the incumbent firm.

In the endogenous theory of entrepreneurship, the spillover of knowledge and the creation of a new, knowledge-based firm are virtually synonymous. Of course, there are many other important mechanisms facilitating the spillover of knowledge that have nothing to do with entrepreneurship, such as the mobility of scientists and workers, and informal networks, linkages and interactions. Similarly, there are certainly new firms started that have nothing to do with the spillover of knowledge. Still, the spillover theory of entrepreneurship suggests that there will be additional entrepreneurial activity as a rationale and cognitive response to the creation of new knowledge. Those contexts with greater investment in knowledge should also experience a higher degree of entrepreneurship, ceteris paribus. Perhaps, it is true that entrepreneurs are made. But more of them will discover what they are made of in a high knowledge context than in an impoverished knowledge context. Thus, we are inclined to restate the conventional wisdom and instead propose that entrepreneurs are not necessarily made, bur are rather a response – and in particular a response to high knowledge contexts that are especially fertile in spawning entrepreneurial opportunities.

By endogenously facilitating the spillover of knowledge created in a different organization and perhaps for a different application, entrepreneurship may serve as the missing link to economic growth. Confronted with a formidable knowledge filter, public policy instruments emerging from the new growth theory, such as investments in human capital, R&D and university research may not adequately result in satisfactory economic growth.

By serving as a conduit for knowledge spillovers, entrepreneurship is the missing link between investments in new knowledge and economic growth. Thus, the knowledge spillover theory of entrepreneurship provides not just an explanation of why entrepreneurship has become more prevalent as the factor of knowledge has emerged as a crucial source for comparative advantage, but also why entrepreneurship plays a vital role in generating economic growth. Entrepreneurship is an important mechanism permeating the knowledge filter to facilitate the spillover of knowledge and ultimately generate economic growth. Entrepreneurship education and the transfer of technology from universities to commercialization in the private sector makes a significant contribution to economic growth by reducing the knowledge filter and facilitating the crucial missing link – entrepreneurship.

NOTES

1. As Gartner and Carter (2003) state, "Entrepreneurial behavior involves the activities of individuals who are associated with creating new organizations rather than the activities of individuals who are involved with maintaining or changing the operations of on-going established organizations".

REFERENCES

Acs, Z. J., Audretsch, D. B., Braunerhjelm, P., & Carlsson, B. (2004). *The missing link: The knowledge filter and endogenous growth* (Discussion paper). Stockholm: Center for Business and Policy Studies.

Aldrich, H. E., & Martinez, M. (2003). Entrepreneurship, networks and geographies. In: Z. J. Acs & D. B. Audretsch (Eds), *Handbook of entrepreneurship research* (pp. 359–400). Boston: Kluwer Academic Publishers.

Arrow, K. J. (1962). Economic welfare and the allocation of resources for invention. In: R. R. Nelson (Ed.), *The rate and direction of inventive activity* (pp. 609–626). Princeton: Princeton University Press.

Audretsch, D., & Keilbach, M. (2004). Entrepreneurship and regional growth: An evolutionary interpretation. *Journal of Evolutionary Economics, 14*, 605–616.

Audretsch, D., & Lehmann, E. (2005). Mansfield's missing link: The impact of knowledge spillovers on firm growth. *Journal of Technology Transfer, 30*, 207–210.

Audretsch, D. B. (1995). *Innovation and industry evolution.* Cambridge: MIT Press.

Audretsch, D. B. (2006). *The entrepreneurial socity.* New York: Oxford University Press, forthcoming.

Audretsch, D. B., Carree, M. A., van Stel, A. J., & Thurik, A. R. (2002). Impeded industrial restructuring: The growth penalty. *Kyklos, 55*, 81–98.

Audretsch, D. B., & Feldman, M. P. (1996). R&D spillovers and the geography of innovation and production. *American Economic Review, 86*, 630–640.

Audretsch, D. B., Keilbach, M., & Lehmann, E. (2006). *Entrepreneurship and economic growth.* Oxford: Oxford University Press, forthcoming.

Audretsch, D. B., & Stephan, P. E. (1996). Company-scientist locational links: The case of biotechnology. *American Economic Review, 86*, 641–652.

Audretsch, D. B., & Thurik, R. (2002). *Linking entrepreneurship to growth.* OECD STI Working Paper 2081/2.

Birch, D. (1979). *The job generation process. MIT Program on Neighborhood and Regional Change.* Cambridge: MIT.

Carree, van Stel A., Thurik, R., & Wennekers, S. (2000). Business ownership and economic growth in 23 OECD countries. Tinbergen Institute Discussion Paper. Available online: http://www.tinbergen.nl/discussionpapers/00001.pdf

Caves, R. E. (1998). Industrial organization and new findings on the turnover and mobility of firms. *Journal of Economic Literature, 36*, 1947–1982.

Coleman, J. (1998). Social capital in the creation of human capital. *American Journal of sociology, 94*, 95–121.

Davis, S., Haltiwanger, J., & Schuh, S. (1996a). *Job creation and destruction.* Cambridge: MIT Press.

Davis, S., Haltiwanger, J., & Schuh, S. (1996b). Small business and job creation: Dissecting the myth and reassessing the facts. *Small Business Economics, 8*, 297–315.

Ericson, R., & Pakes, A. (1995). Markov-perfect industry dynamics: A framework for empirical work. *Review of Economic Studies, 62*, 53–82.

Feldman, M., & Audretsch, D. (1999). Innovations in cities: Science-based diversity, specialization and localized monopoly. *European Economic Review, 43*, 409–429.

Gartner, W. B., & Carter, N. M. (2003). Entrepreneurial behaviour and firm organizing processes. In: Z. J. Acs & D. B. Audretsch (Eds), *Handbook of entrepreneurship research* (pp. 195–222). Boston: Kluwer Academic Publishers.

Gilbert, B., Audretsch, D., & McDoughall, P. (2004). The emergence of entrepreneurship policy. *Small Business Economics, 22*, 313–323.

Glaeser, E., Kallal, H., Scheinkman, J., & Shleifer, A. (1992). Growth in cities. *Journal of Political Economy, 100*, 1126–1152.

Griliches, Z. (1984). *R&D, patents and productivity*. Chicago: University of Chicago Press.

Hofstede, G., Noorderhaven, N., Thurik, A., Wennekers, A., Uhlaner, L., & Wildeman, R. (2002). Culture's role in entrepreneurship: Self-employment out of dissatisfaction. In: *Innovation, entrepreneurship and culture: The interaction between technology, progress and economic growth*. Brookfield, UK: Edward Elgar.

Hopenhayn, H. A. (1992). Entry, exit and firm dynamics in long run equilibrium. *Econometrica*, *60*, 1127–1150.

Jaffe, A. B. (1989). Real effects of academic research. *American Economic Review*, *79*, 957–970.

Jovanovic, B. (1982). Selection and evolution of industry. *Econometrica*, *50*, 649–670.

Klepper, S. (1996). Entry, exit, growth, and innovation over the product life cycle. *American Economic Review*, *86*, 562–583.

Krueger, N. F. (2003). The cognitive psychology of entrepreneurship. In: Z. J. Acs & D. B. Audretsch (Eds), *Handbook of entrepreneurship research* (pp. 105–140). Boston: Kluwer Academic Publishers.

Lucas, R. (1988). On the mechanics of economic development. *Journal of Monetary Economics*, *22*, 3–42.

Lucas, R. (1993). Making a miracle. *Econometrica*, *61*, 251–272.

McClelland, D. (1961). *The achieving society*. Boston: Kluwer Academic Publishers.

Putnam, R. D. (1993). *Making democracy work. Civic traditions in modern Italy*. Princeton: Princeton University Press.

Putnam, R. D. (2000). *Bowling alone: The collapse and revival of American community*. New York: Simon & Schuster.

Romer, P. M. (1986). Increasing returns and long-run growth. *Journal of Political Economy*, *94*, 1002–1037.

Sarasvathy, S. D., Dew, N., Velamuri, S. R., & Venkataraman, S. (2003). Three views of entrepreneurial opportunity. In: Z. J. Acs & D. B. Audretsch (Eds), *Handbook of entrepreneurship research* (pp. 141–160). Boston: Kluwer Academic Publishers.

Shane, S., & Eckhardt, J. (2003). The individual-opportunity nexus. In: Z. J. Acs & D. B. Audretsch (Eds), *Handbook of entrepreneurship research* (pp. 161–194). Boston: Kluwer Academic Publishers.

Shaver, K. G. (2003). The social psychology of entrepreneurial behaviour. In: Z. J. Acs & D. B. Audretsch (Eds), *Handbook of entrepreneurship research* (pp. 331–358). Boston: Kluwer Academic Publishers.

Solow, R. (1956). A contribution to the theory of economic growth. *Quarterly Journal of Economics*, *70*, 65–94.

Thorton, P. H., & Flynne, K. H. (2003). Entrepreneurship, networks and geographies. In: Z. J. Acs & D. B. Audretsch (Eds), *Handbook of entrepreneurship research*. Boston: Kluwer Academic Publishers.

Venkataraman, S. (1997). The distinctive domain of entrepreneurship research. In: *Advances in entrepreneurship, firm emergence and growth*. Greenwich: JAI Press.

NON-DESTRUCTIVE CREATION: HOW ENTREPRENEURSHIP SUSTAINS PROSPERITY [☆]

Amar V. Bhidé

1. INTRODUCTION

Many modern beliefs about entrepreneurship have their roots in Joseph Schumpeter's challenge to the traditional view that growth results from the accumulation of capital. According to the received wisdom of the time, thrifty ants prospered. Spendthrift grasshoppers starved.

Schumpeter argued instead that the development of new "combinations" by entrepreneurs, rather than the steady accumulation of capital, led to long-term growth. Economist Robert Solow's (1956, 1957) papers validated Schumpeter's claim. They reported the "shocking" finding that "most of the growth of the economy over the past century had been due to technological progress" (Stiglitz, 1990). An increase in the use of capital accounted for only 12.5% of the doubling of gross output per man hour from 1909 to 1949; the remaining 87.5% was due to "technical change". And, any technical change requires, as Baumol (1993) points out, entrepreneurial initiative.

☆ Based on a lecture delivered on 17 November 2004 at the Royal Society of Arts (RSA), London.

The Emergence of Entrepreneurial Economics
Research on Technological Innovation, Management and Policy, Volume 9, 55–68
ISSN: 0737-1071/doi:10.1016/S0737-1071(05)09004-9

In this lecture, I will examine how entrepreneurship contributed to economic growth in the 20th century and whether it will continue to make this contribution in the 21st century. My point of departure is Schumpeter's claim that "creative destruction" represents the essence of modern entrepreneurship – that in order to build something new the entrepreneur also has to destroy the old. In fact, I will suggest today, many innovations do not displace existing products and services because they create and satisfy entirely new wants. This non-destructive form of entrepreneurship is as necessary for economic prosperity as creative destruction.

I focus on the entrepreneurial system of the U.S. I believe my general analysis applies to other wealthy countries, but I have nothing to say about the applicability of the U.S. system to other parts of the developed world. And although I briefly discuss the phenomenon of outsourcing from low-wage countries, I do not analyze the role of entrepreneurship in these countries either.

2. SYMBIOTIC RELATIONSHIPS

Sensible people know that over the long run, economic growth requires productivity growth – for per capita living standards to increase, so must per capita output. But we often mistakenly believe that productivity growth comes just from improved efficiency – using fewer resources to satisfy our current wants. We fail to recognize that the creation and satisfaction of new wants can also increase per capita output. For instance, an artist may increase her productivity by developing new techniques that speed up her output of paintings. Alternatively, she may develop a new oeuvre that commands higher prices. She may produce exactly the same number of canvases as before, but, provided her work sells at higher prices, her economic output and productivity increases. Moreover, the new oeuvre may serve as a substitute for more traditional paintings, so innovator's productivity gain comes at the expense of the productivity of artists' who face reduced demand. But it does not have to: the new oeuvre may appeal to completely new sensibilities and find a place on walls that otherwise would have remained bare.

In fact, economies cannot sustain increases in productivity and living standards simply through increasing efficiencies in the satisfaction of existing wants. In the short run, increased efficiencies reduce costs and as costs decline, people consume more of the good or service. But, eventually, the law of diminishing utilities sets in. Sated consumers refuse to buy more even if prices continue to decline. After that, further increases in efficiencies reduce the demand for labor.

In principle, societies could accommodate the reduction in the demand for labor by increasing everyone's leisure. Over the last century, economic growth has helped reduce working hours and increase vacations. But somehow, beyond a certain point, societies seem unable to accommodate reductions in the demand for labor by spreading the work around. Efforts to control unemployment by mandating reductions in work weeks or increasing the number of holidays do not seem to work.

Rather, it is the entrepreneurial activity of creating and satisfying new wants that keeps the system humming. It employs the labor and purchasing power released by increased efficiencies in the satisfaction of old wants. It also creates incentives for continued increases in efficiencies even after demand for old wants has been fully satisfied: Producers who satisfy old wants have to keep economizing on their use of labor because they must compete for employees (and share of consumers' wallets) with innovators who satisfy new wants.

Outsourcing to low-wage countries resembles efficiency improvement in its symbiotic relationship to the satisfaction of new wants. It improves living standards in wealthy countries, provided the human capital released can be used to make new goods and services. Otherwise, like improvements in efficiency, outsourcing can reduce the demand for domestic labor.

3. THE HISTORICAL RECORD

Improvements in efficiency as well as the satisfaction of new wants played significant roles in the economic growth of the 20th century. As is well known, the industrial revolution led to a surge in incomes: According to DeLong (2000), world per capita GDP growth was virtually zero until the 18th century. In the 19th century, per capita incomes more than doubled and then in the 20th century increased more than 8-fold. According to DeLong, although virtually all of humankind saw improvements in its material well-being, growth rates were strongest in the industrial Nations of the West. For the U.S., DeLong estimates a 10.5-fold increase in real per capita GDP in the 20th century.

In part, the growth that followed the industrial revolution resulted from more efficient methods of production of existing goods. For instance, innovations, such as tractors, threshing machines, fertilizers, pesticides and hybrid seeds, led to vast improvements in agricultural productivity. As productivity increases reduced costs and increased the affordability of food, per capita consumption grew. But the increase in the consumption of food or other existing goods does not come close to accounting for the 10.5-fold increase in overall per capita GDP. According to Nordhaus's (1997) estimate, less than 30% of the goods and services consumed in 1991 bear much resemblance to the goods and services of the late 19th century. "Most of the goods we consume today" Nordhaus writes, "were not produced a century ago. We travel in vehicles that were not yet invented that are powered by fuels not yet produced, communicate through devices not yet manufactured, enjoy cool air on the hottest days, are entertained by electronic wizardry that was not dreamt of and receive medical treatments that were unheard of".

Some of the new goods replaced the goods consumed by our forebears. Cars and buses replaced horses and stagecoaches. Steamships grounded sailing ships and ready-to-eat cereal pushed homemade porridge off breakfast tables. As did the improvements in agricultural productivity, many of the new products reduced prices and costs. For instance, candles provided the primary source of artificial light till about the early 1800s. These were followed by lamps that used whale oil, sperm oil, town gas, kerosene and electricity. Nordhaus calculates that these innovations reduced the price of light by 99% – from 40 cents per 1000 lumen hours in 1800 to a 10th of a cent today.

But, in fact, many new 20th century products did not displace existing products – rather they created new markets and satisfied new wants. They were like a new oeuvre of art purchased for spaces that would otherwise remained bare. Air-conditioners reduced temperatures in previously uncooled factories stores and office buildings. Airplanes did not reduce the demand for automobiles – people flew when they would not have driven. New drugs and vaccines offered cures for diseases for which treatments did not previously exist. In 1938, the New York Times observed that the typewriter was "driving out writing with one's own hand", yet Petroski (1990) reports the sale of 14 billion pencils in 1990.

Moreover, even those apparently destructive new products also created new markets because they had features that the products they displaced did not. For instance, automobiles provided much faster and not just cheaper transportation than horse carriages, so people could live in spacious houses located at some distance from their workplace. This helped create demand for suburban housing that did not previously exist. Similarly, incandescent lamps did not merely replace candles and kerosene lamps: their intense luminosity helped create a market for cricket and baseball played at night.

The innovations in information technology (IT) of the late 20th century have followed the same pattern as the electromechanical innovations of earlier decades. According to a U.S. Department of Commerce (1998) report, the share of the IT sector (computing and communications) grew from 4.2% of the gross domestic product of the U.S. in 1977 to 6.1% in 1990 to 8.2% in 1998. This is not because computers have displaced traditional goods and services. Rather, IT has accounted for a disproportionate share of growth: according to the Department of Commerce, IT industries have been responsible for more than one-quarter of real economic growth that is, about 3 times their share of the economy.

The digital revolution has certainly involved some substitution. For instance, calculators displaced slide rules, microprocessor-based workstations displaced minicomputers and CD players displaced cassette tape recorders. But there has also been at least as much non-destructive creation. The personal computer (PC) did not blow away the traditional mainframe computer in a gale of creative destruction. The PC's killer application, the spreadsheet, did not displace any existing mainframe-based applications. Rather, it allowed users, many of whom had not previously used computers extensively, to perform analyses and simulations which they would not have otherwise performed. Similarly, the enormous growth of the home market for PCs did not reduce the demand for mainframe computers.

Over 30 years after the introduction of minicomputers and more than 20 years after the introduction of microcomputers, the mainframe remains an important category. Total worldwide revenues of large-scale computer processors (or mainframes) amounted to USD 16 billion in 1997 compared to USD 16.2 billion in 1982. But, because total demand grew from USD 38 billion to USD 183 billion, mainframes' share of the total computer market dropped considerably, from 42% to about 9% (Bhidé, 2000). The role of PCs in expanding the pie rather than destroying existing markets apparently represents a common feature of the digital revolution. New communication services – e-mail, newsgroups and "chat" – provided a critical mass of users for the Internet and on line services, such as AOL. These services do not however seem to have abated the demand for traditional phone lines – U.S. cities continue to require new area codes. And those new products that have displaced old products, have often done so after they have created a new market. For instance, as I discovered in the course of a consulting study for a now defunct typewriter manufacturer, shipments of word processing units increased 14-fold growth between 1977 and 1981. But, because word processors increased primary demand by satisfying some hitherto unmet want, the sales for typewriters in the U.S.

remained steady at around a million units a year during this period. Similarly, one day (after standards and coverage issues have been resolved) cell phones may make landline phones obsolete. But not before, consumers have purchased hundreds of millions of units in applications where landline phones had not been used.

Innovations that created markets for new goods and services gave lie to predictions that mechanization and mass production would create mass unemployment. Productivity improvements on the farm, which would ultimately allow about 2% of the workforce to feed the entire population, reduced agricultural employment in the U.S. from 11.7 million in 1900 to 5.9 million in 1960. Changes in production technologies also put many highly skilled artisans out of work. But total employment more than doubled – from 29 million in 1900 to 68 million in 1960. The labor released by the farm and workshop was quickly absorbed by factories established to serve new markets. And, the assembly line worker earned more than the farmer or skilled artisan. For instance, by 1900, the average annual manufacturing wage was more than twice the agricultural wage. This gap continued to widen, as real wages in manufacturing increased at 1.7% per year through the first 7 decades of the 20th century.

Products that satisfied new wants also created jobs in new service industries. Refrigerators and air-conditioners had to be transported, advertised, sold by a new kind of retailer, installed and periodically serviced. The transportation, advertising, retailing and other such "service" industries in fact created more jobs than the manufacturing sector. As early as 1920 – long before the term the "service economy" had been coined – employment in trade, transportation and other private service providing sectors was 15% greater than in the manufacturing. By the end of the 1960s, employment was nearly 70% greater.

Although wages in the manufacturing sector stagnated after the 1970s and manufacturing jobs topped out at about 20 million in 1980, overall employment and incomes in the U.S. continued to rise. The number of gainfully employed Americans in 2000, for instance, was 135 million – a nearly 35% increase over the 99 employed individuals in 1980. Real U.S. GDP per capita during this period rose by 57% and disposable personal incomes by nearly 50%. Apparently the growth of businesses in sectors, such as IT, that satisfied new wants more than compensated for the lack of growth in manufacturing. For instance, the production of computers, semiconductors and communications equipment increased 13-fold between 1992 and 2000. Employment in IT services nearly doubled in this period from just over 2 million to 3.6 million. Wages in this sector are about 85% higher than in the economy as a whole. The growth in IT wages has likewise been about 1.6 times faster.

In the latter half of the 20th century, the expansion of markets for new goods and services encouraged – and was facilitated by – imports from low-wage countries. According to Leamer's (2001) calculations, merchandise imports amounted to about 20% of U.S. production between 1900 and 1930. This number then fell to less than 10% after the Hawley–Smoot Act, which imposed tariffs on imports from 15% to 60% and the outbreak of World War II. U.S. imports revived slowly in the 1950s and 1960s before accelerating in the 1970s. Now, more than half of manufactured goods consumed in the U.S. are made abroad.

The resources released by imports fostered the growth of industries that satisfied new wants in the U.S. Cheap TV sets from the Far East allowed U.S. households the wherewithal to purchase PCs powered by Intel microprocessors and Microsoft software. Similarly, engineering graduates who would have otherwise been employed by U.S. TV manufacturers were available for employment by U.S. IT companies. Conversely, the growth in incomes and employment in the new industries helped U.S. consumers pay for the goods produced overseas.

4. DISTINCTIVE FEATURES

To understand what made the entrepreneurial system so good at creating and satisfying new wants, let us examine some differences in the economic performance of the 19th and 20th centuries. As mentioned, growth was slower during the 19th century even though the level of incomes and productivity at the start of the period was lower. The higher "base" at the start of the 20th century should have meant lower rates of growth. Standard supply side arguments would also predict more sluggish growth – tax rates were higher in the 20th century, regulation more extensive and property rights were arguably weaker. Economic activity was less volatile in the 20th century, in spite of two great wars. In the 19th century, several depressions interrupted economic growth. In the 20th century, apart from the Great Depression, downturns were relatively mild and short-lived. Schumpeter attributed booms and depressions to periodic bursts of creative destruction followed by lulls in innovative activity. Why did not this occur in the 20th century? Was it simply because the more effective use of counter-cyclical fiscal and monetary policies eliminated booms and bursts?

Another puzzle. As mentioned, technical progress rather than capital accumulation was the principal source of growth in the 20th century. Crafts's (2000) estimates suggest that in the 19th century capital accumulation made a larger contribution to growth than did technical change. Yet, the new products invented in the 19th century were extraordinary. The inventions credited to the period 1850–1900 include the monorail, the telephone, the microphone, the cash register, the phonograph, the incandescent lamp, dynamite, the electric train, linotype printing, the steam turbine, the gasoline engine, the street car, movies, motorcycles, automobiles, refrigerators, concrete and steel construction, pneumatic tires, aspirin and X-rays. These may well overshadow inventions credited to the entire 20th century.

The entrepreneurial system that evolved during the 20th century has three features that can help explain these puzzles.

4.1. Broad Participation

Participation in the process of creating and satisfying new wants became more broad-based and inclusive. In the 19th century, inventions of new products were made by a few individuals. Edison brought forth a remarkable cornucopia including incandescent bulbs, motion pictures and gramophones, from a small facility in Menlo Park (New Jersey, not California) with fewer employees than the typical Silicon Valley start-up. Alexander Graham Bell had one assistant. Automobile pioneers were one or two man shows – Karl Benz and Gottlieb Daimler in Germany, Armand Peugeot in France and the Duryea brothers of Springfield in Massachusetts.

But small outfits could not develop products for mass consumption. The early automobiles were expensive contraptions, owned, according to Rosenberg (1976), by a few buffs who rode around the countryside terrifying horses. They could not be used for day-to-day transportation because they broke down frequently and lacked a supporting network of service stations and paved roads. One or two brilliant inventors could not solve these problems on their own.

In the 20th century the tasks of converting inventions into mass-market products pervaded society. As often as not, the pioneers paved the way for followers who built on and refined the first offerings. Planned and unwitting collaborations, taking place simultaneously and in sequence made products that initially only kind of, sort of worked commercially viable. For instance, when the first PC, the Altair, was introduced in 1975, its aficionados derived less practical use from their machines than did the turn-of-the-century automobile buffs. Lacking basic input or output devices, such as keyboards and printers, Altairs could not even scare horses. Numerous innovations – such as electronic spreadsheets, the mouse, graphical user interfaces and local area networks – turned this oddity into a ubiquitous artifact. A procession of individuals – Ed Roberts, Gates and Allen, Jobs and Wozniak, Bricklin and Frankston, Mitch Kapor and Robert Metcalf – to name just a few, made all this happen. Only a few of their individual contributions represented breakthroughs, but collectively they created an industry that changed the world.

Similarly, the Internet does not have a solitary Alexander Graham Bell. Rather, many entrepreneurs, venture capitalists, executives of large companies, members of standard setting institutions, researchers in university, commercial and state-sponsored laboratories, and even investment bankers and politicians have revolutionized the way we communicate. Some participants in the revolution have acquired considerable wealth but not fame. Mention of Sir Timothy Berners-Lee's name, for instance, often evokes puzzled looks.

Many consumers – and not just a few well-to-do buffs – have taken chances on products intended to satisfy wants they did not realize they ever had. Although its importance is often overlooked, this "venturesome consumption" has played a critical role. The success of the Japanese consumer electronics industry, I once wrote (Bhidé, 1983), has as much to do with the spirited purchasing habits of Japanese consumers as it does of the innovativeness of Japanese producers. But, while Japanese consumers have been venturesome in just a few spheres, U.S. consumers have been willing to try all sorts of novelties. And with many willing subjects, U.S. entrepreneurs have been able to conduct a large number of experiments.

In turn extensive experimentation, in conjunction with improved monetary and fiscal tools, may have helped eliminate the booms and busts that Schumpeter attributed to innovative activity. When entrepreneurs conduct many different experiments, the probability that at all times some new industry will boom increases. Thus, in the midst of a deep recession in 1982, the PC industry took off and in the current downturn, WiFi sales have surged.

Broad participation in the entrepreneurial system, in turn, was facilitated by an educational system that made literacy nearly universal and provided college educations to about 30 million members of the U.S. workforce. The belief that change is desirable and inevitable also grew beyond a few visionaries. Many came to believe that they could prosper by pursuing the new, new thing, and if they did not, they risked falling behind.

Their growing acceptance turned such beliefs into self-fulfilling prophecies. Consider, for instance, Gordon Moore's famous observation that the number of transistors that built on a chip doubles every 18th month. Semiconductor companies, who believe in this so-called "law", invest the resources needed to make it come true. Downstream customers, such as PC manufacturers, and providers of complementary goods to their customers, such as applications software companies, design products in anticipation of the 18-month cycle. So, when the new chips arrive, they find a ready market, which in turn validates beliefs in Moore's law and encourages even more investment in building and using new chips.

Similarly, the propensity of consumers to open their hearts and wallets to new offerings has involved the dilution of prior beliefs in the moral and economic value of thrift. Through the end of the 19th century, according to Max Weber's thesis, religious convictions about thrift sustained the "spirit of capitalism". Weber argued that merchants and industrialists accumulated capital and believed that they had a moral duty to strive for wealth as well as to lead austere lives. In fact, because venturesome production requires venturesome consumption, excessive thrift injures, rather than helps modern capitalism. As it happens, U.S. consumers have been more inclined to keeping up with the recently acquired baubles of their neighbors than toward excessive thrift. Their venturesome spending has also been sustained by an efficient marketing and distributions system and by a financial system that provides credit to the young and penurious.

4.2. Diversity of the Entrepreneurial Species

A diverse set of organizational forms evolved in the 20th century system that specialized in different kinds of innovation. As mentioned, in the 19th century innovation was undertaken by individuals or very small firms. The large professionally managed corporation became an important contributor to innovation in the first half of the 20th century. In the second half of the century, the diversity of the entrepreneurial species further increased. Researcher laboratories in universities that had hitherto focused just on creating knowledge began to develop commercially useful technologies. Similarly, professionally managed venture capital funds saw explosive growth.

The emergence of new organizations did not make individual entrepreneur extinct. Rather, the old and new entrepreneurial species complemented each other's contributions. The big publicly traded corporation, for instance, has the capacity to undertake very large initiatives that require the advance coordination of many individuals and the pooling of the capital of many investors. Individual entrepreneurs face capital constraints and the coordination of their efforts occurs more through after the fact mutual reaction, rather than through conscious planning. But the same governance mechanisms that give big corporations an advantage in pooling capital and labor also discourages them from undertaking novel initiatives, where it is difficult to reach a consensus about likely outcomes. Individual entrepreneurs in contrast can freely pursue novel projects because they are not answerable to anyone.

Therefore, swarms of individuals often conduct the early experiments from which new industries emerge. Then, after the early uncertainties have been resolved, organizations which can mobilize resources on a larger scale help bring the new products and services into the mainstream. For instance, between 1975 and 1980 individual entrepreneurs, rather than large companies tried to create useful applications for PCs when they were quirky toys. But, after these efforts had borne fruit, it was the launch of IBM's PC in 1981 (when IBM accounted for more than 60% of the worldwide sales of mainframe computers) that "legitimized" the PC with data-processing managers of large companies. The multi-billion dollar investments that Intel and Microsoft made, after that helped carry the PC into virtually every home and office.

Similarly, talk about the potential of nano-technology dates back to at least the early 1990s; but, actual investment by public companies and venture capitalists has been small. Much of the action has come from individual entrepreneurs and university researchers who have been following their dreams and hunches. If and when their efforts succeed, we can expect to see the large capital providers to jump in.

4.3. Incentives for "Non-Destructive" Creation

Entrepreneurial individuals and firms do not have any altruistic concern about the instability of a system that relies just on creative destruction; rather, they undertake non-destructive innovations because creating and satisfying new wants often provides more attractive opportunities. The early technical deficiencies of new products, like automobiles and PCs, make them unsuitable substitutes for existing tried and tested substitutes. Therefore, as Christensen (1997) has pointed out, innovative products usually start up serving a function that existing products do not.

Even, when a new product is technically superior, displacing an existing product is expensive. The innovator has to overcome resistance from the businesses that face the threat of substitution as well as from users who have invested in the old regime. For instance, theaters which now use projectors for celluloid film have been unwilling to incur the costs of switching over to higher quality digital projection systems. Overcoming this resistance reduces the profitability of the enterprise and makes the funding requirements prohibitive for many entrepreneurs.

For large companies, the incentive to favor non-creative destruction is weaker but not absent. They do have the resources to overcome the unwillingness of consumers to incur switching costs. And, where they are the incumbent oligopolists, the issue of competitive retaliation does not arise. But large companies also face pressure from stock markets and employees to keep increasing their revenues. This encourages large companies to develop new sources of revenues, rather that substitutes for their existing revenues. For instance, Cringely (1996) suggests that IBM executives backed its PC initiative in 1980 because they thought PCs would not reduce the demand for IBM's other products, so "every sales dollar brought in to buy a microcomputer would be a dollar that would not otherwise have come to IBM". Similarly, the "rational drug discovery approach" established by Roy Vagelos at Merck stipulated that the company would focus on areas "where there were no therapies or drugs available" (Nichols, 1994).

5. LOOKING AHEAD

The new want machine, which has an excellent record, does not however create jobs at exactly the same rate as increases in efficiency and outsourcing, or cyclical downturns, causes traditional industries to shed them. And indeed, following the boom years in the late 1990s when unemployment reached historic lows, the new want machine appears to have been unable to keep up. Is this a permanent phenomenon that will resurrect luddites and protectionists?

No one can predict when new industries will start adding jobs faster than old industries shed them. Standard macro-economic policies cannot speed things up. Tax cuts and easy money might stimulate "old" economy demand for automobiles and housing, but they cannot overcome the unwillingness of U.S. consumers to use short messaging services (SMS) on their cell phones. Nor can powerful private sector patrons ensure success. In the early 1980s, for instance, venture capitalists and entrepreneurs were much taken by the promise of artificial intelligence. They started so many companies around MIT that a portion of East Cambridge came to be known as Intelligence Alley. To my knowledge, none of these companies survive. Microsoft bet big and wrong on proprietary on line services instead on the Internet. Kleiner Perkins, the venture capital firm that counts Sun Microsystems among its many successes invested in the Segway Human Transporter. A senior partner, John Doerr, said that the Segway would be "as big as the Internet". It is not yet.

But, although it would be foolhardy to make predictions about what great new markets lurk around the corner, we have every reason to believe that that the new want machine remains in excellent shape.

We have not run out opportunities for non-destructive creation. It may be true, because we have run out of "stomach space" (Bresnahan & Gordon, 1997) new food products must replace old food products. We may also have exhausted our "free" time – cellular phones that may not displace landlines, do absorb the time that we might otherwise devote to quiet reverie. Nevertheless the scope for satisfying other kinds of new wants remains ample.

Expenditures on health care, for instance, are almost certain to expand. Modern medicine found cures for many diseases in the 20th century and increased life expectancies in the U.S. for 47 years in 1900 to 77 today. No treatments exist however for a great many other diseases and current life expectancies are well below any theoretical limit for the human life span. The aging of the population similarly provides ample opportunities for goods and services that enhance the quality of the lives of older citizens. Among the young (or would-be young), the desire to look and feel good has sustained many new businesses. The number of health clubs in the U.S. has tripled in the last 20 years and now have 13% of Americans enrolled as members. Cool new ways for altering body parts continue to be found: a doctor in LA has apparently just pioneered the implantation of tiny platinum jewels, shaped like a star into the corner of the whites of the eye (Rundle, 2004). Businesses have created non-destructive sales by finding new ways to tickle the senses, for instance, by selling ringer tones and face plates for cellular phones. Such consumption might not please all tastes, but they have maintained the growth of the modern shopping basket in the past and in all likelihood will continue to do so in the future.

The system for discovering and exploiting these opportunities is in excellent shape; its crucial elements have become stronger over the years, not weaker. The number of individuals who can and want to participate in entrepreneurial activities and the diversity of organizations through which they can participate is greater than ever before. So, whereas the performance of the 20th century economy is a difficult act to follow, we have reasons to hope for an encore.

REFERENCES

Baumol, W. J. (1993). *Entrepreneurship, management and the structure of payoffs*. Cambridge, MA: The MIT Press.

Bhidé, A. (1983). Beyond Keynes: Demand side economics. *Harvard Business Review, 6*(4), 100–110.

Bhidé, A. (2000). *The origin and evolution of new business*. New York: Oxford University Press.

Bresnahan, T. F., & Gordon, R. J. (1997). Introduction. In: T. F. Bresnahan & R. J. Gordon (Eds), *The economics of new goods* (p.16). Chicago: The University of Chicago Press.

Christensen, C. M. (1997). *The innovator's dilemma: When new technologies cause great firms to fail*. Boston: The Harvard Business School Press.

Crafts, N. (2000). *Globalization and growth in the twentieth century*. IMF Working Paper.

Cringely, R. X. (1996). *Accidental empires*. New York: Harper Business.

DeLong, J. B. (2000). *The shape of twentieth century economic history*. NBER Working Paper 7569.

Leamer, E. (2001). Who is afraid of global trade? Unpublished manuscript.

Nichols, N. (1994). Medicine, management and mergers: An interview with Merck's P. Roy Vagelos. *Harvard Business Review, 72*(1), 104–114.

Nordhaus, W. D. (1997). Do real-output and real-wage measures capture reality? The history of lighting suggests not. In: T. F. Bresnahan & R. J. Gordon (Eds), *The economics of new goods* (pp. 29–66). Chicago: The University of Chicago Press.

Petroski, H. (1990). *The pencil: A history of design and circumstance*. New York: Alfred A. Knopf.

Rosenberg, N. (1976). *Perspectives on technology*. Cambridge, U.K.: Cambridge University Press.

Rundle, R. L. (2004). Eye doctor to elite blazes new trail in selling surgery. *Wall Street Journal* (October 26), A1.

Solow, R. M. (1956). A contribution to the theory of economic growth. *Quarterly Journal of Economics, 70*, 65–94.

Solow, R. M. (1957). Technical change and the aggregate production function. *Review of Economics and Statistics, 39*(3), 312–320.

Stiglitz, J. (1990). Comments: Some retrospective views on growth theory. In: P. Diamond (Ed.), *Growth/productivity/unemployment: Essays to celebrate Bob Solow's birthday*. Cambridge, MA: The MIT Press.

U.S. Department of Commerce. (1998). *The emerging digital economy*. Washington, DC.

PART II

HOW PERSISTENT ARE REGIONAL START-UP RATES? AN EMPIRICAL ANALYSIS

Michael Fritsch and Pamela Mueller

ABSTRACT

We investigate regional differences in the level and the development of regional new business formation activity. There is a pronounced variance of start-up rates across the regions. The level of regional new firm formation is rather path-dependent resulting in relatively small changes. The main factors determining the level of regional start-ups are innovative activity and entrepreneurship. These factors are also responsible for changes in the level of regional new business formation. The growth of regional demand and regional unemployment do not play a significant role for the change of regional start-up activity. Steering innovation and creating an entrepreneurial atmosphere could be an appropriate starting point for policy measures that try to promote start-ups. Our empirical evidence strongly suggests that such measures may have significant effect only in the long run.

The Emergence of Entrepreneurial Economics
Research on Technological Innovation, Management and Policy, Volume 9, 71–82
Copyright © 2005 by Elsevier Ltd.
ISSN: 0737-1071/doi:10.1016/S0737-1071(05)09005-0

1. THE PROBLEM

Recent studies have confirmed the popular expectation that new business formation has a positive impact on economic development.[1] Although the determinants of new business formation have been analyzed very well (see for example Armington & Acs, 2002; Audretsch & Fritsch, 1994a; Reynolds, Storey, & Westhead, 1994; Fritsch & Falck, 2002), hardly anything is known about to what extend the level of start-up activity may change. How persistent is the level of regional start-up activity, how can regional start-up activity be stimulated, and to what extend is new business formation suited as a target variable for policy makers to boost economic growth?

In this chapter we analyze the persistence of regional new business formation activity over a period of 20 years in order to assess the magnitude and the pace of changes that have occurred. Furthermore, we identify the factors that determine the development of new business formation activity (Section 4) and draw conclusions with regard to strategy and measures of a policy for stimulating new business formation and entrepreneurship (Section 5). We begin with some basic information on the data and on measurement issues (Section 2).

2. DATA AND MEASUREMENT ISSUES

The information on new business formation and regional employment is from the establishment file of the German Social Insurance Statistics, as described and documented by Fritsch and Brixy (2004).[2] The information for West Germany is currently available on a yearly basis for a relatively long time, ranging from 1983 to 2002. The spatial framework is the level of planning regions. These regions are functional units that consist of at least one core city and the surrounding area (for details, see Bundesamt für Bauwesen und Raumordnung, 2003).

In order to be able to judge if the level of start-up activity in a certain region is relatively high or relatively low compared to other regions, or if some regions are more entrepreneurial than others, the number of start-ups should be related to the economic potential of the respective region. Therefore, we use the start-up rate according to the *labor market* approach, which means that the number of start-ups per period is divided by the number of persons in the regional workforce at the beginning of the respective period, including those persons that are recorded as unemployed.[3] The entry rate according to the labor market approach may be interpreted as the propensity of a member of the regional workforce to start his or her own business.

3. THE EVOLUTION OF NEW BUSINESS FORMATION 1983–2002

Between 1983 and 2002 there were on average 126,000 start-ups per year in the private sector. Over the years, the number of start-ups increased slightly with a relatively distinct rise between 1990 and 1991 and between 1997 and 1999.[4] Compared to the 1983–1989 period, where on average 117,235 new businesses were recorded, the average number of new businesses in the 1990–1997 period increased to 131,651 (+ 12.3 percent) and rose to 153,469 (+ 30.9 percent) in the 1998–2002 period. The majority of the new businesses, about 93,400 per year (74 percent of all start-ups), were in the service sector compared to about 13,800 new establishments per year (11 percent) in manufacturing.[5] There was an overall trend towards an increasing share of start-ups in the service sector and a corresponding decreasing share in manufacturing (Fig. 1). In the service sector, most of the new establishments were set up in wholesale and resale trade, hotels and inns, and the

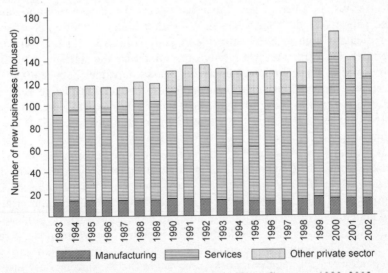

Fig. 1. Number of Start-ups per Year in West Germany 1983–2002.

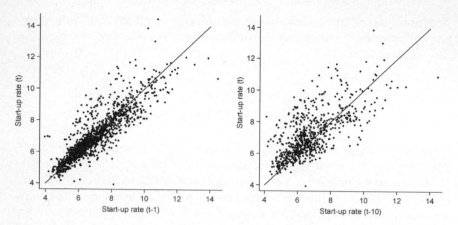

Fig. 2. Relationship between Start-up Rates in Subsequent Years (*t* and *t*−1) and over a 10-Year Period (*t* and *t*−10).

non-specified "other" services. In manufacturing, most start-ups were in electrical engineering, furniture, and food.

The development of new business formation activity is also rather steady on the regional level (Fig. 2). In order to be able to draw a comparison, start-up rates are analyzed. Investigating the relationship between regional start-up rates (number of new businesses per 1,000 employees and unemployed persons) in different years shows rather high correlation coefficients that indicate a high level of path dependency (Fig. 2 and Table A1 in the Appendix). Start-up rates are highly determined by the start-up rates from previous years. The correlation coefficients assume values between 0.95 and 0.98, if start-up rates of subsequent years are considered (Table A1). The relationship is not as close for years that are farther apart, but even over a 10-, 15-, and 19-year period the value of the correlation coefficient always remains above 0.76. There is a slight variation with regard to the closeness of the relationship between the different years, but the basic pattern is remarkably constant. Obviously, entrepreneurial activity is rather persistent over time – on the national and on a regional level.[6] This suggests that entrepreneurial culture has to be regarded as a kind of 'capital' that is accumulated over longer periods of time. In comparison to the persistency of start-up rates over time, we find a high variation between start-up rates over space. The minimum regional start-up rate is about 4 start-ups per 1,000 persons in the regional work force while the maximum start-up rate amounts to a little more than 14 (Fig. 2).

In order to analyze the path dependency of start-up rates in more detail and to determine the magnitude of changes, rank positions were assigned to each region with regard to their level of new business formation activity. Since we are not interested in the short run fluctuations, but rather the developments in the medium and long run, we analyzed the changes of rank positions between 5-year periods; the average start-up rates in the 1984–1987, 1988–1992, 1993–1997, and in the 1998–2002 period. The advantage of taking rank positions is that they display the relative performance of the regions independent of the national trend. Rank 74 is assigned to the region with the highest start-up rate, and rank 1 to the region with the lowest start-up rate in each period.

The analysis reveals that changes in rank positions tend to be relatively modest. The regions hardly ever experience a rank change of more than 20 rank positions between two successive 5-year periods. The number of regions with rank changes of more than 20 rank positions increases with the length of time period. On average, less than half of the regions experienced a change of more than three rank positions between two successive time periods. In more than 85 percent of the regions changes between two successive time periods did not exceed 10 rank positions. The greatest change between two successive periods amounted to 25 rank positions, and the maximum change over four periods (period 1984–1987 to 1998–2002) is 30 rank positions (for details see Fritsch & Mueller, 2005a).

4. WHAT DETERMINES THE LEVEL AND CHANGES OF REGIONAL START-UP ACTIVITY?

It is a prevailing hypothesis in the literature that entrepreneurship is closely linked to innovation activity and structural change. Particularly, the qualification and knowledge of the regional workforce as well as the intensity of entrepreneurial 'spirit' in a region may have a pronounced effect on the level of new business start-ups (see Fritsch & Falck, 2002; Armington & Acs, 2002; Reynolds, Storey, & Westhead, 1994 for an overview). We measure the level of *innovation activity* by the share of employees devoted to research and development.[7] The *share of employees in small and young establishments*, namely businesses with less than 20 employees, which are at maximum 3 years old, stands for the regional level of entrepreneurship. We assume that small and young firms can be regarded as seedbed for entrepreneurship.[8] A high proportion of small firm employment may also indicate low minimum efficient size of the industries in the respective region that can be assumed favorable for entry (Fritsch & Falck, 2002). Moreover, small average establishment size implies that there is a relatively high number of establishments and entrepreneurs located in the region.

The change of real gross value added over 2-year periods is also included since it can be expected that growth of *regional demand* stimulates new business formation activity. *Population density* has the role of a catch all variable that is meant to control for diverse kinds of regional characteristics such as availability of qualified labor, land prices and the level of regional knowledge spillovers, we also include population density. In order to measure the *path-dependency* of regional start-up rates, we used the start-up rate of the previous 2-year period. Spatial autocorrelation is accounted for by including the average value of the residuals for adjacent regions.

The estimates for the determinants of the start-up rate confirm our expectations (Table 1).[9] In the econometric analysis the dependent variable regional start-up rate as well as the independent variables are average values of two successive years, resulting in nine periods. In addition to pooled regression we also applied panel regression with fixed effects in order to exploit the panel character of our data set.[10] According to the results, the level of innovative activity and the level of entrepreneurship as well as regional economic growth have a significantly positive effect on regional start-ups. The coefficient for population density is not significant. The high coefficient and t-value for the lagged start-up rate indicate a strong degree of path-dependency. This path-dependency and the spatial autocorrelation are mainly responsible for the relatively high value of the R^2. Excluding the lagged start-up rate and the control variable for spatial autocorrelation leads to a decrease of the R^2 to about 0.7. Including the start-up rates for more remote time periods shows a significantly positive impact, but the coefficients decrease with the time lag. Because of a high degree of correlation between the regional unemployment rate and regional economic growth in the preceding period, both variables should not be included into the same model. Substituting the growth variable by the unemployment rate did not result in a significant impact of unemployment on new business formation activity.

For an analysis of the factors that determine changes of regional new business formation activity, the percent change of the start-up rate in two successive years was the dependent variable (Table 1). The average percentage change of the regional start-up rate over a 2-year period is 0.42 percent. The maximum increase amounts to $+20.71$ percent and the highest decrease is -27.67 percent. In comparison, the absolute change of the

Table 1. Determinants of the Level and Changes of New Business Formation Activity.

	Start-up Rate		Change Start-up Rate (%)	
	(I)	(II)	(III)	(IV)
	Pooled HWS	Fixed Effects	Pooled HWS	Fixed Effects
Innovation	0.005	0.645**	0.078	0.011
activity $(t-1)$	(0.39)	(6.31)	(1.33)	(0.20)
Change of	—	—	0.498*	8.75**
innovation			(2.30)	(4.20)
activity $(t-1)$				
Entrepreneurial	0.113**	0.106*	0.336**	0.342**
climate $(t-1)$	(5.84)	(2.44)	(3.90)	(7.66)
Change of	—	—	2.416**	4.556**
entrepreneurial			(7.61)	(5.47)
climate $(t-1)$				
Population density	−0.000	0.002	−0.001	0.090**
$(t-1)$	(0.32)	(0.80)	(1.39)	(2.79)
Regional	0.006*	0.015**	−0.302**	−0.074
economic	(2.01)	(4.03)	(5.72)	(1.30)
growth $(t-1)$				
Start-up rate $(t-1)$	0.804**	0.150**	−3.136**	−12.26**
	(32.97)	(4.14)	(8.94)	(14.58)
Change of start-up	—	—	−0.530**	−0.863**
rate, percentage			(16.19)	(20.70)
$(t-1)$				
Spatial error	0.947**	0.952**	1.054**	0.949**
	(25.55)	(21.02)	(19.40)	(14.47)
Constant	0.513**	3.177**	6.608**	6.171**
	(6.00)	(5.37)	(4.84)	(0.61)
R^2-adjusted	0.9442	—	0.7687	—
R^2-within	—	0.6838	—	0.8132
R^2-overall	—	0.0123	—	0.0623
F-Value	1223.20	131.21	111.49	138.80
Observations	444	444	370	370

HWS: Huber-White robust estimator.
t-values in parentheses.
*Significant at 5%-level.
**Significant at 1% level.

regional start-up rates is on average +0.003 with a minimum of −2.08 and a maximum of +1.65. As independent variables, we included the level of innovation activity (share of R&D employees), the level of entrepreneurship (share of small and young establishments), the start-up rate in the preceding period, regional economic growth as well as percent changes of innovation activity, percent changes of entrepreneurship, and percent changes of the start-up rate as compared to the previous period. In order to control for diverse kinds of regional characteristics such as availability of qualified labor, land prices, and the level of regional knowledge spillovers, we again include population density. Moreover, spatial autocorrelation is accounted for by the average value of the average error term of the adjacent regions.

Remarkably, the change of innovation activity as well as the level and the change of entrepreneurship have a positive effect on the change of the start-up rate. This suggests that a high level of regional entrepreneurship fuels new business formation processes. This positive impact of the already existing level of entrepreneurship on the change of start-up activity indicates some self-energizing effects of entrepreneurship in the sense that regions with a pronounced tradition in entrepreneurship are obviously able to perpetuate this tradition over time. The negative coefficient for the lagged start-up variable and the change of the start-up rate in the preceding period indicates a "regression to the mean"-phenomenon. If the level of start-up activity is already high, it is more likely to decrease or remain constant than to further increase in the next period. The lagged start-up rate can also be regarded as a control for reversed causality that might be an issue in this model.[11] The regional growth rate in the preceding period has no stimulating effect on the start-up rate. In fact, the coefficient for this variable turns out to be significantly negative in Model III. Obviously, the level of start-up activity is not driven by demand but by factors that are on the supply side of the economy.

5. HOW FEASIBLE IS ENTREPRENEURSHIP?

We found considerable differences of regional start-up rates, and it is quite likely that these differences have consequences for regional development, albeit in the long run. The analysis showed that the level of regional start-up activity is highly path-dependent and that changes tend to be rather small. This high degree of persistence suggests that there are only weak prospects for rapid change with regard to regional new business formation activity. Therefore, a policy that is aiming at increasing the regional level of entrepreneurship needs enough time and a long-term orientation. According to our results, it appears quite likely that the main benefits of such a policy will arise only for future generations but not for the current one. Our analyses of these factors that determine the development of regional new business for-mation clearly indicate a strong influence of innovation and of the already existing level of entrepreneurship. These two issues should be the main starting points for a policy that would like to stimulate new businesses formation in certain regions. One should, however, be aware that a number of factors that might have a significant impact on the level of entrepreneurial activity such as taxes and welfare arrangements are mainly decided on a national level and in most countries do not differ much between regions (Audretsch, Thurik, Verheul, & Wennekers, 2002).

Future research should focus on at least two questions. First, what kind of measures would be appropriate for stimulating a regional culture of en-trepreneurship? Second, what type of innovation promotion policy would be suited for raising the level of entrepreneurship? If entrepreneurship 'capital' is an important resource for growth we should try to learn much more about ways how it can be created.

NOTES

1. Fritsch and Mueller (2004, 2005b), van Stel and Storey (2004), Mueller, van Stel and Storey (2005), Baptista, Escária and Madruga (2005).
2. This database provides information about all establishments that have at least one employee subject to obligatory social insurance. Therefore, start-ups consisting of only owners are not included. In order to capture regional entrepreneurship, we exclude new businesses with more than 20 employees in the first year of their ex-istence; as a result, a considerable number of new subsidiaries of large firms con-tained in the database are not counted as start-ups.
3. See Audretsch and Fritsch (1994b) for different approaches of calculating start-up rates.
4. The reasons for these two increases are largely unclear. It would not be very farfetched to suspect that the rise of the number of start-ups between 1990 and 1991 was caused by the unification of East and West Germany in the year 1990. However, we could not find any further indication for this hypothesis in the data. The rise between 1997 and 1999 coincides with a change of the sector classification system of the Social Insurance Statistics, but again, it remains unclear how this change could have affected the number of start-ups that was recorded. The rise can be mainly ascribed to an increase in the service sector.
5. The "other private sectors" are agriculture and forestry, fishery, energy and water supply, mining, and construction.
6. A variation of start-up rates over time may have two sources, changes in the number of start-ups (the numerator of the start-up rate) or the regional workforce (the denominator). On average, the coefficients of variation of the number of start-ups are found to be twice as high as the coefficients of variation of the number of employees. This indicates that changes of the regional start-up rates are mainly

caused by variation of new business formation activity and not by a change in the number of workforce.

7. We measure R&D employment as the number of employees with a bachelor's or master's degree in natural science or engineering.

8. Wagner (2004) showed that the propensity of an individual to start a business is rather stimulated by young and small firms than just by the presence of small firms. Mueller (2005) found that a high share of small *and* young firms in a region positively affects the individual decision to become a nascent entrepreneur.

9. Because the value of the start-up rate is restricted at the lower end, the Tobit regression may be the appropriate method of analysis. We found, however, that ordinary least squares regression (OLS) leads to roughly identical results and provide these estimates here.

10. The analysis of the start-up rate by means of fixed effects panel regressions may be rather problematic, since a large part of the path dependency is included into the region specific effect. Accordingly, the estimated coefficient for the lagged start-up rate is considerably smaller here than in the pooled regression.

11. The question is whether x causes y and how much of the current y can be explained by past values of y. If additional lagged values of x improve the explanation, y is said to be Granger-caused by x if the coefficients of the lagged x's are statistically significant (Granger, 1969).

REFERENCES

Armington, C., & Acs, Z. (2002). The determinants of regional variation in new firm formation. *Regional Studies, 36*, 33–45.

Audretsch, D. B., & Fritsch, M. (1994a). The geography of firm births in Germany. *Regional Studies, 28*, 359–365.

Audretsch, D. B., & Fritsch, M. (1994b). On the measurement of entry rates. *Empirica, 21*, 105–113.

Audretsch, D. B., Thurik, R., Verheul, I., & Wennekers, S. (2002). Understanding entrepreneurship across countries and over time. In: D. B. Audretsch, R. Thurik, I. Verheul & S. Wennekers (Eds), *Entrepreneurship: Determinants and policy in a European–U.S. comparison* (pp. 1–10). Dordrecht: Kluwer Academic Publishers.

Baptista, R., Escária, V., & Madruga, P. (2005). *Entrepreneurship, regional development and job creation: The case of Portugal.* Papers on entrepreneurship, growth and public policy June 2005, Max-Planck Institute for Economics, Jena, Germany.

Bundesamt für Bauwesen und Raumordnung – BBR (2003). *Aktuelle Daten zur Entwicklung der Städte*, Kreise und Gemeinden, Band 17. Bonn.

Fritsch, M., & Falck, O. (2002). *New firm formation by industry over space and time: A multi-level analysis.* Working Paper 11/2002, Faculty of Economics and Business Administration, Technical University of Freiberg.

Fritsch, M., & Brixy, U. (2004). The establishment file of the German social insurance statistics. *Schmollers Jahrbuch/Journal of Applied Social Science Studies, 124*, 183–190.

Fritsch, M., & Mueller, P. (2004). The effects of new business formation on regional development over time. *Regional Studies, 38*, 961–975.

Fritsch, M., & Mueller, P. (2005a). *The persistence of regional new Business formation-activity over time – Assessing the potential of policy promotion programs.* Papers on entrepreneurship, growth and public policy February 2005, Max-Planck Institute for Economics, Jena, Germany.

Fritsch, M., & Mueller, P. (2005b). *The effect of new businesses formation on regional development over time: The case of Germany.* Paper prepared for the Workshop "The effects of new Businesses on economic development in the short, medium and long run", Max-Planck Institute for Economics, Jena, Germany, July 11–12 2005 (Mimeo).

Granger, C. W. J. (1969). Investigating causal relations by econometric models and cross-spectral methods. *Econometrica, 37,* 424–438.

Mueller, P. (2005). *Entrepreneurship in the region: Breeding ground for nascent entrepreneurs?* Working Paper 05/2005, Faculty of Economics and Businesses Administration, Technical University of Freiberg.

Mueller, P., van Stel, A., & Storey, D. J. (2005). *The effect of new business formation on regional development over time: The case of Great Britain.* Paper prepared for the Workshop "The effects of new Businesses on economic development in the short, medium and long run", Max-Planck Institute for Economics, Jena, Germany, July 11–12 2005 (Mimeo).

Reynolds, P. D., Storey, D. J., & Westhead, P. (1994). Cross national comparison of the variation in new firm formation rates. *Regional Studies, 27,* 443–456.

van Stel, A., & Storey, D. J. (2004). The link between firm births and job creation: Is there a upas tree effect? *Regional Studies, 38,* 893–909.

Wagner, J. (2004). Are young and small firms hothouses for nascent entrepreneurs? Evidence from German micro data. *Applied Economics Quarterly, 50,* 379–391.

APPENDIX

Table A1. Correlation Matrix of Yearly Start-up Rates 1984–2002.

	Start-up Rate of Year																	
	2002	2001	2000	1999	1998	1997	1996	1995	1994	1993	1992	1991	1990	1989	1988	1987	1986	1985
2001	0.92																	
2000	0.96	0.92																
1999	0.93	0.90	0.97															
1998	0.94	0.89	0.94	0.94														
1997	0.95	0.92	0.95	0.93	0.95													
1996	0.95	0.91	0.96	0.95	0.96	0.96												
1995	0.92	0.88	0.92	0.93	0.95	0.95	0.97											
1994	0.91	0.88	0.92	0.93	0.95	0.95	0.96	0.98										
1993	0.92	0.89	0.93	0.94	0.94	0.96	0.96	0.97	0.97									
1992	0.82	0.88	0.92	0.92	0.95	0.95	0.95	0.96	0.95	0.96								
1991	0.90	0.86	0.89	0.89	0.93	0.92	0.93	0.94	0.93	0.94	0.95							
1990	0.86	0.82	0.88	0.86	0.89	0.90	0.90	0.92	0.91	0.93	0.96	0.91						
1989	0.90	0.86	0.90	0.90	0.93	0.92	0.93	0.93	0.93	0.94	0.97	0.95	0.95					
1988	0.88	0.82	0.86	0.85	0.90	0.88	0.89	0.88	0.88	0.89	0.95	0.93	0.91	0.96				
1987	0.87	0.84	0.88	0.87	0.92	0.90	0.91	0.92	0.91	0.92	0.96	0.94	0.93	0.97	0.95			
1986	0.81	0.76	0.81	0.81	0.88	0.84	0.86	0.88	0.86	0.86	0.92	0.88	0.92	0.94	0.92	0.95		
1985	0.82	0.79	0.84	0.84	0.89	0.87	0.88	0.91	0.90	0.89	0.95	0.91	0.93	0.95	0.92	0.96	0.96	
1984	0.84	0.80	0.86	0.87	0.91	0.88	0.90	0.93	0.91	0.91	0.94	0.92	0.90	0.94	0.89	0.95	0.93	0.97

All coefficients significant at 1% level.

ENTREPRENEURIAL ORIENTATION OF RUSSIAN SME

Tatiana Iakovleva

INTRODUCTION: THE RUSSIAN CONTEXT

The importance of small enterprise to the economy is now widely recognized not only by the Western industrialized world, but also by many countries, which formally had socialistic forms of government. Former Communist countries as well as less developed countries that are working to fuel their economies are expending considerable effort to foster entrepreneurship (Kasadara, 1992).

While entrepreneurship research has a history in the twentieth century focusing on entrepreneurs and their enterprises in the Western countries, the aspects of entrepreneurship in the East with collectivist orientation have received limited attention. There is a real lack of understanding about entrepreneurship in Russia, the country that Winston Churchill called a "riddle wrapped in a mystery inside an enigma" (Ageev, Gratchev, & Hirich, 1995). It is important to clarify, whether Western theories are generally applicable in emerging economy environments and whether existing concepts permit development of new concepts or modification of old ones (Hoskisson, Eden, Lau, & Wright, 2000).

The Emergence of Entrepreneurial Economics
Research on Technological Innovation, Management and Policy, Volume 9, 83–97
Copyright © 2005 by Elsevier Ltd.
ISSN: 0737-1071/doi:10.1016/S0737-1071(05)09006-2

The most interesting and exiting about entrepreneurship in Russia is that it has emerged only 15 years ago. In 1989 the law on 'Entrepreneurial activities' was approved. That means that the history of 'modern' (post-Soviet) entrepreneurship is rather short. Due to the dramatic changes in all spheres of life during the 'perestroika' period – reconstruction of the economy and collapse of Soviet Union – lots of people were forced to or decided freewill to try something new in their life – to open an enterprise. Lots of small, privately owned enterprises appear – newly opened or privatized former state firms. By 2000 more than 891,000 small entrepreneurs operated in Russia (Russian SME Resource Centre). More than 25% of the population of Russia are occupied today in SME, which accounts for 12–15% of GDP of the country (Russian State Statistic Committee Report, 2003).

The first 10 years after 'perestroika' began (end of the 1980s–1990s) is often labelled as years of 'wild capitalism' in popular press. Today, the market relations have stabilized relative to the end of the 1980s. However, 15 years of market is a rather short period. Founders starting new enterprises were and in many cases still are forced to create infrastructure by themselves – no market relationships existed in planned Soviet economy (Ylinenpåå & Chechurina, 2000; Puffer & McCarthy, 2001). The term 'entrepreneur' in Russian business context often has a mixed meaning. From the sociological research on Russian entrepreneurs (Grishenko, Novikova, & Lapsha, 1992; Turen, 1993; Bezgodov, 1999), it follows that not all of those performing entrepreneurial activities perceive themselves as entrepreneurs. At the same time, those labelled themselves as entrepreneurs often combine work for salary and entrepreneurship activities. The term 'entrepreneur' refers more to the fact that individual is somehow engaged in private enterprise as a partner rather than as an employee. In Russian context it does not refer to the degree of novelty in products or services provided on the firm level. This happened because after the collapse of Soviet Union any desire to start enterprise was really entrepreneurial – nobody in the country did it before. In people's mind, the perception of 'entrepreneurs' in the society is still mixed – positive towards value-creating efforts and negative while some associate entrepreneurs with mafia and oligarchs (Babaeva, Babaev, & Neslon, 1993; Bezgodov, 1999; Iakovleva, 2001). To start an enterprise in Russia is, in itself, an action, which is new, different, and innovative and risk-taking desire.

Both for theorists and for practitioners it is important to know about superior firm performance in Russia.

THEORY AND HYPOTHESES

Resources of the Firm and Performance

According to the resource-based view (RBV) a firm may be perceived as an aggregation of resources, which are translated by management into strengths and weaknesses of the firm (Lerner & Almor, 2002). Barney described resources as "all assets, capabilities, organizational processes, firm attributes, information, knowledge, etc. controlled by a firm that enable the firm to conceive of and implement strategies that improve its efficiency and effectiveness" (Barney, 1991, p. 101).

The RBV suggests that differences in performance among firms may be best explained through differences in firm resources and their accumulation and usage (Penrose, 1959; Andrews, 1980; Barney, 1991; Grant, 1991; Peteraf, 1993). Numerous studies have shown that different kinds of resources contribute to firm performance. Peteraf (1993) claims that a major contribution of the RBV is to explain longlived differences in firm profitability, which cannot be attributed to differences in industry conditions. Empirical studies show existence of relationship between organizational resources and performance, including resources such as human capital of the firm (Birley & Stockley, 2000; Erikson, 2003); organizational capital – competences and capabilities of the firm (Chandler & Hanks, 1994b; Chasten & Mangles, 1997; Heeley, 1997); social capital – organizational or individual networks (Donckels & Lambrecht, 1994; Hansen, 1995), availability of financial capital (Cooper, Gimeno-Gascon, & Woo, 1994; Bamford, Dean, & McDougall, 1997).

Several studies show that access to financial capital influences the performance and growth of the small firm (Cooper & Gascon, 1992; Storey, 1994; Wiklund, 1999). Financial capital provides a buffer against unforeseen difficulties that may arise due to plenty of different reasons (Castrogiovanni, 1996). Financial capital also provides organizational financial slack, facilitating the necessary response to changing conditions and increasing the willingness of the firm to innovate and change (Zahra, 1991).

Hypothesis 1. Financial capital is positively related to the firm performance.

Entrepreneurial Orientation and Performance

Entrepreneurship scholars have attempted to explain performance by investigating a firm's entrepreneurial orientation (EO). EO refers to a firm's strategic orientation, capturing specific entrepreneurial aspects of decision-making styles, methods and practices (Lumpkin & Dess, 1996). Besides the tradition strategies the firm can choose from, the EO of the firm is supposed to influence the firm growth and performance (Wiklund, 1998; Lumpkin & Dess, 2001). EO consists of several terms, such as innovativeness, risk-taking and proactiveness. Schumpeter (1934) was among the first to emphasize the role of innovation in the entrepreneurial process. Innovativeness reflects a firm's tendency to engage in and support new ideas, novelty, experimentation and creative processes that may result in new products, services or technological processes (Lumpkin & Dess, 1996). The concept of risk-taking is a quality that is frequently used to describe entrepreneurship (Shane, 1994; Lumpkin & Dess, 1996). Richard Cantillon, one of the first authors who used term 'entrepreneur' as early as in the beginning of the 18th century, argued that uncertainty and riskiness of self-employment is the principal factor that separated entrepreneurs from non-entrepreneurs. Proactivness suggests a forward-looking perspective characteristic of a marketplace leader that has the foresight to act in anticipation of future demand and shape the environment (Lumpkin & Dess, 2001). Proactive forms can introduce new goods and services ahead of their competitors. A first-mover can control access to the market by dominating distribution channels. By introducing new products and services, firms can establish industry standards. All this can positively influence performance of the firm, and some empirical findings support this proposition (Zahra, 1991; Zahra & Covin, 1995).

Hypothesis 2. EO is positively related to firm performance.

Firm Resources, EO and Performance

Resources alone are not sufficient to achieve competitive advantage. In the resource-based perspective, managers have to select an appropriate strategy in order to make the most effective use of the firm's resources and capabilities (Grant, 1991). The extent to which core resources and capabilities are identified and exploited in appropriate ways by the firm's strategy will influence its performance. Because of constant environmental changes, managers do have choices to make about strategic alternatives, but their options might be limited within the established framework of available resources (Spanos & Lioukas, 2001). EO is the way of how strategies can be organized, it refers to a firm's strategic orientation, capturing specific entrepreneurial aspects of decision-making styles, methods and practices. Several studies show the interaction effect EO has towards external environment and performance (Covin & Slevin, 1989; Zahra & Covin, 1995). Recent studies show contingency effect that EO has towards firm's knowledge-based resources and performance (Wiklund & Shepherd, 2003). Following Wiklund and Shepherd's (2003) call for further research on the moderating effect of EO and internal firm resources towards firm's performance, the following hypothesis is proposed:

Hypothesis 3. EO moderates the relationship between financial capital and firm performance. In other words, EO will enhance the positive relationship between firm resources and performance.

SAMPLE

To test the hypotheses a sample of Russian small- and medium-sized enterprises was used. The objective of the survey was to collect data from the heads of or owners of privately owned small enterprises (less than 100 employees), which were independent enterprises. Because of the difficulties with data collection in Russia, it was decided to use 152 Russian students from the Baltic State Technical University of St. Petersburg to contact the enterprises. Initially, a database of 800 small privately owned enterprises, established in 2000 and representative to the industry structure of entire population of small enterprises in St. Petersburg was obtained. However, during the data-gathering process it became evident that it was not possible to obtain information from chosen enterprises. The main reason was that enterprises refused to participate in the research and to fill in questionnaires. Also, the database was not as good as expected – one-third of enterprises that were on the list could not be found on the addresses provided. It was decided then that students can use their contacts – family members or friends to find owners or heads of small enterprises in St. Petersburg and to ask them to fill in questionnaires. The requirements of industry and firm age could not be met insofar. Entire number of students was increased to 600. Each of them received between one and six questionnaires. Totally 466 questionnaires were received. Questionnaires were filtered on several criteria – only persons responsible for the decision making on the enterprise were considered, and only independent enterprises (not a subsidiary of other firms) were chosen to the analysis. This was done for two reasons. First, the key decision makers have a better understanding of the firm's strategies. Second, firm should be free to chose and follow its strategy, otherwise it can be led by the head office. Also, firm size was checked – only firms that have less than 100 employees were considered. In Russia, enterprises are considered as small if the number of employees does not exceed 100 employees. The students were required not to contact sole proprietorships as lot of them in Russia are just registered and do not work in reality, that makes it impossible to use statistics on sole proprietorships in my study. Based on that criterion, 30 questionnaires were removed from the sample. In addition, five questionnaires were removed due to high percentage of missing data. This resulted in 281 usable questionnaires.

In regard to representativity of sample, the only test I can make is to check the industry structure of sample and to compare this with population of SMEs in St. Petersburg. Approximately 39% of firms from the sample were within service industry (including construction), 32% were within sale and distribution and 26% were production companies. As of 2002, there were 131,447 small enterprises in St. Petersburg. The initial structure of the small enterprises in St. Petersburg in 2002 was as follows: services including construction, transport, education 30%, sale and distribution 48% and production 15% (Leontief Centre Report, 2002). Majority of firms participated in the research have either one (37%) or two (33%) partners. Only 32% have reported that they are family firms. With regard to the legal status of the enterprises, 74% were limited liability companies, 20% were closed joint-stock companies and 6% were open joint-stock companies. Approximately 9% of firms were new enterprises (12% changed their status and 8% re-opened after bankruptcy), with a mean firm age of 6 years. However, 50% of firms are between 1 and 5 years old, and 42% of firms are between 6 and 12 years old. That means that approximately 92% of responded firms are not older than 12 years, which is not surprising since entrepreneurship in Russia was officially allowed just 15 years ago.

MEASURES

The measurement of the variables/concepts is to a considerable extent based on previously developed measures used in the entrepreneurship literature.

Dependent Variables

Performance is measured with the help of importance and satisfaction questions on certain items. Respondents were asked to indicate the degree of importance their enterprise attaches to the sales level, sales growth, market share, profitability, net profit, gross profit and to the ability to fund enterprise growth from profits over the past 3 years. Then, they were asked how satisfied they have been with the same indicators over the past 3 years. Questions were partly taken from Chandler and Hanks (1993) and partly from Westhead, Ucbasaran, and Wright (2005) and transformed after the consultation with Russian entrepreneurs. Based on these 16 questions, the Composite performance index was constructed following the principle used in expectancy theory and later in Theory of Planned Behaviour (Ajzen, 1991). First, important questions were rescaled from 7-point Likert scale (1–7) to scale (−3–3), and then satisfaction and importance scores were multiplied, which resulted in factor with 0.91 Chronbach's α (see Table 1). Summated scale index was used in the regression.

To validate the measure of performance, the correlations between the composite performance and two other measures of performance (performance in broad categories (based on different questions) and satisfaction with performance index (based on the same questions)) were calculated, 0.65 ($P<0.01$) and 0.98 ($P<0.01$), respectively.

Table 1. PCA for Composite Performance.

Variables	Factor Loadings	Communality
Composite performance		
Net profit satisfaction∗importance	0.88	0.77
Gross profit satisfaction∗importance	0.84	0.71
Sales growth satisfaction∗importance	0.84	0.71
Profitability satisfaction∗importance	0.83	0.69
Sales level satisfaction∗importance	0.83	0.69
Market share satisfaction∗importance	0.74	0.54
Ability to fund business from the profit satisfaction∗importance	0.71	0.50
Eigenvalue	4.62	
Percentage variance explained	65.93	
Chronbach's α	0.91	

Note: Factor loadings 0.3 or smaller are suppressed. KMO = 0.885, Bartletts's test of sphericity app. $\chi^2 = 1260.38$; df = 21, Sig. 000.

Independent Variables

Financial capital ($\alpha = 0.73$) refers to capital availability from banks, suppliers or customers and capital availability relative to competitors. First two questions are taken from Shane and Kolvereid (1995) and the last is taken from Borch et al. (1999). Factor loadings and communality, as well as Chronbach's α could be seen from Table 2.

EO ($\alpha = 0.87$) was measured with the help of seven items: (1) tendency to be ahead of competitors; (2) strong emphasis on R&D (Lumpkin & Dess, 2001); (3) we initiate actions which competitors then respond to; (4) first enterprise to introduce new product or service (Covin & Slevin, 1989); (5) stress on new product development; (6) availability of new products (Chandler & Hanks, 1994b); and (7) bold, wide-ranging acts are common practice (Miller & Friesen, 1982). Factor loadings and communality, as well as Chronbach's α could be seen from Table 2.

Control Variables

Environment affects firm performance regardless of its strategic orientation or its resources (Lumpin & Dess, 1996). Past results also suggest that EO is not equally suitable in all environments (Miller & Friesen, 1982; Covin & Slevin, 1989; Zahra, 1993). That is why environment should be always entered into the model as a control variable, while investigating the effect of other factors towards EO or performance. The dynamics of demand, sometimes expressed as market attractiveness, environment munificence or dynamism, appears to be the most important variable in the environment to enhance performance (Wiklund, 1999). In highly dynamic environment opportunities emerges, which small firms can take advantage of (Chandler & Hanks, 1994a; Zahra, 1993). Especially market munificience, operationalized as market growth, is stressed as being important to small firm performance (Chandler & Hanks, 1994b; Lumpkin & Dess, 1996; Wiklund, 1999). It was also proven that industry growth has positive impact towards performance independently of the EO of the firm (Lumpkin & Dess, 1996).

Perceived external environment was operationilized with the help of four items, first three taken from Miller and Friesen (1982), and the last is taken from Zahra (1993). Dynamism ($\alpha = 0.64$) – actions of competitors easy to predict, demand and consumer tastes easy to forecast, product technology is not subject to change; Hostility ($\alpha = 0.65$) – price competition, competition in product quality; dwindling markets; Heterogeneity

Table 2. PCA for All Independent Variables.

Variables/Varimax-Rotated Components	1	2	3	4	5	Communality
Entrepreneurial orientation						
D1 We strive to be the first to have new products available	0.74					0.62
D2 Bold, wide-ranging acts are common practice	0.65					0.54
D3 Initiate actions which competitors then respond to	0.76					0.60
D4 First business to introduce new product/service, etc.	0.77					0.65
D5 We stress new product development	0.80					0.74
D8 Tendency to be ahead of other competitors/new products	0.80					0.68
D9 Emphasis on R&D, technological leadership and innovation	0.71					0.60
Hostility						
C10_r Price competition is not a great threat		0.75				0.53
C12_r Competition in product quality or novelty is not a great threat		0.77				0.61
C13_r Dwindling markets for products is not a great threat		0.65				0.66
Finance resources						
F2 Bank loans are easily available for us			0.84			0.74
F7 Capital from suppliers or customers is easily available for us			0.82			0.72
F10 Relative to competitors we have advantageous financial resources			0.66			0.52
Dynamism						
C5_r Actions of competitors are quite easy to predict				0.68		0.49
C6_r Demand and consumers tastes are fairly easy to forecast				0.82		0.70
C7_r The product/service technology is not subject to very much change				0.67		0.54
Heterogeneity						
C3 Customer-buying habits for different products we offer differ sign.					0.89	0.82
C4 Nature of competition for different products we offer differ sign.					0.85	0.78
Eigenvalue	4.08	1.97	1.96	1.79	1.62	
Percentage variance explained	22.68	10.94	10.90	9.92	8.98	
Cumulative percentage of variance	22.68	33.62	44.52	54.44	63.42	
Chronbach's α	0.87	0.65	0.73	0.64	0.74	

Note: KMO = 0.793, Bartlett's test of sphericity app. χ^2 = 1515, 031; df = 153, Sig. 000.

($\alpha = 0.74$) – customer-buying habits; the nature of competition; Munificence – growth opportunities in industry.

Firm-age and industry effects (dummy variables for sale/distribution and for service) were used as additional control variables.

RESULTS

Table 3 provides mean values, standard deviations and correlations for all continuous variables. Skewness and Kurtosis statistics of all the variables were investigated; social capital and organizational capital summated indexes were transformed to achieve normality.

The hypotheses were tested using hierarchical regression analysis (see Table 4). Test for detecting multicollinearity was carried out and results have not identified any multicollinearity (except interaction model, which is allowable).

The base model (control variables only) explains a statistically significant share of the variance in firm performance ($r^2 = 0.06$, $P<0.01$). The independent model makes a significant contribution over and above the model ($\Delta r^2 = 0.09$, $P<0.001$). The positive significant effect of financial capital and EO support Hypotheses 1 and 2. The interaction term makes a significant contribution over and above the main effects ($\Delta r^2 = 0.02$, $P<0.05$). That supports Hypothesis 3 and means that EO enhances positive impact that availability of financial resources had on performance.

DISCUSSION AND CONCLUSION

The primary contribution of this chapter is that EO moderates the relationship between availability of financial capital and firm performance. That means that entrepreneurial decision-making style-innovativeness, risk-taking and proactiveness – enhance the positive influence of the availability of financial resources. Findings are complement with both Cockburn, Henderson, & Stern (2000) and Wiklund and Shepherd (2003) and suggest that not only availability of resources, but also strategic style implemented by the firm is important. Being ahead of competitors, constantly innovative towards products, services and routines allow better utilization of resources and leads to superior firm performance. This finding stress the importance of the firm organization and strategic management style and allow more

Table 3. Mean Values, Standard Deviations and Correlations.

Variables	Mean	SD	1	2	3	4	5	6	7	8	9	10
1 Performance	1.30	3.17	1									
2 EO	3.43	0.83	0.24**	1								
3 Social capital	199.29	20.03	0.10	0.12	1							
4 Organizational capital	18.45	5.28	0.21**	0.14*	0.15*	1						
5 Financial capital	2.99	0.98	0.29**	0.21**	0.10	0.19**	1					
6 Human capital	64.33	27.09	0.13*	0.07	-0.03	-0.01	0.06	1				
7 Dynamism	2.83	0.91	0.01	0.07	-0.19**	-0.08	-0.08	0.06	1			
8 Hostility	3.01	0.93	-0.14*	-0.06	0.01	-0.09	-0.29**	0.00	0.36**	1		
9 Heterogeneity	3.38	0.92	-0.05	0.29**	0.15*	0.02	0.00	-0.01	0.07	0.14*	1	
10 Munificence	3.53	0.83	0.16*	0.28**	0.15*	0.09	0.11	0.02	0.10	-0.06	0.27**	1
11 Firm age	6.46	3.94	-0.17**	-0.29	-0.06	-0.03	0.00	-0.02	0.03	0.05	-0.00	-0.08

*$p < 0.05$.
**$p < 0.005$.

Table 4.   Interaction Effect – Financial Resources∗EO towards
Performance.

	Base Model		Independent Model		Contingency Model	
	St. B, list.	t-statistic	St. B, list.	t-statistic	St. B, list.	t-statistic
Dynamism	0.06	0.84				
Hostility	−0.09	−1.37				
Heterogeneity	−0.09	−1.42				
Munificence	0.17**	2.67				
(one variable – (c8))						
Industry sale/distribution	−0.09	−1.16				
Industry service	−0.67	−0.89				
Firm age	−0.19**	−3.00				
Financial capital			0.25***	3.79		
EO			0.18**	2.64		
Financial capital∗EO					0.89*	2.53
r^2	0.89		0.19		0.21	
Adjusted r^2	0.06**		0.15***		0.17***	
F		3.23		5.64		5.84
Change in r^2			0.09***	12.93	0.02*	
Change in F						6.39

*$P<0.05$.
**$P<0.01$.
***$P<0.001$ ($n = 239$).

complete explanation of the firm performance rather than explanation just based on the resource availability.

Studying the moderating effect of EO and internal firm characteristics complements those studies that have found a contingent relationship between EO and knowledge-based resources (Wiklund & Shepherd, 2003) and EO and external environment (Covin & Slevin, 1989; Zahra & Covin, 1995). Still unexplored is the presence or absence of contingency effect of EO towards individual-level variables such as entrepreneur competencies and firm performance.

One more contribution of this chapter is that results allow concluding that performance of Russian enterprises can be explained with the help of Western theories. Finding on positive main-effect-only between firm resources and firm performance and of firm EO and firm performance confirms this.

These findings open a road for the researchers in former Soviet-based economies, facilitating the research on such important for the development of any economy phenomena as entrepreneurship.

REFERENCES

Ageev, A., Gratchev, M., & Hirich, R. (1995). Entrepreneurship in the Soviet Union and post-socialist Russia. *Small Business Economics*, *7*, 365–367.

Ajzen, I. (1991). The theory of planned behavior. *Organizational Behavior and Human Decision Processes*, *50*, 179–211.

Andrews, K. (1980). *The concept of corporate strategy*. Homewood, IL: Richard D. Irwin.

Babaeva, L., Babaev, R., & Neslon, L. (1993). Perspectives of entrepreneurship and privatisation in Russia: Policy and attitudes [Перспективы предпринимательства и приватизации в России: политика и общественное мнение]. *Sociological Review* [Социологические исследования], *1*, 7–17.

Bamford, C. E., Dean, T. J., & McDougall, P. P. (1997). Initial strategies and new venture growth: An examination of the effectiveness of broad vs. narrow breadth strategies. In: D. Reynolds, W. D. Bygrave & N. M. Carter, et al. (Eds), *Frontiers of entrepreneurial research*. Wellesley, MA: Babson College.

Barney, J. (1991). Firm resources and sustained competitive advantage. *Journal of Management*, *17*, 99–120.

Bezgodov, A. (1999). *Entrepreneurship sociology (Очерки социологии предпринимательства)*. St Petersburg: Petropolis (СПБ, «Петрополис»).

Birley, S., & Stockley, S. (2000). Entrepreneurial teams and venture growth. In: D. Sexton & H. Landstrom (Eds), *The Blackwell handbook of entrepreneurship*. Oxford: Blackwell.

Borch, O. J., Morten, H., & Senneseth, K. (1999). Resource configuration, competitive strategies, and corporate entrepreneurship: An empirical examination of small firms. *Entrepreneurship Theory and Practice*, *42*, 49–71.

Castrogiovanni, G. J. (1996). Pre-startup planning and the survival of new small businesses: Theoretical linkages. *Journal of Management*, *22*(6), 801–823.

Chandler, G. N., & Hanks, S. H. (1993). Measuring the performance of emerging businesses: A validation study. *Journal of Small Business Management*, *8*, 391–408.

Chandler, G. N., & Hanks, S. H. (1994a). Founder competence, the environment, and venture performance. *Entrepreneurship Theory and Practice*, *18*, 223–237.

Chandler, G. N., & Hanks, S. H. (1994b). Market attractiveness, resource-based capabilities, venture strategies and venture performance. *Journal of Small Business Management*, *12*, 27–35.

Chasten, I., & Mangles, T. (1997). Core capabilities as predictors of growth potential in small manufacturing firms. *Journal of Small Business Management*, *35*, 47–57.

Cockburn, I. M., Henderson, R. M., & Stern, S. (2000). Untangling the origins of competitive advantage. *Strategic Management Journal*, *21*(Special Issue), 1123–1145.

Cooper, A., & Gascon, F. (1992). Entrepreneurs, processes of founding, and new-firm performance. In: D. Sexton & J. Kasarda (Eds), *The state of the art of entrepreneurship*. Boston, MA: PWS Kent Publishing Company.

Cooper, A., Gimeno-Gascon, F. J., & Woo, C. (1994). Initial human and financial capital as predictors of new venture performance. *Journal of Business Venturing, 9*, 371–395.

Covin, J., & Slevin, D. (1989). Strategic management of small firms in hostile and benign environments. *Strategic Management Journal, 10*, 75–87.

Donckels, R., & Lambrecht, J. (1994). Networks and small business growth: An explanatory model. *Small Business Economics, 7*, 273–289.

Erikson, T. (2003). Towards of taxonomy of entrepreneurial learning experiences among potential entrepreneurs. *Journal of Small Business and Enterprise Development, 10*, 106–113.

Grant, R. M. (1991). The resource based theory of competitive advantage: Implications for strategy formulation. *California Management Review, 33*, 114–135.

Grishenko, G., Novikova, L., & Lapsha, I. (1992). Social portrait of entrepreneur [Социальный портрет предпринимаеля]. *Sociological Review* [Социологические исследования], *10*, 53.

Hansen, E. L. (1995). Entrepreneurial networks and new organisation growth. *Entrepreneurship Theory and Practice, 19*, 7–19.

Heeley, M. B. (1997). Appropriating rents from external knowledge: The impact of absorptive capacity on firm sales growth and research productivity. In: D. Reynolds, W. D. Bygrave & N. M. Carter, et al. (Eds), *Frontiers of entrepreneurship research*. Wellesly, MA: Babson College.

Hoskisson, R., Eden, L., Lau, C. M., & Wright, M. (2000). Strategy in emerging economies. *The Academy of Management Journal, 43*, 249–267.

Iakovleva, T. (2001). *Entrepreneurship framework conditions in Russia and in Norway: Implications for the entrepreneurs in the agrarian sector*. Hovedfagsoppgaven, Bode Graduate School of Business.

Kasadara, J. (1992). Introduction. In: D. Sexton & J. Kasarda (Eds), *The state of the art of entrepreneurship*. Boston, MA: PWS Kent Publishing Company.

Leontief Center Report. (2002). www.leontief.ru.

Lerner, M., & Almor, T. (2002). Relationships among strategic capabilities and the performance of women-owned small ventures. *Journal of Small Business Management, 40*, 109–125.

Lumpkin, G. T., & Dess, G. (2001). Linking two dimensions of entrepreneurial orientation to firm performance: The moderating role of environment and industry life cycle. *Journal of Business Venturing, 16*, 429–451.

Lumpkin, G. T., & Dess, G. G. (1996). Clarifying the entrepreneurial orientation construct and linking it to performance. *Academy of Management Review, 21*, 135–172.

Miller, S., & Friesen, P. (1982). Innovation in conservative and entrepreneurial firms: Two models of strategic momentum. *Strategic Management Journal, 3*, 1–25.

Penrose, E. (1959). *The theory of the growth of the firm*. London: Basil Blackwell Publisher.

Peteraf, M. (1993). The cornerstones of competitive advantage: A resource-based view. *Strategic Management Journal, 14*, 179–191.

Puffer, S. M., & McCarthy, D. J. (2001). Navigating the hostile maze: A framework for Russian entrepreneurship. *Academy of Management Executive, 15*, 24–36.

Russian SME Resource Centre. http://www.rcsme.ru.

Russian State Statistic Committee Report. (2003). http://www.gks.ru/wps/portal.

Schumpeter, J. (1934). *Theory of economic development: An inquiry into profits, capital, credit, interest and business cycle*. Trans. Redovers Opie. Cambridge.

Shane, S. (1994). The effect of national culture on the choice between licensing and direct foreign investments. *Strategic Management Journal, 15*, 627–642.

Shane, S., & Kolvereid, L. (1995). National environment, strategy and new venture performance: A three country study. *Journal of Small Business Management, 33*(2), 37–50.

Spanos, Y., & Lioukas, S. (2001). An examination into the causal logic of rent generation: Contrasting Porter's competitive strategy framework and the resource-based perspective. *Strategic Management Journal, 22*, 907–934.

Storey, D. J. (1994). New firm growth and bank financing. *Small Business Economics, 6*(2), 139–151.

Turen, A. (Ed.). (1993). *Russian entrepreneurship: Experience of sociological analysis.* Moscow.

Westhead, P., Ucbasaran, D., & Wright, M. (2005). Decisions, actions and performance: Do novice, serial and portfolio entrepreneurs differ? *Journal of Small Business Management*, forthcoming.

Wiklund, J. (1998). *Small firm growth and performance.* Doctoral dissertation, Jönköping University.

Wiklund, J. (1999). The sustainability of the entrepreneurial orientation – performance relationship. *Entrepreneurship Theory and Practice, 24*, 37–48.

Wiklund, J., & Shepherd, D. (2003). Knowledge-based resources, entrepreneurial orientation, and the performance of small and medium-sized businesses. *Strategic Management Journal, 24*, 1307–1314.

Ylinenpää, H., & Chechurina, M. (2000). Perceptions of female entrepreneurs in Russia. In: D. Deschoolmester (Ed.), *Seminar Proceedings of Entrepreneurship under difficult circumstances*, 30th European Small Business Seminar, Gent, Belgium.

Zahra, S. A. (1991). Predictors and financial outcomes of corporate entrepreneurship: An exploratory study. *Journal of Business Venturing, 6*, 259–286.

Zahra, S. A. (1993). Environment, corporate entrepreneurship and financial performance. *Journal of Business Venturing, 8*, 319–340.

Zahra, S., & Covin, J. (1995). Contextual influence on corporate entrepreneurship – performance relationship: A longitudinal analysis. *Journal of Business Venturing, 10*, 43–58.

SURVIVAL AND GROWTH OF START-UPS IN INNOVATION- AND KNOWLEDGE-BASED BRANCHES: AN EMPIRICAL ANALYSIS OF THE FRENCH ICT SECTOR

Frank Lasch, Frédéric Le Roy and Saïd Yami

INTRODUCTION

The ICT sector in France is characterized by intense firm birth rates, but also by a high mortality. Five years after the start-up, only 38.7% of the firms survived, comparing to 51.0% in the middle high technology and 46.3% in non-innovative branches (Lasch, 2003a). The high growth potential of ICT firms is linked to specific problems, such as a higher risk of failure, a difficult financing, the lack of knowledge in firm management of new entrepreneurs, etc. (Pleschak, 1997). Mostly SMEs, young ICT firms are extremely fragile, so the present chapter proposes to discuss the crucial topic of survival and growth in innovation and knowledge-based sectors.

   This research is based upon the assumption that firms are not alike and that differences between them will affect survival and growth. The main objective is to search for key factors of success[1] of new firms in the promising, but particularly complex ICT sector. So, why do certain entrepreneurs

The Emergence of Entrepreneurial Economics
Research on Technological Innovation, Management and Policy, Volume 9, 99–127
Copyright © 2005 by Elsevier Ltd.
All rights of reproduction in any form reserved
ISSN: 0737-1071/doi:10.1016/S0737-1071(05)09007-4

fail while others succeed? And what are the determinants that can be linked to growth? We analyze the impact of several factor groups: human capital and working experience of the entrepreneur, preparation and pre-founding activities, initial organizational characteristics, and inter-firm cooperation.

1. THEORETICAL BACKGROUND

1.1. Determinants of Survival and Growth of ICT Firms

A large number of studies have been devoted to the identification of success factors of new ventures.[2] Most authors classify success factors in three groups: the entrepreneur, the firm and the socio-economic environment (cf. Appendix A). There is agreement in literature that all three of these main elements of entrepreneurship are interrelated. But explaining these differences in successful entrepreneurship, as the results of various combinations of individual, organizational and environmental factors, is a difficult task. So, many variables are used to produce predictive models for the survival and the growth, but results from prior studies are heterogeneous, bringing various results and often contradicting findings.

Some authors even compare and balance the impact of each of the three factor groups. They stress that individual attitude and characteristics have twice the effect upon the success as has the firm's characteristics, and environmental influences are supposed to be relatively minor (Solmossy, 2000, p. 80). But others affirm the importance of the local context and underline that regional conditions and opportunities for entrepreneurial activities, competition and interactive relationships are the main factors in starting and developing new firms (Littunen, Storhammer, & Nenonen, 1998). These authors stress that differing regional conditions will reflect not only in different levels of start-up activity, but also in different structural characteristics of the new firms and can so produce an environmental impact on the success (Tödtling & Wanzenböck, 2003).

In the present study, we focus our analysis on individual and organizational factors to explain the survival and the growth of new ICT firms.

1.2. The Impact of Individual Factors on Survival and Growth

A number of variables are used to explain the impact of the characteristics and the background of the entrepreneur. These factors can be classified in four groups: motivation and entrepreneurial orientation (EO), general human capital, work experience, preparation, and pre-founding activities. A number of studies mainly relate the success of new firms to personality characteristics of the entrepreneur, as a strong motivation, for example ("trait models"; Bellu, 1993; Chell, Haworth, & Brearly, 1991; McClelland, 1961). The relationship between intentional behavior and the success of new firms has been largely demonstrated in literature (Wiklund, 1999; Wiklund & Shepherd, 2001; Delmar & Wiklund, 2003). So, to some extent, success belongs to those who believe it in the strongest and the longest.

For our study, we do not link EO to new entry and performance. We make the assumption that starting up an innovation and knowledge-based firm demands not only a high level of qualification and particular technical skills, but also a strong motivation and a positive intentional behavior (Brüderl, Preisendörfer, & Ziegler, 1996; François, Goux, Guellec, Kabla, & Templé, 1999; Nerlinger, 1998; Seeger, 1997). As a result, entrepreneurs in the ICT sector are supposed to be particularly motivated and to fulfill the key criteria of EO: a propensity to act autonomously, a willingness to innovate and to take risks, and a tendency to be aggressive toward competitors and proactive relative to marketplace opportunities (Lumpkin & Dess, 1998, p. 137).

General human capital is one of the most used factors in literature and it includes age, education level, unemployment, gender, and ethnicity. Age is highly correlated to the education level; in fact, entrepreneurs in innovation and technology are in average 2 to 5 years older than those in non-innovative sectors and start-up at an age between 36 and 39 (Lasch, 2003a; Pleschak & Rangnow, 1995; Seeger, 1997). Authors explain these differences in age with a higher level of education of entrepreneurs in knowledge-based sectors.

While some studies observe a positive relationship between age at start-up and the success of the firm (Wicker & King, 1989), others present negative results (Pleschak, 1997) or find no significant differences at all (Brüderl et al., 1996). So, various viewpoints are possible, on the one hand, young entrepreneurs are considered to be more ambitious and motivated, on the other, older ones have developed stronger networks, are more experienced and can raise easier funding and capital. Even if there is no agreement in literature about this relationship, age is correlated to a high qualification level, which is pointed out as to be one of the key success factors in most of the studies (Brüderl et al., 1996; Cooper et al., 1994; Dahlqvist et al., 2000; Wiklund & Shepherd, 2001).

Previous researches also stress that the impact of gender and ethnicity concerns more the growth performance than the survival of new firms

(Brüderl et al., 1996; Cliff, Langton, & Aldrich, 2004; Dahlqvist et al., 2000). Firms founded by women and ethnic minorities do not fail more often than other, but they start high-performance ventures to a less extent. Similar findings are stressed for entrepreneurs that started their business from a situation of being unemployed, but authors are more convinced that chances of failure are greater for this type of firm.

Different authors attach considerable value to the experience of the entrepreneur. Relevant work experience contributes to success (Wiklund & Shepherd, 2001), especially when there is similarity between the new firm's business and the organization in which the entrepreneur worked before (Brüderl et al., 1996; Cooper et al., 1994).

The size of the firm in which an entrepreneur worked before is a rarely studied variable, but nevertheless crucial for the learning process of managerial abilities. Authors stress that employees in SMEs have more opportunities to gain entrepreneurial and managerial knowledge than those in large firms, by nature characterized by a higher division of labor (Greenan, 1994). Employees in SMEs fulfill more often managerial tasks, are more involved in different activities and their employment security depends directly on the performance and the success of the firm (Schmude, 1994a). They can so develop a more entrepreneurial attitude and some authors stress that firms founded by entrepreneurs having worked in large firms before, fail more often (Pleschak, 1997). But there are also some push factors that explain higher spin-off activities from SMEs than from large firms: a higher risk of failure for SMEs, lower wages' level and in average more weekly work time hours (Nerlinger, 1998; Schmude, 1994a).

The importance of industry-specific knowledge is generally admitted in literature, but for other specific experience more contradictious findings prevail. So, management experience is crucial for certain authors (Cooper et al., 1994; Pleschak, 1997), but not for others (Brüderl et al., 1996). Previous start-up experience seems not to be a clear precondition for success and some authors even find a negative correlation for this factor. Different viewpoints can be used to explain this relationship. Experienced founders can profit from their entrepreneurial knowledge and realize more rapidly an unsuccessful future of their business. They, thus, hesitate less to close down than inexperienced ones (Dahlqvist et al., 2000). Or does a large number of entrepreneurs that have not the qualities to lead an entrepreneurial project to success but that do not hesitate to start-up (and fail) again ("recidivists") bias research results?

Finally, social and personal networks (family) can facilitate the access to different kinds of knowledge (tacit knowledge, specific knowledge, entrepreneurial knowledge) and thus contribute to the success of the new firm, especially when they present opportunities for networking (Aldrich & Zimmer, 1986; Aldrich & Cliff, 2003; Brüderl et al., 1996; Greve & Salaff, 2003; Hansen, 1995; Johannisson, 1998; Nijkamp, 2003; Varamäki & Veslainen, 2003). We consequently hypothesize a positive relationship between general human capital and the success of ICT firms.

Hypothesis 1. Survival and growth of ICT firms are positively related to the general human capital and the working experience of the entrepreneur.

1.3. The Impact of Pre-Founding Activities on Survival and Growth

Intense pre-founding activities are supposed to increase the success, but as for most of the discussed factors, prior researches present ambiguous findings. Indicators for a well prepared project are numerous: start-up training, having a business plan, having studied the technical and the financial feasibility of the project, number of relevant contacts, first file of potential clients, etc.

While Castrogiovanni (1996) insists on the importance of a well prepared start-up and Brüderl et al. (1996), Schutjens and Wever (2000), Hansen (1995) give empirical evidence that support pre-founding entrepreneurial activities, Dahlqvist et al. (2000) do not confirm this relationship. Nevertheless, the starting up of an innovation and knowledge-based firm should demand a far higher extent and quality of pre-founding activities comparing to non-innovative ventures. This leads us to the following hypothesis:

Hypothesis 2. Survival and growth of ICT firms are positively related to the extent and quality of the pre-founding activities.

1.4. The Impact of Initial Organizational Factors on Survival and Growth

Organizational characteristics are another explanation for differences between successful firms and failures. In literature, there is agreement that a significant firm size and financing increase the chances of success. The amount of capital in the start-up period and sufficient financing in the critical first 3 years are, in a certain way, a guarantee for the continuous development of the young firm and a buffer for hazardous or unforeseen events (Brüderl et al., 1996; Cooper et al., 1994; Dahlqvist et al., 2000; Wiklund, 1999).

There are many indicators for financial capital used in previous researches: the amount of capital raised at the start-up, the availability of venture capital

(Engel, 2002; Dahlqvist et al., 2000), allocated subventions and public aids (Brüderl et al., 1996; Dahlqvist et al., 2000). The availability of significant financial capital gives the entrepreneur the possibility to start his business from the beginning with a certain firm size in terms of employment. Therefore, the number of employees at the start determines, to some extent, the performance of the firm and increases the chances of success.

A number of authors stress that the chances of success increase, when the founder is assisted in his decision-making process by a business partner or an entrepreneurial founding team (Ruef, Aldrich, & Carter, 2003; Brüderl et al., 1996; Pleschak, 1997; Schutjens & Wever, 2000; Teal & Hofer, 2003). But the theoretical competitive advantage of an entrepreneurial founding team (complementarities, a broader "knowledge-base", an efficient task division) is not totally supported by certain authors that point out possible risks that can lead to failure, like disharmonies between partners (Almus, Egeln, & Engel, 1999; Nerlinger, 1998; Seeger, 1997). Nevertheless, complementarities should prevail and produce positive effects especially in innovation and knowledge-based firms.

Starting with a certain number of possible customers or a file of clients may reduce the risks of failure, especially for innovation and knowledge-based firms that have to support additional costs due to a high R&D intensity and time-expensive development of innovative market ideas or high-tech products (Kulicke, 1990). Some authors (Koschatzky, 1997; Seeger, 1997) also stress the importance of the number of clients (degree of dependence) and the type of clients (private customers, public institutions, other firms).

The success of new firms may also depend on the regional market orientation (local, national, international markets), but for this variable, various viewpoints exist. So, certain authors stress that firms with a high degree of specialization should diversify regionally their markets (Bathelt, 1992) and, especially for innovation-based firms, competing from the start-up at a national level increases the chances of success (Koschatzky, 1997). In fact, some authors point out higher survival risks for firms that follow from the beginning internationalization strategies (Bürgel, Fier, Licht, & Murray, 2001; Sapienza, Autio, & Zahra, 2003).

The choice of location is mostly motivated by private reasons of the entrepreneur, as proximity to the place of residence (Schmude, 1994b). Innovative firms have specific needs concerning their location, but also a particular interaction with the local economy, thus the choice of localization may also affect the success. In literature a number of authors stress the importance of these innovation- and technology-based externalities (localization and agglomeration effects) as well as the role of the regional context as a source of particular kind of knowledge and expertise, that promotes (or inhibits) new technology-based start-ups (Audretsch, 1998; Collinson & Gregson, 2003; Lasch, Le Roy, & Yami, 2005; Nguen & Vicente, 2003).

Several researches note that knowledge spill-overs are far more important than agglomeration effects for the new firm formation in innovation-based sectors (Armington & Acs, 2002; Capello, 2002; Lasch et al., 2005). Consequently, we can suppose that access to market and resources (agglomeration effects), knowledge-spillovers (localization effects) and other cost-reducing reasons should determine the choice of localization of an entrepreneur in the ICT sector far more than personal reasons. Following the previous discussion, we consider that initial organizational factors determine the success of new firms.

Hypothesis 3. Survival and growth of ICT firms are positively related to the initial organizational factors.

1.5. Inter-Firm Cooperation and Firm Growth

Against this background, cooperation, network activities and knowledge externalities are considered as crucial, in particular for knowledge-based businesses like those in the ICT sector. In fact, the modern entrepreneur tends to increasingly become a creative network operator and manager (Nijkamp, 2003). Often cooperation leads to cooperation, once entered in the first agreement (Varamäki & Veslainen, 2003). Entrepreneurs in knowledge-based firms, compared with traditional firms generally invest more time in networking (Johannisson, 1998). ICT firms are required by the development, the production and the marketing of their products or services to pursue permanent innovation activities, intense and enduring contacts and cooperation (formal or contractual) with R&D infrastructure and firms in their "glocal" network.

Several studies show that the more new firms are integrated in regional networks of relationships as far as consulting, transfer, finances, and businesses are concerned, the more their chances of success increase (Butler & Hansen, 1991; Camagni, 1991, 1995; De Propris, 2002; Fromhold-Eisebith, 1995; Grabher, 1993; Koschatzky, 1997; Park, 1996). Regarding their fragility, such integration is crucial for ICT firms and far more important than for non-innovative ventures, which lead us to the following hypothesis:

Hypothesis 4. Growth of ICT firms is positively related to the extent of inter-firm cooperation.

2. METHOD

2.1. Databases

In this chapter, we use a data set that offers the opportunity to gather information of the firms at their start and once again 3 and 5 years later. This is a dataset collected by the French national institute of statistics and economic studies, INSEE, that considers cohorts of new firms since 1994 ("enquête SINE"), where one firm out of five is observed during 5 years (in average three questionnaires). For our study, the first wave was used (first questionnaire at the start-up in 1994 and second questionnaire in 1997). The results of the second wave (1999 to 2004) are soon available. In this database, questionnaires of 24.191 firms (all sectors) were available and, as we focus on the ICT sector, 498 firms of this branch constitute our sample.

2.2. Defining the ICT Sector

The definition we mobilize is similar to what is used in most of the recent publications in France (Heitzmann & Rouquette, 1999; Lasch et al., 2005; Rouquette, 1999; see Appendix B) but excludes the national telecommunication sector (France Télécom) and the aeronautic/space industries as well as pharmaceutical industries (both sectors are not considered as ICT activities). The delimitation of the ICT sector is realized by using the actual French sector classification ("Nomenclature d'Activités Française, Naf700" – SIC four digit code). According to our definition, the ICT sector is composed by three sub sectors that split in 20 divisions (see Appendix B *high tech industries* (first category of the OECD definition), *ICT services* (computer/software services and telecommunications, except "France Télécom"), as well as *other knowledge intense services* (non-university R&D, technical studies, analysis, testing, and inspections).

2.3. Measuring the Variables

The main objective of our study is to examine the success of new firms in terms of survival, but also to answer the question if certain characteristics of the start-up period still have an effect after the critical first 3 years. In a first research step, we divided the firms in two groups: those who continued their activity after 3 years (*survivors*) and those who closed down (*exitors*). As the basis for an analysis of success factors, we look first at the differences between these two groups in terms of initial conditions (individual and organizational characteristics).

The different determinants of success linked to the analyzed factor groups "general human capital and work experience", "preparation and pre-founding activities", "initial organizational start-up characteristics" are supposed to be interrelated and should differentiate significantly more from the less successful entrepreneurs. So, in a second research step, a multivariate analysis is used as a refinement and focuses on the growth[3] of the survivors. In this model, we introduce the most significant variables of step one (initial start-up conditions), as well as some other variables that proxy firm activities of the first 3 years.

The independent variables respond to the hypothesis emitted in Section 1 and proxy four factor groups (cf. Table 1).

2.4. Statistical Tests

In order to test the Hypotheses 1–3 (determinants of survival), we split the sample in those who survived the *three first years* ($n = 278$), and those that quit the market during the same period ($n = 220$). For Hypotheses 1–3 (determinants of growth), we naturally consider only the survivor firms and limited our analysis to the most important subsector, the "ICT services". Future research steps will use a broader sample and consider the whole ICT sector (knowledge intense services and high tech industry included).

We use a multiple regression model crossing each independent variable with an index of growth (number of employees between 1994 and 1997). For hypothesis 4 (impact of inter-firm cooperation), we have also limited our analysis on the survivor group ($n = 278$). Their growth rate is compared with the cooperation intensity.

3. RESULTS: WHY DO FIRMS FAIL WHILE OTHERS SUCCEED?

3.1. Determinants of Survival

3.1.1. Human Capital, Working Experience and Survival
Hypothesis 1 postulates a positive link between the human capital of the entrepreneur and the chances of survival. At the first look, survivors and

Table 1. Proxies of Survival and Growth (Success Factors).

Success Factors	Proxies
Human capital and working experience (Hypothesis 1)	
General human capital	Age of founder; university or high school graduation; start-up from a situation of unemployment; academic spin-offs
Working experience	Working experience of 3 years minimum
Firm size of last employment	Firm size of former employment (<3, 3–9, 10–49, 50–199, >200)
Industry-specific knowledge	Start-up in the same activity/sector as former employment
Management experience	Experience as manager, cadre
Prior start-up experience	Previous start-up experience
Social and personal networks	Examples of entrepreneurs in the social and personal network
Preparation and pre-founding activities (Hypothesis 2)	
Preparation and pre-founding activities	Contacts with consultants; start-up training; clients approached or file of clients; competitors or market analysis; financing plan; technical feasibility
Initial organizational characteristics (Hypothesis 3)	
Business relations	Business relations with former employer
Start-up capital	Amount of start-up capital ($<15.000€$, 15.000–40.000€, 40.000–75.000€, 75.000–150.000€, $>150.000€$), public subventions
Firm size	Number of employees at start-up
Founding team	Entrepreneurial founding team
Subcontractor	Essentially subcontractor activities
Number of clients	Number of clients (1–2, 3–10, >10)
Type of clients	Private, firms, great distribution, public sector
Local market	Clients essentially in local market
National market	Clients essentially in national market
International market	Clients essentially in international market
Location choice for economic reasons	Market proximity, supplier proximity, client proximity, location choice by opportunity, cost reduction, local infrastructure, public aids
Location choice for private reasons	Proximity to residence, other private reasons
Inter-firm co-operation (Hypothesis 4)	
Inter-firm cooperation	Inter-firm cooperations
R&D cooperation	R&D cooperations

exitors have similar human capital characteristics and reveal no significant difference (cf. Table 2). So, the education level, starting-up from a situation of unemployment or starting-up directly after graduation (academic spin-offs) does not seem to affect the survival of the new firm. The only difference is in age: successful founders are in average 1 year older than those who did not pass the critical first 3 years threshold.

But real differences appear when work experience is analyzed. Even if working experience in general seems not to be significant, starting up a business in the same sector as the former employment increases the chances of survival. The firm size of the former employment situation also reveals to be important and the results point out that when successful founders worked

Table 2. Human Capital and Working Experience.

Human Capital and Working Experience of the Entrepreneur	Survivors ICT Firms ($n = 278$)	Exitors ICT Firms ($n = 220$)
Age	39.5	38.5
Education level (university/ high school graduation)	32.5%	33.5%
Starting-up from a situation of unemployment	10.3%	11.0%
Academic start-up	4.0%	4.0%
Start-up in the same activity/ sector as former employment	87.0%	82.6%
General working experience (minimum 3 years)	87.1%	87.5%
Last employment in firm (size)...		
<3 employees	9.1%	10.2%
3–9 employees	21.2%	19.0%
10–49 employees	30.8%	26.5%
50–199 employees	16.2%	11.6%
>200 employees	22.7%	32.7%
Total	100.0%	100.0%
Specific working experience (manager, cadre)	45.2%	46.0%
Entrepreneurial experience (minimum 1 start-up)	27.7%	32.3%
Examples of entrepreneurs in social and personal network	63.8%	65.2%

more often before the start-up in SMEs, exitors came rather from large companies. As a surprise, successful founders have less specific experiences (as a manager, firm founder, and cadre) and have fewer examples of entrepreneurs in their social network. An interesting result is also the fact that experienced founders fail more often than entrepreneurial newcomers.

3.1.2. Pre-Founding Activities and Survival

A well prepared start-up is supposed to be one of the most important key factors to success (Hypothesis 2). Our results globally confirm this relationship (cf. Table 3). So, the successful entrepreneurs prepare intensively the start-up and realize more often than exitors specific pre-founding activities (contacts with consultants, clients approached or file of clients, financing plan established). Nevertheless, we obtain no significant differences for activities like start-up training and analysis of market or competitors. A surprising result for ICT firms is the negative relationship between failure and pre-founding activities like "having checked the technical feasibility". Existing business relations to the former employer seem also to increase the chances of survival. In conclusion, these findings give strong support to Hypothesis 2.

3.1.3. Initial Organizational Characteristics and Survival

Initial organizational characteristics at the start-up are the third factor group where differences between survivors and exitors clearly appear (cf. Table 4). Successful entrepreneurs start with a bigger size, more financial capital, obtain more often public aids and their chances of survival increase when the start-up is realized by a founding team.

The results for competitive advantages linked to the factor "clients" are ambiguous. First, being essentially a subcontractor from the start-up does

Table 3. Pre-founding Activities.

Pre-founding Activities	Survivors ICT Firms ($n = 278$)	Exitors ICT Firms ($n = 220$)
Contacts with consultants	59.4%	50.5%
Start-up training	21.9%	19.5%
Clients approached or file of clients	68.7%	64.1%
Competitors or market analysis	38.1%	38.2%
Financing plan established	71.9%	68.6%
Technical feasibility checked	44.2%	50.0%
Business relations with former employer	21.2%	17.7%

Table 4. Initial Organizational Characteristics.

Pre-founding Activities	Survivors ICT Firms ($n = 278$)	Exitors ICT Firms ($n = 220$)
Public aids obtained	36.0%	24.5%
Capital at start-up...		
<15.000€	44.6%	52.3%
15.000–40.000€	41.0%	36.8%
40.000–75.000€	8.3%	6.8%
75.000–150.000€	2.5%	1.8%
>150.000€	3.6%	2.3%
Total	100.0%	100.0%
Firm size at start-up (number of employees)	3.38	1.93
Entrepreneurial founding team	42.1%	40.5%
Essentially subcontractor activities	28.8%	27.3%
Number of clients (total sales)		
1 or 2 clients	16.2%	33.6%
3–10 clients	51.4%	24.1%
>10 clients	32.4%	42.3%
Total	100.0%	100.0%
Type of clients		
Private customers	12.6%	20.9%
Other firms, commercials	65.5%	57.7%
Great distribution	6.5%	6.8%
Administration or public sector	15.5%	14.5%
Total	100.0%	100.0%
Geographical location of clients (total sales)		
Local or regional	61.8%	63.2%
National	31.3%	25.5%
International	6.9%	11.3%
Total	100.0%	100.0%
Choice of location motivated by...		
Proximity to market	15.8%	15.7%
Proximity to supplier	2.4%	1.9%
Proximity to client	5.4%	1.9%
Opportunity	11.3%	9.0%
Cost-reduction	12.8%	11.2%
Local infrastructures	5.4%	6.4%
Local public aids	1.5%	1.5%
Proximity to residence	28.3%	32.2%
Other private reasons	17.3%	20.2%
Total	100.0%	100.0%

not seem to have an impact on the survival. Second, a small number of clients increase the risk of failure, but paradoxically entrepreneurs that quickly made business with many clients are more often exitors than survivors. So, having a "reasonable" number of clients (3–10) seems to affect most the chances of survival. Third, differences between survivors and exitors also appear when the type of client is analyzed. So, exitors make more often business with private clients than survivors that prefer dealing with other firms. Both groups deal to the same extent with the great distribution and public institutions. Finally, successful firms are rapidly present on the national market, but they seem to prepare their international business more slowly (and carefully?). In fact, firms that internationalize from the start are exposed to high risks and prove to have much higher mortality rates. Finally, exitors deal more often with local or regional clients than survivors.

The chances of survival should improve with the quality of the location (business opportunities, market proximity, externalities of agglomeration and localization, etc.). Therefore, a successful entrepreneur should be sensitive to regional conditions and not choose the location for private reasons only. But our results do not confirm that these findings are as clear as they are supposed to be. Even if the exitors implanted their business more often motivated by private reasons or in proximity to their residence than the survivors, both groups do not significantly differ in their choice of location when economic reasons are analyzed. Only the proximity to clients, and to some extent cost-reduction reasons, seem to be success factors that characterize the survivors. Market proximity, local infrastructures and financial aids do not significantly increase the survival of the new firm.

3.2. Determinants of Growth

Even if there are many studies of the determinants of survival and the growth of new firms, there is no real agreement in literature about the key factors of success (proxied by growth) and different studies produce different results. One explanation given in literature is that sector specificities are often neglected and can thus bias the findings. The literature review has shown that determinants of success may even differ between subsectors. This is particularly true for an emerging, very dynamic but heterogeneous sector like the ICT branch. Indeed, some authors point out important differences between ICT subsectors in firm characteristics, location needs, new firm formation dynamics and regional differences in firm formation rates (Lasch, 2003a, b; Lasch et al., 2005).

But, for our purpose, we concentrate on the most important subsector, the ICT services and we exclude knowledge intense services as well as high tech industries. So, a regression model is built where the independent variables proxying human capital, pre-founding activities, initial organizational characteristics, and inter-firm cooperation are crossed with an index of growth (growth of employees between 1994 and 1997). For the ICT services, 5 variables out of 26 are significant to a 5% level and 4 to a 10% level.

Human capital and working experience seems not to influence at all firm growth for ICT services (all proxies are insignificant). No significant results were obtained for the other variables like education level, working experience in SMEs, or specific experience (founder, manager). Starting-up a business in the same sector as the last employment is also not automatically related to success. The importance of pre-founding activities is confirmed, in particular when the new firm starts up with a file of clients. But, start-up training seems not to have any sustainable effect on the performance of the firm.

Initial organizational characteristics can produce sustainable effects and are positively related to firm growth, especially when a high start-up capital is available. Starting with a small firm size reduces the chances of growth for ICT services and public aids obtained at start-up have no further effects on the growth of the firms (cf. Table 5).

Hypothesis 4 underlines the importance of networking and cooperation. So, we introduced in our analysis one of the most important success factors stressed by literature, especially for knowledge-based firms: inter-firm cooperation. At the difference to the analysis of the other success factors mentioned above, we naturally consider the survivor group only and focus on the impact of inter-firm cooperation activities in the first 3 years on the performance (proxied by the evolution of total sales). Our findings are twofold and support Hypothesis 4. High-performing firms cooperate more and invest more especially in R&D cooperation (cf. Table 6).

In our regression model, we observe also the evolution of some initial organizational characteristics over time and measure their impact on the growth chances of the firms. So, financing performances, like the introduction of capital from other companies, tend to increase the growth of ICT services. To our surprise, (R&D) cooperations with other firms increase the chances of survival but not of growth. The same result is obtained for a diversification of products and services (10% level), but the chances of growth increase strongly with the number of clients. Nevertheless, they decrease when the file of clients is mainly constituted by private customers. Finally, a high degree of internationalization is linked to high risks, as well

Table 5.   Results of the Multiple Regression Model.

Dep. Variable: Growth of the Number of Employees Between 1994 and 1997 (log.)	
Variables	ICT Services[a]
Human capital and working experience	
Education level (university or high school graduation)	0.0877
Start-up in the same activity/sector as former employment	0.0102
[b]Specific working experience (manager, cadre)	−0.0253
Last employment in firm with less than 3 employees	−0.0315
Last employment in firm with 3–9 employees	0.0216
Last employment in firm with 50–199 employees	−0.1330
Last employment in firm with more than 200 employees	−0.0936
Pre-founding activities	
Start-up training	0.0647
Clients approached before start-up or file of clients	0.1697***
Initial organizational characteristics	
Public aids	−0.1306*
Capital raised at start-up less than 15.000 €	−0.0361**
Capital raised at start-up between 40.000 and 74.999 €	0.2936*
Capital raised at start-up more than 75.000 €	0.4020**
Firm size at start-up (number of employees)	−0.0140***
Entrepreneurial founding team	−0.2330***
Activities and characteristics of the firm in the second and third year after start-up	
Capital from other firms incorporated	0.2165**
Mainly subcontractor activities	0.0904
Evolution of number of clients	0.2960****
Clients mainly private customers	−0.4002***
Clients mainly other firms (SME)	0.0312
Clients mainly other firms (large firms)	0.1733°
Clients mainly in locale/regional market	−0.0616
Clients mainly in international market	−0.3889**
Diversification of products and services	0.1280*
R&D cooperations	−0.1388*
Other cooperations	−0.0127

*sign. 20%.
**sign. 10%.
***sign. 5%.
****sign. 1% level.
[a]$R^2 = 0.4406$ (adj. $R^2 = 0.2776$).
[b]$R^2 = 0.4290$ (adj. $R^2 = 0.2365$).

Table 6. The Impact of Inter-firm Cooperation on Performance.

ICT Firms (Survivors) Nature of Cooperation	Cooperation Intensity	— ← Evolution of Total Sales → +				
		Extremely Diminished (%)	Lightly Diminished (%)	Stable (%)	Lightly Increased (%)	Extremely Increased (%)
Developing of products/services	14.1%	8.7%	21.2%	8.0%	17.3%	18.8%
Fabrication of products/services	5.6%	8.7%	0.0%	5.3%	7.1%	6.3%
Other cooperations (organization, logistics, etc.)	21.3%	26.1%	19.6%	16.0%	19.5%	28.0%
No cooperations	59.0%	56.5%	59.2%	70.7%	56.1%	46.9%
Total	100.0%	100.0%	100.0%	100.0%	100.0%	100.0%

as starting-up a business with an entrepreneurial founding team. For all the other variables, we obtain no significant effect.

4. DISCUSSION

We share with many predecessors the experience that discussing our research results in making the link with the existing literature is a very difficult and complex task. The previous researches are too heterogeneous and additionally, to our knowledge, success factors for the very specific ICT sector have not yet been sufficiently studied. Prior research also often neglected sector-specific analysis and when some studies focus on survival, others seek to identify predictors of growth or high performance. Consequently, we concentrate on two points where, to our eyes, the present chapter can advance existing knowledge: designing a, in some way idealistic, profile of successful entrepreneurs in the ICT sector (survival), and linking variables to performance (growth).

4.1. Towards a Profile of Successful Entrepreneurs in the ICT Sector

A typical starter of a successful knowledge and innovation-based firms certainly does not exist. Nevertheless designing an idealistic profile, based upon our results, can offer a first, deeper insight in qualities that could influence more than others the survival of new firms of this type. This information is not only important for policy measures, but it can also be used as a starting point for future research. So, based on our research results, we can describe successful ICT entrepreneurs in the following way:

Entrepreneurs of survivor-firms are in general older (experienced founders), are team-founders, are academic or industrial spin-off's (no significant period of unemployment) and are more successful when they built up their business in the branch of their (last) professional experience. Successful entrepreneurs come from SMEs, whereas founders that quit the competition worked rather in large firms. As a surprise, successful founders have less specific experience (as a manager, firm founder, and cadre) and have fewer examples of entrepreneurs in their social network. They do prepare intensively their entrepreneurial project, start with a bigger size and more capital and obtain more often subventions and public aids. Additionally, starting a business in the ICT sector has more chances to survive when potential clients have been found before the creation, especially business relations with the firm of the last employment or being a subcontractor prime. Successful firms make business with other firms and less with private customers, they compete rapidly on the national market, but they seem to prepare their international business more slowly (or carefully?). In fact, firms that started directly international ventures prove to have a higher mortality. The location choice of successful founders is less motivated by personal criteria (proximity to the residence, family), professional criteria prime (proximity to the market, clients/customers, environmental economies). Finally, mobilizing external knowledge sources (R&D cooperation, informal contacts) improve significantly the survival and success of new ICT firms.

4.2. Linking Determinants of Survival to Growth

Determinants of survival have often been linked to performance (cf. Section 1). So, authors try to identify predictors of success and indicators of risk that allow to classify the new firms in those who should be, from the start, on routes to success and those engaged in dead ends. In fact, four variables influence both survival and both growth of ICT firms: starting a business with a file of existing clients, a high starting capital, a capital from other companies incorporated and an increasing the number of clients. But, human capital in general, a high education level in particular, as well as working experience seem not to be a guarantee for survival and growth.

For the other ones our multiple regression model points out, that predictors of survival are in part different from predictors of growth (cf. Table 6). Our regression model did not confirm the importance of R&D cooperations for growth, as well as start-up training and the advantage to start as a subcontractor. Public aids obtained increase the chances of survival, but does not seem to have any impact on the growth of the firms.

To simplify, predictors of growth for young ICT firms are mainly capital- and customer-specific variables.

CONCLUSION

Advancing the perception of entrepreneurship in innovation and particularly in an ICT sector with a high growth potential is crucial, regarding how relatively little research has been undertaken into its specificities. In this chapter, an empirical leap forward was made in using a data set that permitted to gather information of the firms at their start and once again

3 years later (one firm out of five of the 1994 generation). A conceptual lead forward was made by analyzing not only the successful firms (in terms of survival), but also the firms that quit the competition in the first 3 years. Beneath the comparison between the survivors and the firms that quit the competition, the results were used to construct a multiple regression model measuring the impact of some key determinants on the growth of the firms.

The main objective of the present chapter was to deal with the crucial topic of survival and growth an emerging sector characterized by high firm birth rates, but also high risk of failure. Against this background we analyzed 498 newly founded ICT firms of the 1994 generation in France. The basic question was twofold, first, to understand why certain entrepreneurs fail, while others survive and, second, to identify variables that influence not only survival but also the successful development of the new firms in terms of growth. So, based upon a literature review, we discussed the impact of four factor groups: human capital and working experience of the entrepreneur, pre-founding activities, initial organizational characteristics (hypothesis 1–3) and inter-firm cooperation (hypothesis 4).

The comparison of the group of survivors and the exitors helps us to design a first, idealistic, profile of successful entrepreneurs.

But, predictors of survival are in part different from predictors of growth. The positive influence of only four factors was measured in a significant way: starting with a file of clients, a high capital at start-up, additional capital from other companies and an increasing number of clients. The factors noted in literature which are associated with the survival and the growth of new firms do only conform in part to expectations. Growth factors which are often stressed in literature point out to be of no significant importance in the ICT sector, this is the case for a high education level. To simplify, a good preparation is also important for new ICT firms, but human capital and working experience are less crucial than expected. A high start-up capital and continuous financing are key success factors.

These results clearly portray the significant influence on the survival and the growth of a number of variables. Implications for management practice are numerous and our results may be useful for practitioners who are involved in new firms, such as venture capitalists, bankers, but also for those of the public authorities.

Our study opens some directions for future research. Results from previous researches are heterogeneous; bring various results and contradicting findings. In order to increase understanding of the complexity of a new venture's survival and success, especially in emerging sectors like the ICT, future studies should be based on broader empirical samples, should integrate all of the four studied factor groups and deal separately with different types of firms (industry specific criteria, performance criteria as self-employment vs. growth oriented ventures, etc.). To consider deeper the heterogeneity of the ICT sector, pointed out in prior research work, could help to advance our understanding of this sector. A distinction between the main branches of the sector (ICT services, other knowledge intense services and high tech industry) would help us to get more detailed results.

Future research should also consider more multiple-level designs. In connecting with this point, we put particular focus on the need for transferring results obtained on an aggregate level to an individual level (for example the impact of regional contingency variables). So, a number of our findings could be detailed and our results give a first idea of the possibilities. In so doing, we see a great potential for further research, for a better understanding of the key determinants of new firm birth but also of those of the survival and growth in general and especially for the ICT sector.

NOTES

1. To simplify our purpose, in this section we use "success" as a synonym for survival and growth.
2. See precisely: Brüderl and Preisendörfer (2000); Brüderl, Preisendörfer, and Ziegler (1996); Brüderl and Schüssler (1990); Castrogiovanni (1996); Cooper, Gimeno-Gascon, and Woo (1994); Dahlqvist, Davidsson, and Wiklund (2000); Delmar and Wiklund (2003); Engel (2002); Greve and Salaff (2003); Heiss and Köke (2001); Johannisson (1998); Lasch (2003a, b); Lechner and Dowling (2003); Littunen, Storhammar, and Nenonen (1998); Lumpkin and Dess (1998); Nerlinger (1998); Schutjens and Wever (2000); Wiklund (1999); Wiklund and Shepherd (2001).
3. The index of growth, our dependent variable, is defined as the growth of employees' number in the first 3 years.

REFERENCES

Aldrich, H. E., & Cliff, J. E. (2003). The pervasive effects of family on entrepreneurship: Toward a family embeddedness perspective. *Journal of Business Venturing, 18*, 573–596.

Aldrich, H. E., & Zimmer, C. (1986). Entrepreneurship through social networks. In: D. L. Sexton, & R. W. Smilor (Eds), *The Art and Science of Entrepreneurship* (pp. 3–23). Ballinger, New York.

Almus, M., Egeln, J., & Engel, D. (1999). *Determinanten regionaler Unterschiede in der Gründungshäufigkeit wissensintensiver Dienstleister*. ZEW Discussion Paper, n°99-22. Mannheim [ZEW].

Armington, C., & Acs, Z. J. (2002). The determinants of regional variation in new firm formation. *Regional Studies*, *36*(1), 33–45.

Audretsch, D. (1998). Agglomeration and the location of innovative activity. *Oxford Review of
Economic Policy*, *14*(2), 18–29.

Bathelt, H. (1992). Erklärungsansätze industrieller Standortentscheidungen. Kritische Best-
andsaufnahme und empirische Überprüfung am Beispiel von Schlüsseltechnologie-
Industrien. *Geographische Zeitschrift*, *80*, 191–213.

Bellu, R. R. (1993). Task role motivation and attributional style as predictors of entrepreneurial
performance: Female sample findings. *Entrepreneurship & Regional Development*, *5*,
331–344.

Brüderl, J., & Preisendörfer, P. (2000). Fast-growing businesses. Empirical evidence from a
German study. *International Journal of Sociology*, *30*(3), 45–70.

Brüderl, J., Preisendörfer, P., & Ziegler, R. (1996). *Der Erfolg neu gegründeter Betriebe: Eine
empirische Studie zu den Chancen und Risiken von Unternehmensgründungen*. Berlin:
Betriebswirtschaftliche Schriften, Vol. 140.

Brüderl, J., & Schüssler, R. (1990). Organizational mortality: The liability of newness and
adolescence. *Administrative Science Quarterly*, *35*, 530–547.

Bruneau, E., & Lacroix, M. (2001). *Towards the construction of information in activities and
products classifications in* 2007. Working Paper, INSEE Ile-de-France, Paris.

Bürgel, O., Fier, A., Licht, G. & Murray, G. (2001). *Internationalization of high-tech start-ups
and fast growth evidence for UK and Germany*. Discussion Paper no. 01-35, Zentrum für
Europäische Wirtschaftsforschung (ZEW) Mannheim.

Butler, J. E., & Hansen, G. S. (1991). Network evolution, entrepreneurial success and regional
development. *Entrepreneurship and Regional Development*, *3*, 1–16.

Camagni, R. (1991). *Innovation networks: Spatial perspectives*. London/New York: Belhaven-
Pinter.

Camagni, R. (1995). Espace et temps dans le concept de milieu innovateur. In: A. Rallet &
A. Torre (Eds), *Economie industrielle et économie spatiale* (pp. 193–210). Paris: Economica.

Capello, R. (2002). Entrepreneurship and spatial externalities: Theory and measurement. *The
Annals of Regional Science*, *36*, 387–402.

Cases, C., Favre, F., & François, J.-P. (1999). L'innovation technologique dans les services aux
entreprises. *Le 4 Pages des Statistiques Industrielles*, Vol. 105.

Castrogiovanni, G. (1996). Pre-startup planning and the survival of new small businesses:
Theoretical linkages. *Journal of Management*, *22*(6), 801–822.

Chell, E., Haworth, J. M., & Brearly, S. A. (1991). *The entrepreneurial personality: Concepts,
cases and categories*. London: Routledge.

Cliff, J. E., Langton, N., & Aldrich, H. E. (2004). Walking the talk? Gendered rhetoric vs.
action in small firms. *Organization Studies*, *26*(1), 63–91.

Collinson, S., & Gregson, G. (2003). Knowledge networks for new technology-based firms: An
international comparison of local entrepreneurship promotion. *R&D Management*,
33(2), 189–208.

Cooper, A. C., Gimeno-Gascon, F. J., & Woo, C. Y. (1994). Initial human and financial capital
as predictors of new venture performance. *Journal of Business Venturing*, *9*(5), 371–395.

Dahlqvist, J., Davidsson, P., & Wiklund, J. (2000). Initial conditions as predictors of new
venture performance: A replication and extension of the Cooper et al. study. *Enterprise
& Innovation Management Studies*, *1*(1), 1–17.

De Propris, L. (2002). Types of innovation and inter-firm cooperation. *Entrepreneurship and Regional Development, 14*, 337–353.

Delmar, F., & Wiklund, J. (2003). *Growth motivation and growth: Untangling causal relationships.* Academy of Management Best Conference Paper 2003 ENT: H1.

Engel, D. (2002). *The impact of venture capital on firm growth: An empirical investigation.* Discussion Paper no. 02-02, Zentrum für Europäische Wirtschaftsforschung (ZEW) Mannheim.

François, J.-P., Goux, D., Guellec, D., Kabla, I., & Temple, P. (1999). Décrire les compétences pour l'innovation. Une proposition d'enquête. In: D. J. Foray (Ed.), *Mairesse: Innovations et performances. Approches interdisciplinaires* (pp. 283–304). Recherches d'histoire et de sciences sociales/Studies in History and Social Sciences. Paris: Economica.

Fromhold-Eisebith, M. (1995). Das "kreative Milieu" als Motor regionalwirtschaftlicher Entwicklung. *Geographische Zeitschrift, 83*, 32–47.

Grabher, G. (Ed.) (1993). *The embedded firm – on the socio-economics of industrial networks.* London/New York: Routledge.

Greenan, N. (1994). L'organisation du travail dans les PMI se distingue-t-elle de celle des grandes enterprises? *Economie et Statistiques, 271–272*, 87–103.

Greve, A., & Salaff, J. W. (2003). Social networks and entrepreneurship. *Entrepreneurship Theory and Practice*, (Fall), 1–22.

Hansen, E. L. (1995). Entrepreneurial networks and organizational growth. *Entrepreneurship Theory and Practice*, (Summer), 7–19.

Hauknes, J. (1999). *Knowledge intensive services – What is their role?* Paris: OECD.

Heiss, F., & Köke, J. (2001). *Dynamics in ownership and firm survival: Evidence from corporate Germany.* Discussion Paper no. 01-63, Zentrum für Europäische Wirtschaftsforschung (ZEW) Mannheim.

Heitzmann, R., & Rouquette, C. (1999). Les technologies de l'information et de la communication. *INSEE Première*, Vol. 648.

Johannisson, B. (1998). Personal networks in emerging knowledge-based firms: Spatial and functional patterns. *Entrepreneurship and Regional Development, 10*, 297–312.

Koschatzky, K. (Ed.) (1997). *Technologieunternehmen im Innovationsprozess: Management, Finanzierung und regionale Netze.* Heidelberg: Technik, Wirtschaft und Politik. Schriftenreihe des Fraunhofer-Instituts für Systemtechnik und Innovationsforschung/ISI, no. 23.

Kulicke, M. (1990). *Entstehungsmuster junger Technologieunternehmen.* Karlsruhe, Fraunhofer-ISI.

Lasch, F. (2001a). Les technologies de l'information et de la communication en Languedoc-Roussillon en 2001: Forte concentration sur la zone d'emploi de Montpellier. *INSEE, Repères pour l'Economie du Languedoc-Roussillon – Synthèse*, Vol. 12.

Lasch, F. (2001b). *Les technologies de l'information et de la communication (TIC) en France et en Languedoc-Roussillon: Concentration géographique et création d'établissements de 1993 à 2001.* Working paper, INSEE-Languedoc-Roussillon – Série Documents de Travail, www.insee.fr/lr.

Lasch, F. (2003a). *Innovations- und technologieorientierte Neugründungen in Frankreich. Eine Untersuchung von Einflussfaktoren auf regionale Disparitäten im Gründungsgeschehen in Informations- und Kommunikationstechnologien (1993 bis 2001) – La création d'entreprises dans le secteur des technologies de l'information et de la communication (TIC) en France. Une analyse des facteurs déterminants de la création régionale et une étude des déterminants de la survie et du succès des jeunes entreprises (1993 à 2001)*. Regensburg: Beiträge zur Wirtschaftsgeographie Regensburg, Vol. 4.

Lasch, F. (2003b). Les technologies de l'information et de la communication en Languedoc-Roussillon. Des besoins spécifiques pour une filière jeune à forte intensité de création. *INSEE Repères-Synthèse pour l'économie du Languedoc-Roussillon*, Vol. 1.

Lasch, F., Le Roy, F., & Yami, S. (2005). New firm formation in ICT sectors in France (1993–2001). In: M. Dowling, J. Schmude & D. Zu Knyphausen-Aufsess (Eds), *Advances in Interdisciplinary European Entrepreneurship, Research*, (Vol. 2, pp. 199–230). London/New Brunswick: Transaction Publishers.

Lechner, C., & Dowling, M. (2003). Firm networks: External relationships as sources for the growth and competitiveness of entrepreneurial firms. *Entrepreneurship & Regional Development, 15*, 1–26.

Littunen, H., Storhammer, E., & Nenonen, T. (1998). The survival of firms over the critical first 3 years and the local environment. *Entrepreneurship & Regional Development, 10*, 189–202.

Lumpkin, G. T., & Dess, G. G. (1998). Clarifying the entrepreneurial orientation construct and linking it to performance. *Academy of Management Review, 21*(1), 135–172.

McClelland, D. C. (1961). *The achieving society*. Princeton, NJ: Van Nostrand.

Nerlinger, E. (1998). *Standorte und Entwicklung junger innovativer Unternehmen: Empirische Ergebnisse für West-Deutschland*. Baden-Baden: Schriftenreihe des Zentrum für Europäische Wirtschaftsforschung (ZEW), Vol. 27.

Nguen, G. D., & Vicente, J. (2003). Réseaux métropolitains, formes locales d'organisation et ancrage de l'activité économique. *Géographie, Economie, Société, 5*(3–4), 287–310.

Nijkamp, P. (2003). Entrepreneurship in a modern network economy. *Regional Studies, 37*(4), 395–405.

Nivlet, J.-M. (2001). Le secteur du contenu et la révision des nomenclatures d'activités. Working Paper, Groupe de Voorburg sur les statistiques de services, 16ème reunion – Session 1 – Société de l'information, Paris.

Park, S. O. (1996). Networks and embeddedness in the dynamic types of new industrial districts. *Progress in Human Geography, 20*, 476–493.

Pleschak, F. (1997). Entwicklungsprobleme junger Technologieunternehmen und ihre Überwindung. In: K. Koschatzky (Ed.), *Technologieunternehmen im Innovationsprozess: Management, Finanzierung und regionale Netze:* 13-33. Heidelberg: Schriftenreihe des Fraunhofer-Instituts für Systemtechnik und Innovationsforschung/ISI-Technik, Wirtschaft und Politik, Vol. 23.

Pleschak, F., & Rangnow, R. (1995). *Ergebnisse des BMFT-Modellversuchs "technologieorientierte Unternehmensgründungen in den neuen Bundesländern" der Jahre 1990 bis 1994*. Karlsruhe, Fraunhofer-ISI.

Rouquette, C. (1999). Les statistiques des TIC. *Courrier des Statistiques, 89*, 43–49.

Ruef, M., Aldrich, H. E., & Carter, N. M. (2003). Homophily, strong ties, and isolation among U.S. entrepreneurs. *American Sociological Review, 68*, 195–222.

Sapienza, H. J., Autio, E., & Zahra, S. (2003). *Effects of internationalization on young firms' prospects for survival and growth*. Academy of Management Best Conference Paper 2003 ENT: G1.

Schmude, J. (1994a). Qualifikation und Unternehmensgründung. Eine empirische Untersuchung über die Qualifikationsstrukturen geförderter Unternehmensgründer in Baden-Württemberg. *Geographische Zeitschrift, 82*, 166–179.

Schmude, J. (1994b). *Geförderte Unternehmensgründungen in Baden-Württemberg. Eine Analyse der regionalen Unterschiede des Existenzgründungsgeschehens am Beispiel des Eigenkapitalhilfe-Programms (1979–1989)*. Stuttgart: Erdkundliches Wissen, Vol. 114.

Schutjens, V., & Wever, E. (2000). Determinants of new firm success. *Papers of Regional Science, 79*, 135–159.

Seeger, H. (1997). *Ex-Post Bewertung der Technologie- und Gründerzentren durch die erfolgreich ausgezogenen Unternehmen und Analyse der einzel- und regionalwirtschaftlichen Effekte*. Münster: Hannoversche Geographische Arbeiten, no 53.

Solmossy, E. (2000). Entrepreneurial Dimensions: The relationship of individual, venture and environmental factors to success. *Entrepreneurship, Theory & Practice,* (Summer), 79–80.

Teal, E. J., & Hofer, C. W. (2003). New venture success: Strategy, industry structure, and the founding entrepreneurial team. *The Journal of Private Equity,* (Fall), 38–51.

Tödtling, F., & Wanzenböck, H. (2003). Regional differences in structural characteristics of start-ups. *Entrepreneurship & Regional Development, 15*, 351–370.

Varamäki, E., & Veslainen, J. (2003). Modelling different types of multi-lateral cooperation between SMEs. *Entrepreneurship and Regional Development, 15*, 27–47.

Wicker, A. W., & King, J. C. (1989). Employment, ownership and survival in microbusinesses: A study of new retail and service establishments. *Small Business Economics, 1*, 137–152.

Wiklund, J. (1999). The sustainability of the entrepreneurial orientation-performance relationship. *Entrepreneurship, Theory & Practice,* (Fall), 37–48.

Wiklund, J., & Shepherd, D. A. (2001). *Intentions and growth: The moderating role of resources and opportunities*. Academy of Management Proceedings 2001 ENT: F1.

APPENDIX A

A large number of studies have been devoted to the identification of success factors of new ventures (Table A1).

Table A1. Synopsis of Previous Research Results.

Entrepreneur-Associated Factors	Positive Relationship to Start-up Activities, Survival or Success	Negative Relationship to Survival or Success	Not Significant
General human capital	Brüderl et al. (1996); Dahlqvist et al. (2000); Cooper et al. (1994); Wiklund and Shepherd (2001); Wicker and King (1989); Pleschak (1997)		Schutjens and Wever (2000)
Unemployment		Smallbone (1990)	Brüderl et al. (1996); Dahlqvist et al. (2000)

Table A1. (*Continued*)

Entrepreneur-Associated Factors	Positive Relationship to Start-up Activities, Survival or Success	Negative Relationship to Survival or Success	Not Significant
Work experience in general	Schutjens and Wever (2000); Wiklund and Shepherd (2001)		
Industry specific knowledge	Brüderl et al. (1996); Cooper et al. (1994)		Dahlqvist et al. (2000)
Specific experience (manager or founder)	Cooper et al. (1994)	Dahlqvist et al. (2000)	Brüderl et al. (1996)
Social and personal networks	Greve and Salaff (2003); Johannisson (1998); Brüderl et al. (1996); Aldrich and Cliff (2003)		
Preparation and pre-founding activities	Schutjens and Wever (2000); Brüderl et al. (1996); Castrogiovanni (1996)		Dahlqvist et al. (2000)
Strong motivation (EO)	Wiklund (1999); Wicklund and Shepherd (2001); Delmar and Wiklund (2003)		Schutjens and Wever (2000)
Ownership	Heiss and Köke (2001)		
Size	Schutjens and Wever (2000); Heiss and Köke (2001); Brüderl et al. (1996); Wiklund (1999)		
Presence of business partner, entrepreneurial team	Shepherd (1999); Schutjens and Wever (2000); Brüderl et al. (1996); Ruef et al. (2003); Teal and Hofer (2003); Pleschak (1997b)		Nerlinger (1998); Seeger (1997); Almus et al. (1999)
Capital availability	Brüderl et al. (1996); Dahlqvist et al. (2000); Cooper et al. (1994); Wiklund (1999)		

Table A1. *(Continued)*

Entrepreneur-Associated Factors	Positive Relationship to Start-up Activities, Survival or Success	Negative Relationship to Survival or Success	Not Significant
Venture capital	Engel (2002); Dahlqvist et al. (2000)		
Subventions, public aids	Brüderl et al. (1996); Dahlqvist et al. (2000)		
Business relations	Brüderl et al. (1996)		
Market	Bürgel et al. (2001)		
Networking and cooperation	Nijkamp (2003); Hansen (1995); Lechner and Dowling (2003)		
Localization choice	Kangasharju (2000); Schmude (1994b)		
Local socio-economic environment	Littunen et al. (1998); Tödtling and Wanzenböck (2003)		Dahlqvist et al. (2000)

APPENDIX B. DEFINING THE ICT SECTOR: CORE BRANCHES AND EXTENDED DELIMITATIONS

This review gives an overview of what can be considered as "core activities" and "extensions" in the definition of the French ICT sector (see Table B1). Extended delimitations can be explained by the difficulty to identify a certain number of ICT firms in using the Naf700 classification, being the only instrument for the quantification of all firms, but which is not a hundred percent precise instrument for this new and dynamic branch. Even if nearly all ICT firms can be identified, the example of the national telecommunications (Naf subsector code 642A) illustrates this methodological problem: in this sector the activities linked to new information and communication technologies cannot be separated from the ones based on ordinary, "traditional" telephone services. Other businesses based on future technologies, like biotechnologies, are, on the other hand, dispersed about several subsectors of the pharmaceutical industry and the R&D in natural sciences (i.e. 241AEGL, 242ACD, 731Z). A number of studies analyze the ICT sector in a more global way, integrating not only the core subsectors but also new prospering activities like the "contents" (Bruneau & Lacroix, 2001;

Table B1.   The ICT Branch Divided in Subsectors.

Code NAF700	
High tech industry	
246J	Fabrication of data support
300A	Fabrication of business machines
300C	Fabrication of computer and hardware
321A	Fabrication of passive electronic components and condensators
321B	Fabrication of active electronic components
322A	Fabrication of radio emitting and transmitting components
322B	Fabrication of telephones
323Z	Fabrication of equipments for the reception, recording and reproduction of sound and image
Telecommunications (services)	
642B	Other providers except national (France Télécom)
Computer services	
713E	Location of business machines and computer system
721Z	Consulting in information and computer systems
722Z	Software development
723Z	Data administration and use
724Z	Development and administration of data bases
725Z	Repair and services for business machines and computer systems
726Z	Other computer related services
Other knowledge intense services	
731Z	R&D in natural and physical sciences
732Z	R&D in human sciences
742C	Engineering and technical studies
743B	Technical analysis, testing and inspections

Nivlet, 2001); other business services where specific knowledge is needed or certain innovation and technology-based services (i.e. R&D, technical studies and analysis; Lasch, 2001a, b). Indeed, networking and relaying on external competences is one of the main characteristics of ICT firms. In this context, two subsectors play an important role: technical studies (code 742C) and technical analysis, testing and inspections (743B). These knowledge-intense services are increasingly the object of recent research studies and provide for a good part of the economic growth drifting from industry to the service sector (Hauknes, 1999). Moreover, the concentration of innovative firms in a regional economy stimulates and promotes the formation of other, new local ICT firms. These services demand a very high qualification and form a high potential of future firm founders, which mostly implant their new businesses in the region of their last employment. Our delimitation of the ICT sector is similar to what is used in most of the recent publications (see among many: Cases et al., 1999; Heitzmann & Rouquette, 1999; Rouquette, 1999; Table A1), but excludes the national telecommunication sector. Those firms basically making business with what is called ICT "contents" are not part of the definition, because the actual French classification does not allow their specification and clear identification (similar problem as for the national telecommunications). As discussed above a few numbers are dispersed in subsectors, which are not part of the ICT branch. That can be the case for firms in biotechnology, multimedia or even industries classified as middle-high technologies by the OECD but which are innovation and technology-based producers of specialized products, very similar to high technology firms. Finally, remember that two high technology sectors, the aeronautic and space industries (code 353ABC) as well as pharmaceutical industries, are not considered as ICT branches.

STRUCTURE OF SUSTAINABLE ECONOMIC VALUE IN SOCIAL ENTREPRENEURIAL ENTERPRISES

Tom G. Strothotte and Rolf Wüstenhagen

1. INTRODUCTION

Social Entrepreneurial Enterprises (SEEs) are companies that are founded with the mission to change the world in a specific socially oriented way rather than to provide an (economic) ROI (Bornstein, 2004). The social mission is usually accomplished incrementally by convincing other members of society of their cause. The degree to which the social mission is accomplished is the function which an SEE tries to optimize while at the same time remaining economically viable and independent. As SEEs are entrepreneurial enterprises, they are associated with a high risk of failure, yet at the same time they empower their leaders through independence.

The activities of SEEs are often financed by manpower that is generously given free of charge by individuals who are convinced of the social mission. The only cash flows available are generally from charitable contributions. In rare cases, these are augmented by government grants. Some SEEs eventually provide themselves with cash flows by selling products related to their businesses. For example, the World Wildlife Fund (WWF), albeit no longer an entrepreneurial enterprise, funds part of its socially minded activities through the sale of its own line of cuddly animals, and it remains true to its mission by selling replicas only of such animals as are threatened by extinction.

The Emergence of Entrepreneurial Economics
Research on Technological Innovation, Management and Policy, Volume 9, 129–140
Copyright © 2005 by Elsevier Ltd.
ISSN: 0737-1071/doi:10.1016/S0737-1071(05)09008-6

Financing of SEEs is always a problem, since an SEE can usually do better at achieving its social mission with cash than without. In this chapter, we will demonstrate that indeed SEEs, under certain circumstances, can produce economic value added and can convert this into a stream of cash flows which can be used to fund the SEE. However, such income is not without its problems, since social entrepreneurs often do not want to see themselves 'making money', but emphasis instead their role in 'changing the world'. Even if they are willing to endeavour in activities to produce income to fund their SEE, the places in which economic value added is generated are often overlooked. This chapter deems to close this gap.

The chapter is organized as follows. Section 2 discusses the sustainability of SEEs by first setting up requirements for the social mission of an SEE. It is shown that only if this mission is sustainable can the SEE itself be sustainable. Next, Section 3 outlines where economic value added is generated in an SEE. A 'customer value' approach is taken to examine the activities of an SEE and to derive where the value is harboured. The latent nature of such value is not uncommon in the 'customer value' approach, and Section 4 then turns to methods of converting such value added into a stream of cash flows. Finally, concluding remarks and suggestions for future work are given in Section 5.

2. SUSTAINABILITY

Most authors nowadays use the notion of sustainability in the sense of Brundtland (1987), which proposes that "sustainable development is development that meets the needs of the present without compromising the needs of future generations to meet their own needs". Corporate Sustainability has also been conceptualized as a triple-bottom line (Elkington, 1998), i.e., simultaneous creation of economic, environmental and social value. While much research has been done to operationalize environmental sustainability (Wackernagel & Rees, 1996; Schönwandt, 2004; Hockerts, 2003a, b), the concepts of economic and social sustainability and their interrelationships are relatively less well researched (Emerson, 2000, 2003). We look at these aspects in our chapter, with a particular focus on the activities of SEEs. At the outset, we shall analyse the circumstances under which an SEE is in itself 'sustainable' in the original sense of the word, i.e., long-term viable. This in turn has implications for its financing. We propose the notion of the sustainability of a (social) mission and suggest that an SEE is only sustainable if its mission is sustainable.

2.1. Sustainability of a Mission

We can observe that once a company's *raison d'être* vanishes, it will cease to exist. While a company whose goal is to generate economic value can, in principle, go on operating indefinitely, an SEE must be analysed to see if it too can do so. The *raison d'être* of an SEE is its (social) mission, and once this is accomplished the SEE ceases to exist. We say that an SEE with a mission, which can be accomplished in an overseeable amount of time, has an unsustainable mission, while an SEE whose mission will probably never be accomplished, or at least not for a long time, has a sustainable mission.

Examples of unsustainable missions are:

(1) Abolish the production of products using polyvinylchloride (PVC) all over the world (this mission was eventually accomplished).
(2) Achieve a high market penetration of green freezer technology in Germany (this mission was also accomplished).

It should be noted that once a mission is accomplished, a new mission may be to monitor that the mission actually remains accomplished and backlashes do not occur. Also accomplishing a mission to 100% may be exorbitantly expensive, whereas a lower degree of accomplishment (e.g., 90%) may be much less expensive. Hence, a trade-off between the degree of accomplishment of a mission and the cost will have to be considered.

Examples of sustainable missions in the sense outlined above are:

(1) To raise awareness of human rights violations by governments. The reason why this is sustainable is that there will probably always be governments that will violate human rights – in particular since the definition of human rights is not generally agreed upon and may change over time.
(2) To save all animal species existing today from extinction. The problem is so large and diverse that it probably cannot ever be solved, hence the mission is sustainable.
(3) Provide each child in the developing world with a sponsor in the developed world. This is a goal which is unattainable in the foreseeable future, hence the mission is sustainable.

It is useful to treat the sustainability of a social mission as a continuum depending on the length of time or the amount of resources necessary to accomplish the mission. This continuum will then be divided into 'low sustainability' and 'high sustainability'. We shall use these notions later on in this chapter.

2.2. Economic Sustainability

Economic sustainability should be the goal of any enterprise, including SEEs, even though in their case the social mission has the higher priority. We refer to economic sustainability as a state in which an enterprise can pay for its own activities through its income, i.e., has a viable business plan. This goal will have a lower priority for an SEE than for a regular commercial venture, and indeed those involved in an SEE may not see nor want to achieve economic sustainability.

Fig. 1 shows the relationship between economic sustainability and sustainability of the social mission. Note that if the SEE's mission is not sustainable, a change or exit strategy must be devised so as to cover the situation that arises when the mission is accomplished or – in the worst case – if it cannot be accomplished. In the situation that the SEE produces low economic value added, also an exit strategy or a change strategy must be developed so as either to provide funding for the SEE through new economic value added, or a change strategy which adjusts the mission or business plan to make the SEE sustainable.

Pertaining to Fig. 1, horizontal transitions come about as a result of a change in social mission. The transition may also come about as a result of

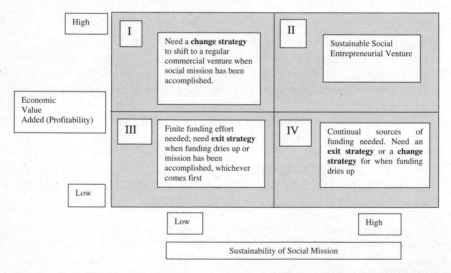

Fig. 1. Relationship between Economic Value Added and Sustainability of the Mission for SEEs.

the SEE's environment changing, i.e., the sustainability of the mission changes in its perception in either direction.

Vertical transitions come about as a result of changes in the success of the implementation of the business model or as a result of changes in the business model itself.

2.3. Sustainability of SEEs

We shall now turn to SEEs based on the definition of SEEs and their dichotomy given above. According to the dichotomy of the missions of SEEs there will be differences in the SEEs depending on the sustainability of the mission upon which they are based. The other factor which influences the sustainability is the economic viability as an enterprise.

(1) SEEs based on sustainable missions are sustainable SEEs if they have an adequate business plan; and
(2) SEEs based on unsustainable missions are unsustainable SEEs.

We shall study such SEEs in turn.

An example of a company which was unsustainable – we conjecture due to the unsustainability of its mission – is Foron Haus- und Kühltechnik GmbH, which was active in East Germany in the early 1990s (Hockerts, 2004). This company started as an SEE whose mission was to change the world in the sense of convincing people to use a specific greener technology for freezers. This is an unsustainable mission because eventually other freezer producers will offer and push green freezers. By choosing the method of producing, marketing and sell such freezers it positioned itself in QIV. It completed its mission when the other freezer makers decided to get into this market, too; the business moved into QI/QIII. At this point, all that was left was an entrepreneurial enterprise with a poor business plan that was doomed to failure. Eventually, it became evident that it had landed in QIII and ultimately went bankrupt.

Consider the society Hochbegabte e.V. (Berlin) as an example of a sustainable SEE. This society has as its mission to make a contribution to the education of gifted children. Such children have an intelligence quotient (IQ) of over 140 (representing about 2% of the population) and often cause problems in school because they are bored. The mission is sustainable because there is a constant supply of new gifted children, and because public policy in Germany is unlikely to change quickly enough for the state to handle the education of these children by itself.

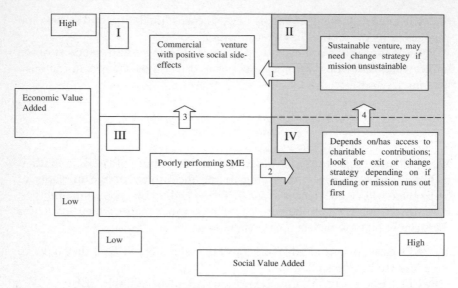

Fig. 2. Relationship between Economic Value Added and Social Value Added. Companies used on the Right Half of the Diagram are SEEs. Some of the Transitions between Quadrants can be Explained with Respect to the Sustainability of the Social Mission on which the SEE is Based.

Fig. 2 now summarizes the situation of SEEs with respect to the fulfilment of the social mission (referred to as 'social value added') and their economic value added (as their ability to fund themselves).

Note that any SEE will be somewhere on the plane of Fig. 2. The primary goal will be to be as far to the right as possible; however, the higher up the better, as this gives the SEE income to continue its work.

Some of the transitions between quadrants of Fig. 2 are of interest in the present context.

(1) QII to QI (decreasing social value added at a high level of economic value added, arrow No. 1): In this transition, a successful SEE changes into a commercial venture. This is a necessary transition if the mission is unsustainable (Foron GmbH after the other freezer makers entered the market). The transition is also made in the case that the mission is sustainable, but the leaders of the firm are losing their social touch (for whatever reason). This transition may require an exit strategy for the initiators of the SEE because they may not want to work for a purely commercial venture.

(2) QIII to QIV (increasing social value added at a low level of economic value added, arrow No. 2): In this transition, a poorly running commercial venture takes on a social mission in order to get access to charitable contributions (perhaps as a way to survive). This can only be a stop-gap measure, as ventures in QIV may not last very long in their own right. An example is a software company offering image-processing software which is not doing well and tries to save itself by beginning to adapt its software for use by blind computer users, even though the number of clients is too small to yield a viable business case.

(3) QIII to QI (increasing economic value added at a low level of social value added, arrow No. 3): Such a transition is the job of management consultants (they may, as a side effect, position the company even lower on the social value added scale).

(4) QIV to QII (increasing economic value added at a high level of social value added, arrow No. 4): The SEE is implementing a change strategy, having discovered how to fund its social mission. For instance, the WWF going into the business of selling stuffed animals. This makes particular sense for SEEs with sustainable social missions, but can also apply to ones with unsustainable missions.

Having looked at the sustainability of SEEs, we can see the need for sustainability both with respect to the mission as well as the economic value added. Hence, in the next section, we will turn to a method of identifying the economic value added by an SEE and how this can be used to fund the SEE itself.

3. ECONOMIC VALUE OF SEEs: A CUSTOMER VALUE PERSPECTIVE

Having examined the relationship between economic value added and social value added, we are now in a position to take a step further and ask the question where this economic value is harboured. The background to this question is twofold: Ultimately, we will want to try to convert this economic value added into cash flows which can be harvested. While the previous section pointed to difficulties with this approach, we consider it to be a necessary step on the way to realizing the social mission set out for the SEE. Indeed, we will turn to this topic in the next section. In the meantime, the current section will assess the structure of this economic value.

Our approach to determining where the economic value added is harboured is based on the notion of customer value (Belz & Bieger, 2004). Underlying this approach is the assumption that a company can increase its shareholder value (thus its economic value) by focusing on increasing the value of its products and services for its customers. The logic of this approach makes use of a value chain as follows: (1) Creating customer value leads to (2) increased cash flows on the part of the customer. These cash flows can be viewed as (3) an increase in customer equity. Thereby increasing the (4) customer portfolio value. This in turn increases the (5) shareholder value of the company offering the product or service.

Two important challenges lie on this chain. On the one hand, customer value created by the company providing the product or service must actually lead to increased cash flows on the part of the customer. For example, if a service is provided more quickly, this must be turned into an economic benefit. Second, part of the enhanced cash flows must flow back to the company providing the product or service. Otherwise, economic value may actually be destroyed because providing the customer value is often associated with increased costs. To stay with the example, to provide a product or service more quickly presumably increases the costs to the company providing this product or service; at least this amount must be recovered from the customer for it to be a worthwhile proposition.

In this section, we shall concentrate on the first element on this chain, i.e., identifying how an SEE enhances customer value. How to convert this customer value into economic value for the SEE will then be the topic of Section 4.

3.1. An SEE's Customers

First, we must define who the customer of an SEE really is, taking into account the peculiarities of SEEs. We note that SEEs may not have customers in the traditional sense of someone who pays a market price for a product or a service. Instead, recall that an SEE's primary goal is to achieve a social mission rather than to create economic value. Hence, for the analysis, it is appropriate to choose a wider definition of the term 'customer' encompassing all persons or companies with direct or indirect contact with the SEE.[1] Among these are persons and companies who

(1) use products or services of the SEE,
(2) influence the decisions of the aforementioned with respect to the products or services of the SEE or its social mission,

(3) are potential users of the products or services, and
(4) are the SEE's suppliers and their own staff (including honorary work-
    ers).

Indeed, each customer can be seen as an SEE's chance to take an incremental step towards achieving its social mission.

3.2. An SEE's Customer Value

We are now in a position to identify a number of areas where an SEE's
customer's value may be harboured. At the outset, it is important to note
that the value which we are searching for is, for the present instance, generated implicitly in the course of the SEE's work towards achieving its social
mission and is not cultivated explicitly. Hence, this customer value ought to
be compatible with any social entrepreneur's social mission – indeed, we
shall contend that it may not even be possible to generate some of this
economic value, even if were not desired. But we shall return to this point
later on in Section 4.

One area in which an SEE generates economic value is in the way its
activities carry out an inherent market segmentation. For example, the customers of an enterprise promoting green energy will have certain attributes
in common with a much higher probability than a random sample of the
same size taken from the general population. These customers may, for
example, also drive or be interested in driving cars which use fuel very
efficiently; they may be interested in other products which are environmen-
tally preferable, hence opening up cross-marketing opportunities.

An SEE such as alluded to must find people ('customers') who are sus-
ceptible to the notion of green energy as a first step towards promoting its
use. This process of identifying its (potential) customers is otherwise called
market segmentation. It costs money to segment a market appropriately and
to find customers. Once these customers have been identified, their identity
has a certain economic value assuming that someone is willing to pay for
their identity.

Another aspect of customer value created by SEEs lies in the social status
of actually being a customer. For example, persons donating money for a
particular cause (as for the tsunami victims in Asia early in 2005) may receive
decals which can be displayed for others to see. Another example was the
movement against violence toward foreigners in which persons supporting
this cause wore buttons with texts such as *"Ne touche pas à mon pot"*.

The point in time at which someone becomes a customer of an SEE may also have an inherent social status associated with it. Some social missions develop as bandwagons and it is no longer a distinction to be a customer. However, it may still be a distinction to belong to the first few customers who 'discovered' the SEE. For example, to have a small membership number in a society with many members may have some inherent value.

Yet another aspect of social status of being a customer arises when it is a particular privilege to be a customer. This situation comes up when certain prerequisites have to be fulfilled before one can become a customer. For example, one cannot simply become a member of a Rotary Club; membership is attained only by nomination from within the club and is restricted to highly recognized members of the community. An example of an SEE in this regard is Hochbegabten e.V., a society for the advancement of highly intelligent persons. In order to become a member of this society, proof must be provided that the prospective member's intelligence quotient (IQ) is at least 140. Membership in such clubs or societies thus implies social prestige.

Finally, customers of SEEs often get to know one another through their activities related to the SEE. This contributes to the personal network of each customer – a network which can be leveraged for other purposes and thus has an inherent value.

4. FROM CUSTOMER VALUE TO CASH FLOWS

As indicated at the outset of the previous section, one of the particular challenges of the 'customer value' approach to creating economic value is that it is effective only if it is possible to actually create cash flows for the SEE. This is the point where social entrepreneurs or even their customers may be alienated because they believe in the non-profit nature of their mission. While it is important not to alienate these stakeholders, it is a reality that most SEEs can make better progress toward fulfilling their mission with free cash flows than without. Hence, the sources of economic value alluded to in the previous section should be taken seriously.

Nonetheless there remains the question how an SEE's customer value can be converted into cash flows, assuming that this is desired.

Table 1 provides a rather generic list of possible sources of economic value added. Of course, in each specific situation, an SEE should be analysed with the goal of identifying other such possible sources and devising methods of converting them into cash flows.

Table 1. How to Realize Economic Value Added of SEEs.

Type of Economic Value Added	How to Realize the Economic Value Added
Market segmentation	Provide visibility of other companies interested in this market segment
Social status of being a customer	One-time and annual membership fees appropriate to social status
Social status of being an early customer	Exclusive special events (with fees) for such customers
Limited customer base	
Network among customers	Maintain registry of customers (members) and charge a fee for access to it

5. CONCLUDING REMARKS

In this chapter, we have outlined a method of systematically identifying possible sources of economic value added in social entrepreneurial enterprises. The method is based on the sustainability of the social mission, which is the basis of the SEE's activities.

In the chapter, we have assumed that the economic value added, which is to be converted into cash flows is generated as a by-product of the SEE's activities. It would be interesting to investigate whether or how this value can be developed systematically so as to provide more income for the SEE. This would move an SEE from being a strictly non-profit organization into one which also has commercial interests – even though these will likely be used exclusively to further the SEE's social mission.

While commercial activities by SEEs may be seen as a necessity on the part of a professional manager, they face resistance on the part of social entrepreneurs who carry out their activities on the basis of idealism. Ways of convincing them that their goals are best served by generating capital, which can be used to further their cause, will have to be developed in the future to provide a basis for an improvement of the funding situation of SEEs.

NOTES

1. We could also refer to this group as the SEE's stakeholders.

REFERENCES

Belz, C., & Bieger, T. (2004). *Customer value–Kundenvorteile schaffen Unternehmensvorteile.* Thexis, St Gallen.

Bornstein, D. (2004). *How to change the world. Social entrepreneurs and the power of new ideas.* Oxford.

Brundtland, G. (Ed.). (1987). *Our common future: The World Commission on Environment and Development.* Oxford.

Elkington, J. (1998). *Cannibals with forks: The triple bottom line of the 21st century.* Oxford.

Emerson, J. (2000). *The nature of returns: A social capital markets inquiry into elements of investment and the blended value proposition.* Harvard Business School working paper. www.blendedvalue.org

Emerson, J. (2003). The blended value proposition: Integrating social & financial returns. *California Management Review,* (Summer), 35–51.

Hockerts, K. (2003a). Sustainability innovations, ecological and social entrepreneurship and the management of antagonistic assets. Ph.D. thesis, University of St Gallen, St Gallen.

Hockerts, K. (2003b). *Case study: Mobility car sharing – from ecopreneurial start up to commercial venture.* Winner of the 1st Oikos Sustainability Case Writing Competition. http://www.oikos-stiftung.unisg.ch/homepage/case.htm

Hockerts, K. (2004). Bootstrapping social change – towards an evolutionary theory of social entrepreneurship. *Academy of Management Review,* submitted.

Schönwandt, C. (2004). *Sustainable entrepreneurship im sektor erneuerbare energien.* Munich, Mering. Ph.D. thesis, University of Kassel.

Wackernagel, M., & Rees, M. (1996). *Our ecological footprint. New catalyst bioregional ser.* (Vol. 9). Gabriola Island, BC: New Society Publishers.

WHERE AND HOW DO INNOVATIVE FIRMS FIND NEW BUSINESS OPPORTUNITIES? AN EXPLORATORY STUDY OF NEW ZEALAND FIRMS

Thomas Schibbye and Martie-Louise Verreynne

INTRODUCTION

In today's competitive environment firms can seldom rely on their current products and services to secure their future success (Miller, 1983; Zahra, 1993; Lumpkin & Dess, 1996). Neither can they ignore their position in the market vis-à-vis their current and potential competitors (Barney, 2002). To win in the competitive global market, firms also have to continuously improve their internal processes in order to ensure that operations are efficiently performed (Carpinetti & Martins, 2001; Tompkins, 2001). These challenges may seem overwhelming and even threatening, but by generating more opportunities firms can increase the possibility of obtaining successful outcomes. This is based on the assumption that the discovery of new opportunities helps leverage a firm's value creation and ensures that the firm remains vital (Stevenson, 1983).

The Emergence of Entrepreneurial Economics
Research on Technological Innovation, Management and Policy, Volume 9, 141–163
Copyright © 2005 by Elsevier Ltd.
All rights of reproduction in any form reserved
ISSN: 0737-1071/doi:10.1016/S0737-1071(05)09009-8

Both Drucker (1985) and Barringer and Bluedorn (1999) emphasise that it is not enough to passively wait for opportunities to arise. Drucker (1985) says that successful innovations are a result of a conscious and purposeful search for innovation opportunities. Barringer and Bluedorn (1999) conclude that opportunity recognition is "often associated with a flash of genius, but in reality is probably more often than not the end result of a laborious process of environmental scanning and industry awareness" (p. 436). They also recommend that all entrepreneurially minded firms should scan the environment to recognise opportunities. Therefore, firms should be proactive when searching for new opportunities and should systematically manage their innovation.

Schibbye and Verreynne (2004) suggest that business opportunities can be defined as:

Attractive, durable and timely chances for a firm to improve its competitive position and performance in order to generate profit, given that a relevant market exists or can be created for a firm's products and/or services.

This definition embraces a broad range of business opportunities and points out that an opportunity does not necessarily have to lead to a competitive advantage (Shrivastava, 1994) to be an opportunity. Instead, every chance a firm has to improve its position and performance, even if such performances are marginal, are in the true sense opportunities (Bellon & Whittington, 1996).

Although the question of the sources of opportunities has been addressed by many authors (Baghai, Coley, & White, 1999; Drucker, 1985; Hargadon & Sutton, 2000; Stevenson & Gumpert, 1985; Timmons, 2002), few have devoted specific attention to this area. Neither does any consensus exist as to where to look for opportunities. Therefore, it appears that there is a gap in the literature about the sources of opportunities. Consequently, there seem to be no guidance for firms in this regard. Moreover, few studies have been conducted to examine where firms actually find new business opportunities. To gain further knowledge about this area, an exploratory study was conducted by in-depth interviewing managers of leading innovative firms in New Zealand.

This chapter begins by presenting the sources of opportunities described in existing theory. Second, the methodology is briefly explained. Third, the authors present the findings, and finally conclusions are drawn, limitations of the study are discussed and the authors suggest areas for future research.

SOURCES OF OPPORTUNITIES

Sources of opportunities are areas that individuals or groups can study to find new entrepreneurial opportunities, or to discover new optimalisation choices that the firm can realise to improve its competitive position and performance (Schibbye & Verreynne, 2004). The sources of opportunities discussed in this chapter aim to create awareness of where potential opportunities may be discovered. All the sources of opportunities offer multiple perspectives on where to find new opportunities. This chapter adopts Drucker's (1985) advice on how to interpret the different sources of opportunities by taking a metaphorical perspective. Each source symbolises a window exposing an area where opportunities can be found. By looking through the different windows, some of the same opportunities can be seen from more than one window. However, the angle is always different, and each window shows its own unique scenery, making it useful to look out of all the windows if one wishes to discover which opportunities are hidden. Such an approach is desirable since new opportunities are likely to appear when one is thinking in new and creative ways. Such thinking should occur if a firm explores sources of opportunities that are not typically studied in that industry. As a result, firms should explore all the different sources of opportunities and not just those sources that at first glance seem relevant to the firm.

Schibbye and Verreynne (2004) propose that there are 16 different sources of opportunities organised into three different groups – macroenvironmental sources of opportunities, industry- and firm-level sources of opportunities and finally universal sources of opportunities (exist at both the micro-, industry-and firm level). All the 16 sources are briefly described below.

Macroenvironmental Sources of Opportunities

According to Drucker (1986), macroenvironmental sources of opportunities are external to the firm in that a firm has little or no chance of influencing them. Such sources are government actions, demographics, geographies, perceptional and sociological changes and finally consumer economics, though it may be argued that in some instances the firm can affect consumer perception.

Stevenson and Gumpert (1985) suggest political action and regulatory standards as a source of opportunity. This is what Eckhardt and Shane (2003) describe as government action. This action can be divided into three broad categories, political, legal and economic actions. Saloner, Shepard, and Podolny (2001) provide examples from the macroeconomic environment where the government's intervention includes taxes and subsidies, international trade rules, regulations, price controls, antitrust laws and information provision. Clearly, these external factors represent opportunities.

Drucker (1985) suggests demographic changes to be the most reliable source of opportunity outside the firm or industry because demographic events have known lead times. Eckhardt and Shane (2003) illustrate this by describing the aging of the baby boomers to bring about new opportunities. Firms aware of this aging follow the distribution of age and will act proactively by reallocating resources from products and services aimed at children to tailor products and services for the elderly.

Geographies can also be categorised as a source of opportunity because there are many opportunities to be found within this area. Czinkota and Ronkainen (1990) suggest a variety of reasons why firms should internationalise, which is one suggestion of how to interpret geographies. First, international sales may be a source of higher profit margins or of more added-on profits. A second stimulus emanates either from unique products or from a technological advantage. A firm may produce goods or services that are not widely available from international competitors or may have made technological advances in a specialised field. Another motivation could be if the firm holds exclusive information about foreign customers, market places or market situations that is not widely shared by other firms. Finally, Czinkota and Ronkainen (1990) suggest that firms may wish to go abroad to obtain tax benefits (Larkins & Jacobs, 1996) or utilise economies of scale. Other reasons may be to improve the firm's competitiveness or achieve favourable publicity and recognition. Geographies can also refer to a product or service, which is imported and can be replaced by producing a similar product at the local destination. In other words geographies should be interpreted as any movement of goods and businesses that can result in new opportunities, both regarding import and export.

Change in perception of current or potential new customers is suggested by Drucker (1985) as a source of opportunity. He argues that when such a change takes place, the facts do not change. Instead a person's view changes, moving from seeing a glass as half empty towards perceiving it as half full. By studying aspects of sociology, such as fashions and trends, firms can look for opportunities. Stevenson and Gumpert (1985) emphasise social values as one of the sources of opportunities arguing that "social values define new styles and standards of living" (p. 87). It is not necessarily economics that dictate such changes, and in many cases it does not have anything to do with economics. Such an example is the growing health consciousness of consumers (Goldman, 2002). A range of industries, among them, soft drinks suppliers, have began to exploit this trend (Leverett, 2003). Soft drinks suppliers have experienced a tremendous increase in the sales of bottled water (www.bottledwaterweb.com). As this has proven to be a huge opportunity, the same providers have exploited this opportunity further by not only providing regular water, but also flavoured sparkling water free of disadvantages such as the high levels of sugar like soft drinks usually contain (Leverett, 2003). Obviously, change in perception can be the catalyst for the growth of whole industries. Through market research firms increase their chances to discover these changes.

Stevenson and Gumpert (1985) suggest consumer economics as a source of opportunity. It affects both the ability and willingness to pay for new products and services. For example, during economic periods of prosperity, consumers typically increase their demand for luxury goods.

Industry- and Firm-Level Sources of Opportunities

The industry- and firm-level sources of opportunities (Drucker, 1985) emerge within an industry or a firm. Six sources of opportunities exist at this level. These are presented below: Industry changes entail opportunities that arise due to the requirements of reallocating resources to respond to a new industry structure (Drucker, 1985). Barney (2002) explains that the kinds of opportunities a firm can expect to discover at the industrial level depend on the industry structure and life stage. While a niche strategy may be a suitable opportunity for firms competing in declining industries, such a strategy may be destructive to firms operating in emerging industries because niche strategies often exclude certain customers.

Process needs are described to exist whenever a demand arises to innovate or answer a particular need, such as health foods and time-saving devices (Kuratko & Hodgetts, 2001). It "perfects a process that already exists, replacing a link that is weak and redesigns an existing old process around newly available knowledge. Sometimes it makes possible a process by supplying the missing link" (Drucker, 1986, p. 85). Typically for process needs, everybody in the firm is aware of the need to improve the process, but it is seldom that anyone reacts to this need. Hence, when someone solves the problem and presents the new innovation, everybody instantly accepts the innovation as being obvious and as a result, it becomes the standard. Opportunities discovered through process needs are often a result of a task-oriented approach rather than adapting a situational orientation (Drucker,

1986). This means that opportunities from process needs are a result of solving a specific problem rather than satisfying a customer need.

Suppliers present a source of opportunity in the sense that they can provide the company with vital inputs such as technical advice, expertise about raw materials and they can gather information which would not have been easily accessed by the firm alone (Wright, 1999). In addition, a firm's performance depends on the quality of the supplier's materials, the supplier's capacity and ability to deliver (Monczka, Trent, & Callahan, 1993). Consequently, every possibility that could enhance joint performance should be initiated. Batson (2002) notes that co-operation between suppliers and customers, for instance customer–supplier partnerships, can result in drastic cost reductions within the value chain. Reduced costs may cause the firm's strategic position to improve, and thus the performance is likely to increase or at least be maintained (Barney, 2002).

The traditional marketing approach perceives customers as a source of opportunity. Both Flores (1993) and Thomke and von Hippel (2002) highlight the importance of listening to customers and responding to their needs. Their recommendations are supported by Hills and Shrader's (1998) empirical research revealing that the vast majority of the 218 entrepreneurs included in their study agreed that they listen extremely hard to what customers say as a way of identifying opportunities. Customers cannot usually identify solutions to their problems, but they can identify their problems, and this is the firm's opportunity (Havener & Thorpe, 1994). However, the firm often has to identify where the opportunities are without receiving specific complaints, suggestions or requests from the customers.

Rivalry-related sources of opportunities target all opportunities which arise as a result of the interrelationship between the firm and its rivals. This rivalry can involve competitors, substitutes, suppliers and customers (Porter, 1980). Such a focus opens up a wide variety of opportunities since every industry possesses its own particular features. For example, the telecommunication industry is dominated by few giant firms enjoying an oligopoly situation (Thiagarajan, 2003), in contrast to the architecture industry, which can be described as experiencing perfect competition. Forming alliances, mergers and acquisitions are examples of opportunities that can be exploited through rivalry-related sources of opportunities.

While rivalry-related sources of opportunities have an external focus on creating new opportunities, internal-directed sources of opportunities relate to areas of improvements within the firm, that is the Kaizen approach (Masaaki, 1986). This involves improving the quality of products and services, decreasing lead-time, reducing costs, improving work processes and getting rid of waste. Robinson and Schroeder (2003) emphasise that every employee should be engaged in this work by suggesting and implementing ideas at a continuous basis.

Universal Sources of Opportunities

The authors suggest that five different sources of opportunities can be labelled as universal sources of opportunities. These sources of opportunities are new knowledge, technology, unexpected occurrences, incongruities and old ideas. These are shortly presented below.

Innovations inspired by new knowledge can result in the creation of new goods and services, the introduction of methods of production, the utilisation of new sources of supply, the restructuring of industries and the creation of new markets and regions (Schumpeter, 1934). However, innovations based on new knowledge do not need to be scientific or technical, for example new knowledge about how to organise a firm better may be just as valuable as a technical innovation. The authors propose that firms should systematically analyse new knowledge both created outside and within to determine whether new information can lead to the discovery of new opportunities.

Shane (2000) suggests that opportunities arise due to technological change. For those firms that manage to respond to the changes by adjusting their business operations and/or business structure, technological change represents a great opportunity. A typical example is found in the case of disruptive technology (Bower & Christensen, 1995). Here, the technological changes have such a dramatic impact that the incumbent firms are likely to go out of business because they are not able to adapt to the changes. On the other hand, for those firms, often small, low costs providers entering this industry, this disruptive technology represents a great opportunity (Utterback, 1994). However, technological changes do not have to be as drastic as those caused by disruptive technology for opportunities to arise. In fact, small and simple ideas may in many instances be transformed into great opportunities, such as the build-to-order principle adopted by Michael Dell has been the main catalyst behind Dell Computer's success even though all his competitors understand how Dell Computers operates (Shah & Serant, 2002).

Based on empirical research, Franklin (2003) explains that the most successful innovations are based on unexpected occurrences, which are described as serendipitous moments when innovators stumble on something they are not looking for, but immediately recognise its significance. Neither "need spotting" (actively looking for an answer to a known problem), "solution spotting" (find a new way of using an existing piece of technology), "mental inventions" (things dreamed up in the head with little reference to the outside world), market research or trend following provides as many successful innovations as unexpected occurrences (Franklin, 2003). Consequently, it is very important that firms are aware of these unexpected occurrences, and quickly take advantage of them (Robinson & Stern, 1997). For example, managers study the firm's balance sheet as deviations occur frequently in most firms' accounts.

Another source of opportunity, incongruities, is defined as discrepancies and dissonances "between what is and what ought to be, or between what is and what everybody assumes it to be" (Drucker, 1986, p. 72). They are described as qualitative rather than quantitative because incongruities do not manifest themselves in the firm's accounts (Drucker, 1986). This means that incongruities may be quite difficult to discover. An example of an incongruity is illustrated by Monem's and Collin's (2000) study of Australian apple exporter's poor performance in Malaysia. Their study revealed that the suppliers thought that size rather than colour determined whether the Malaysian consumers would buy the apples or not. However, this assumption was wrong. Consumers had strong preferences for red apples, especially the Chinese customers, while size was considered less important. This shows that the suppliers' perception of consumers' preferences did not match reality because the suppliers had not conducted proper market research. The solution in this case would simply have been to investigate the market more closely before entering it.

To find new opportunities, it is also advisable to revise old ideas. This approach is widely adopted for example by the fashion industry. Designers often find their inspiration from old trends, which they then modernise and present as new and revolutionary ideas. Based on their research, Hargadon and Sutton (2000) suggest that the best innovators systematically use old ideas as the raw materials to find new ideas. They recommend that firms take one idea which is common place in one area and move it to a context where it is not common at all. This is referred to as knowledge brokering (Bissell, 1997; Hargadon, 1998). To exploit this source of opportunity, Hargadon and Sutton (2000) advise firms to systemise the process of "playing around" with and passing around old ideas in the organisation so that they can be applied to less obvious contexts. This can lead to the discovering new opportunities.

METHODOLOGY

Having identified the different sources of opportunities suggested by theory, it seemed reasonable to research whether practise and theory do harmonise. Briefly explained, the authors decided to carry out an exploratory study involving in-depth interviews with top managers from innovative firms. An innovative firm is defined as a firm that creates something unique by using new methods or ideas. This is typically described as radical innovations (Ethan, Mckeough, Ayers, Rinehart, & Alexia, 2003), and is commonly associated with the launching of completely new products and the creation of new markets (Kuratko & Hodgetts, 2001). An innovative firm can also be a firm that systematically improves on existing products, services and processes. This can be to develop extensions, improve existing products and finding better ways of doing business, which is commonly referred to as incremental innovations (Henderson & Klark, 1990). Obviously, the difference between these two approaches is substantial. For the purpose of this chapter, firms having adapted either of these approaches are defined as innovative firms.

The focus was upon gaining insight and familiarity with the topic so more rigorous investigation could be conducted later on. The need to explore the topic, and gain rich data and insights into an otherwise underdeveloped area of the entrepreneurship literature, lead to the use of in-depth interviews. An interview protocol was developed consisting of both carefully worded open-ended questions and a topic guide in addition to closed questions to gather categorical data.

To identify firms characterised as innovative, business professionals with comprehensive knowledge about New Zealand firms were contacted to obtain information about which firms are famous for being innovative in New Zealand. In addition, secondary information was collected through governmental rapports. Also non-profit organisations were contacted such as The Foundation for Research, Science and Technology to identify potential participants. To control the information provided by these third parties, the researcher also examined the firms' internet home pages, and discussed with firm representatives whether they had launched completely new products or services last year, entered new business areas or made significant improvements to work processes, products or services. In all cases the information on the firms' home pages was consistent with the information provided by the third parties. Eight firms were included in the final sample for this study. The findings from the interviews were content analysed and compared to the information gained from the literature review. These two sources of information were used to develop a framework of opportunity sources, which can potentially be used by firms to facilitate their search for opportunities, or provide a framework for future research.

FINDINGS

This section provides a brief background to the firms included in the sample of this study after which the sources of opportunities utilised by these firms are presented.

Firm Characteristics

Table 1 (Appendix A) provides a schematic summary of the studied firms' profiles. All eight firms represented by a letter from A to H. Below each letter is a column, which describes the firm. The column to the left shows which characteristics are presented at the different rows.

These characteristics suggest innovative firms cannot be categorised or recognised based on the industry, the industry life cycle stage or age. Earlier studies (Banbury & Mitchell, 1995; McGahan & Silverman, 2001) suggest that the explanation might be that innovative firms are opportunity seekers all their lives. If the study had been a large-scale research project including many more firms, the results might have been different. Most of the firms in this study classified their environments as dynamic. This is also supported by existing literature which suggests that in order for firms to grow or at least survive when operating in rapidly changing environments, they have to re-engineer themselves (Kloot, 1996; Vickery, 1999).

A clear pattern that arises from the data in Table 1 is how the respondents described their firm's culture. All the respondents described their firms' organisational culture as informal. Dubin (1958, 1974) suggests that the term informal culture in a firm can refer to the ways tasks are carried out that are not outlined in official, formal descriptions and the social interrelationships between the people in the firm. Morand (1995) proposes that an informal culture can be described as entailing "loose, spontaneous, more casual social intercourse and comportment" (p. 831). Groat (1997) adds that it allows and encourages open relationships and interaction between people as individuals more than as "post-holders". Both the results and literature (Miller, 1971; Wickisier, 1997) therefore indicate that innovative firms tend to adopt an informal organisational culture. Stevenson and Gumpert (1985) point

Table 1. Profiles of the Firms Studied.

Appendix	A	B	C	D	E	F	G	H
Industry	Agritech	Biotech	Several/forest products	Several	Biotech	Electronics	Education	Clothing/design
Number of FTEs (Full time equivalents)	>19 large	>19 large	>19 large	>19 large	>19 large	>19 large	>19 large	<5 small
Age of the firm	Around 40	<15	>100	<15	<15	Around 40	>100	<15
Organisational culture	Informal	Informal	Informal	Informal	Informal	Informal	Informal	Informal
Organisational structure	Decentralised	Decentralised	Hierarchical	Hierarchical and decentralized	Decentralise	Matrix org	Divisionalised form	Decentralised
Industry life cycle stage	Introductory/ Growth and mature	Introduction and growth	Mature	Reinventing/ growth	Discovery	Exponential growth	Growth	Mature
Number of innovations introduced last year	7	6	8 (in 2000)	Not measurable	5	10	8	70% were completely new
Nature of the environment	Dynamic	Dynamic	Stable	Dynamic	Dynamic	Dynamic	Dynamic	Dynamic
Responsible for finding new opportunities	Marketing, engineers + mngt.	Scientists, S and D + R and D	New venture division and top mngt.	Business development	Scientists and management	Mngt, sales department and engineers	Random, bus development manager	Management
Involvement level of top management	Actively involved	Actively involved	Actively involved	Actively involved	Actively involved	Actively involved	Actively involved	Actively involved
Encouraged to find new opportunities	Everybody	Everybody	Everybody	Everybody	Everybody	Everybody	Everybody	Everybody

out that such a structure is favourable when one wants to find new opportunities.

A last comment based on the demographical characteristics of the firms in this study is the involvement of top management in finding opportunities for seven of the eight firms incorporated in the research. McCosh, Smart, Barrar, and Lloyd (1998) suggest that top management should be directly involved in finding new opportunities. However, to what degree it is a common practice that the top management is directly involved in finding new opportunities needs to be explored further. This involvement can be extended to other employees with firms claiming that management, scientists and engineers seemed to be mentioned particularly as the ones who were prioritised, and who received the most resources to assist them in searching for and pursuing opportunities. Nevertheless, it appears that the attitude of the firms is that everybody should be allowed to have their say and should be listened to. The next section briefly describes where these firms find new opportunities.

Where do Firms Find New Opportunities?

Participants were first asked which sources of opportunities they use by asking open-ended questions. Thereafter, respondents were provided with a list of potential sources of opportunities based on the review of the literature presented earlier in this chapter.

The first question led participants to identify opportunities, such as the demand side and the rivalry arena as the most frequently employed sources of opportunities. Technology, old ideas and new knowledge were second. Politics, demographics, sociology, incongruities and unexpected occurrences were only mentioned once or twice. The remaining sources of opportunities were not referred to by any of the respondents. It was also revealed that the non-technological firms only referred to macroenvironmental sources of opportunities and two industry-and firm-level sources of opportunities as to where they find new opportunities. In contrast, the technology-driven firms did not mention the macroenvironment at all as an area they explore when they search for opportunities. Instead, they reported that only the industry and firm level and the universal sources of opportunities were applied.

The second question lead to almost three times as many sources of opportunities being identified by participants. Table 2 provides a summary of all the sources of opportunities identified by participants in both questions. This list is more extensive than the list provided without any prompt. It

Table 2. Sources of Opportunities Identified in Both the Literature Review and Interviews.

	A Tech	B Tech	C Non-tech	D Non-tech	E Tech	F Tech	G Non-tech	H Non-tech
Geographies			X	X		X	X	
Government action	X	X	X	X		X	X	X
Demographics		X		X		X	X	X
Sociology				X			X	X
Consumer economics		X	X				X	X
Industry changes				X			X	X
Process needs		X	X	X	X	X	X	
Supply side				X	X	X	X	X
Demand side	X	X	X	X	X	X	X	
Rivalry arena	X	X	X	X	X	X	X	
Internal processes			X	X	X	X	X	
Technology	X	X	X	X	X	X	X	X
Old ideas	X	X	X	X	X	X	X	X
Incongruities				X			X	X
Unexpected occurrences	X					X	X	X
New knowledge		X	X	X	X	X	X	X

does, however, only present those sources that were already explained in the literature review.

In addition to the 16 sources of opportunities identified through a literature review and summarised in Table 2, the participants suggested a range of other potential sources to be included in the list. The most relevant ones were business economics, competitors, missed opportunities and business models. As respondent F said, "I interpret the source consumer economics as being individual consumers. While consumers in New Zealand these last years have generally been very well off, many businesses have gone through quite tough times, including our own. So business and the consumer economics do not always line up in time. I think business and consumer economics are two independent things and they can be completely different". These additional sources of opportunities are included in the discussion and framework below.

DISCUSSION

The findings show that the respondents answered very differently when asked open-ended questions and when asked to confirm whether they apply any of the sources recognised by the researcher when they are searching for new opportunities. Although this result in itself is interesting this discussion focuses on the sources of opportunities identified in the literature and empirical parts of this study.

First, when comparing the findings between where non-technological firms and technology-driven firms find opportunities few differences were found. Even though the non-technology firms identified more opportunities than the technology-driven firms, the researchers do not interpret this as sufficient evidence to say that a pattern has occurred. The results may reflect a trend, namely that technology-driven firms consciously examine information regarding technology, and to a lesser extent focus on opportunities in the macroenvironment when they are searching for new opportunities, and vice versa for non-technological firms. How much emphasis one should place on these answers is uncertain. Therefore, only limited conclusions can be drawn about who are likely to apply which sources of opportunities before more firms have been included in the study.

Overall, it appears from the findings that several patterns occur. For instance, every source of opportunity identified in the literature review should be included in the opportunity-source framework because the findings from the research show that all the sources were applied by at least three out of eight firms. When reviewing the sources of opportunities, the firms become aware of where they find opportunities. Some firms also expressed the opinion that through this process they learnt where they can search to find new opportunities. Firm D for example, suggested that the interview was a "useful eye-opener". Furthermore, when looking at Table 2, the distribution of positive responses seems to be fairly equal for the three groups, macroenvironmental, industry and firm level and universal sources of opportunities. This suggests that firms should pay equal attention to the three kinds of sources of opportunities. Also, innovative firms seem to apply a wide range of sources to find new opportunities.

Second, sources of opportunities additional to those discussed in the literature review were identified by participants. For instance, missed opportunities may be an area to explore to find new opportunities. On the one hand, it can be argued that this area is closely related to old ideas as one explores areas that have already been considered and/or pursued. On the other, by including missed opportunities in the model, one can facilitate employees thinking differently than about old ideas. By looking at why the firm did not manage to take advantage of an opportunity the firm may discover areas in which they can improve so that new opportunities can be exploited. Therefore, missed opportunities should be an area to consider when searching for new opportunities. Thus, it is recommended that missed opportunities should be included as a separate source in a framework such as the one included in this section.

Business models were another possible source of opportunities suggested by participants. "Business models are abstracts about how inputs to an organisation are transformed to value-adding outputs" (Betz, 2002, p. 21) and Porter's (1985) value-chain model is one of the most famous versions. Chapman, Soosay, and Kanampully (2002) point out that new business models can provide alternative approaches to business practices for firms to consider, in which it can lead to greater efficiency. They discuss particularly how logistics firms are redesigning their business models to fit the "new economy" (Webber, 1993; Sweet, 2001). In this regard, Byrne and Brandt (1992) suggest three noticeable opportunities to shift the business model to become a virtual corporation. By reorganising the firm as a virtual corporation, firms can share costs, skills and get access to global markets. Linder and Cantrell (2001) argue that by choosing the "right" business model, one can expect the firm's performance to improve. Hence, it seems that business models should be included in the opportunity source model in contrast to the Internet which should not be a separate source in the model. Like all the other sources, all firms should examine business models as a source of opportunity as new business models are becoming commonplace in almost "every industry" (Boulton, Libert, & Samek, 2000).

Respondent F suggested the inclusion of business economics as a separate source of opportunity in an overall framework. Business economics here refers to fluctuation in businesses' profits. For example, during depressions many firms cut costs to survive (McDonald, 1995). The result is that business-to-business suppliers face the same depression as their customers' purchase power decreases. On the other hand, when firms experience growth, they tend to leverage the number of investments. It is especially this period that represents an opportunity for the business-to-business suppliers. By examining statistics regarding business and consumer economics from different countries it seems clear that businesses and consumers do not necessarily experience economical difficulties and growth at the same time. This supports the idea of including business economics as a distinct source of opportunity in the model. Moreover, none of the other sources of opportunities directly involve the same areas as business economics. Therefore, it seems appropriate to include business economics as a separate source of opportunity in the opportunity-source model.

The next section proposes an opportunity-source framework that is developed based on the literature review and primary research.

The Opportunity-Source Framework (OS Framework)

Fig. 1 provides a summary of the sources of opportunities that were identified in the literature review and interviews. It provides a clear overview of
how the different sources of opportunities are organised and related to each
other. The framework is not constructed to be industry specific, but rather is
a tool that can assist all firms to find new opportunities. The framework is
intended to be used as a creative brainstorming tool as to where new opportunities can be discovered by firms, and as a method for framing future
research by researchers. The opportunity-source framework consists of two
different levels, the macroenvironmental and the industry and firm level. All
the sources of opportunities have been placed within this framework at the
level at which they seem most relevant.

As stated earlier, all the sources of opportunities offer multiple perspectives on where to find new opportunities. Consequently, firms should explore all the different sources of opportunities and not just those sources
that at first glance seem relevant to the firm.

	Missed opportunities	New Knowledge	Unexpected occurrences	Incongruities	Old Ideas	Technology
Macro environmental sources of opportunities						
Geographies						
Politics, legislation and economics / government action						
Demographics						
Sociology / change in perception						
Consumer economics						
Business economics						
Industry and firm level sources of opportunities						
Industry changes						
Process Needs						
Supply side (Suppliers)						
Demand side (Customers)						
Competitors						
Rivalry arena						
Internal processes						
Business models						

Fig. 1. The Opportunity-Source Model.

Application of the Opportunity-Source Framework

The opportunity-source framework can be used by both firms and researchers. For instance by applying the opportunity-source framework during strategic planning and as part of the development of a business plan for a new product/service idea, such a formalised tool can be of assistance to bring structure to the search for new opportunities as suggested by several respondents. Here the sources of opportunities can be used as a checklist for areas one should consider when looking for new opportunities. This increases the chances that one will not overlook any opportunities while developing business plans or during strategic planning. Accordingly, it seems as the opportunity-source model can be useful in this matter. The researchers suggest that to benefit the most from the opportunity-source framework, one should combine it with creative thinking techniques (Michalko, 1991; Root-Bernstein & Root-Bernstein, 1991; Tanner, 1992; Higgins, 1994; Epstein, 1995), such as brainstorming sessions, Lotus Blossom Technique, Delphi and Scenario techniques. If one knows how to think differently the researcher suggests that one is more likely to find new and unique opportunities while exploring the sources of opportunities. Thus, the application of creative techniques should be employed to get the maximum out of the time spent exploring sources of opportunities. To academic researchers, this framework organises the literature and provides a starting point for future research.

Limitations

Any study inevitably has limitations and/or implications depending on the deliberate and unconscious choices made. These implications and limitations are discussed below.

Firstly, the opportunity-source framework does not include any information about cognitive mechanisms, for example why some people and not others recognise and create new opportunities, how people perceive opportunities differently (Baron, 1998), and how opportunities are identified and evaluated (Kaish & Gilad, 1991; Keh, Foo, & Lim, 2002). This means that the framework guides firms into where to search for opportunities, but not how people should think to recognise the opportunities. This framework is furthermore only a first step towards exploiting new opportunities. Since the exploitation of opportunities causes change, for the outcome to be successful, it is required that the firm has the ability to implement such changes

(Wright, 1999). For example, the firm needs an organisational culture supporting the exploitation of new ideas (Jarve, 1996; McCosh et al., 1998; Searle & Ball, 2003). In addition, as recommended by Barringer and Bluedorn (1999), innovation also requires that the firm's strategic management practices support the exploitation of opportunities. Carnall (1999) therefore suggests that firms implementing major changes need to take an organisational-wide approach to successfully carry out the changes.

Secondly, the framework may not include all kinds of sources of opportunities. It is a first step towards systematising the sources of opportunities, making them more visible, and creating awareness of where one can search for new opportunities. For example, depending on which perspective one has, it can be argued that employees are a source of opportunity equivalent to customers and suppliers (DeSimone, Hatsopoulos, O'Brian, Harris, & Holt, 1995). Other related sources may be business reviews, strategic planning and the Internet.

This research is highly exploratory, but even so, the decision to study only eight firms can be viewed as a limitation. Because the sample size is small it is impossible to draw any conclusion about characteristics of the innovative firms. By including such a small number of firms in the study, the generalisability decreases. On the other hand, results from previous research indicate that the findings may be representative for a larger population after all (Markides, 1997; Hills & Shrader, 1998; Hargadon & Sutton, 2000; Franklin, 2003).

Finally, it seems clear that firms less experienced at finding opportunities can learn about where and how to search for opportunities from the innovative firms included in the study. However, while doing so, it is important to carefully consider the results of the study because some firm practices may work well for some firms and may not be applicable to other firms. Hence, a firm should not simply follow the practices employed by the innovative firms described in this chapter. Instead, a firm should adopt only those practices that appear to be of value to that firm.

Future Research

The implications and the limitations discussed above indicate which areas should be further exploited. In general, there are four major areas that logically flow from the previous discussions.

First, there is a need to replicate the research where the only change should be to include a considerably higher number of firms in the study so that the patterns can be confirmed or rejected. This exploratory research succeeded in discovering several patterns, and clearly confirmatory research is a purposeful second step. The second obvious area to examine further is to empirically test and retest the opportunity-source framework to reveal how useful it is. By testing the model, adjustments can be made so that it becomes more applicable. Moreover, such a study may also reveal elements which should be included to improve the model, and areas which restrict its use may also be discovered. Third, it should be possible to apply the framework in a broader context including areas such as cognitive processes, strategic innovation and the underlying elements within each source of opportunities as mentioned above. Such an approach would totally revitalise the model, in other words, using an old model/idea to create a new and improved model. Lastly, it may also be an idea to tailor the framework to only be applicable to one specific industry. This was not the original intention behind the model, but it is possible that firms can find more opportunities if the model is tailor-made for every industry. Thus, this is an area which needs to be examined further.

CONCLUSION

In conclusion, the results of this study indicate that there are at least 20 sources of business opportunities that firms can examine to find new opportunities. The findings reveal that sources of business opportunities exist at three separate levels, namely the macro-, industry-and firm level. Within the specific levels, it is proposed that the macro level comprises government action, demographics, geographies, changes in consumer perception, consumer economics and business economics sources of opportunities, while the industry and firm level consists of industry changes, process needs, suppliers, customers, competitors, rivalry-related sources of opportunities, internal-directed sources of opportunities and finally business models sources of business opportunities. In addition, six sources of business opportunities are found to exist at all levels; namely technology, new knowledge, unexpected occurrences, incongruities, old ideas and missed opportunities.

The research found that innovative firms apply a wide range of sources of opportunities when they search for new opportunities. This supports the idea that firms should explore all 20 sources of opportunities identified in this chapter and not simply those sources which at first glance seem most applicable. An analysis of the findings indicates that many innovative firms may share a set of common characteristics. To begin with, it seems that innovative firms cannot be recognised based on the size and age of the firm or the industry they operate in. Further, it was proposed that innovative firms remain innovative during their whole lifespan as the results showed that these firms can be found at all stages in the industry life cycle. Next, innovative firms appear to have an informal culture and more often than not elements of a decentralised structure. In addition, such firms seem to introduce about five to ten innovations every year. The results also point towards the idea that such firms can often be spotted in rapidly changing environments. Moreover, three groups, namely the management, scientists and engineers were found to be perceived as responsible for finding opportunities. The findings also suggest that everybody working in innovative firms is encouraged to bring forth their ideas. Finally, the results clearly imply that the vast majority of innovative firms have an active top management.

It was found that the respondents are involved in general search for opportunities that can lead to competitive advantage. However, the respondents agreed that a broader focus could be purposeful, and could open up for new opportunities to be discovered. This chapter offers an exclusive tool to enhance creativity, labelled as the opportunity-source framework. It was suggested that such a framework can facilitate firms search for opportunities in a more systematic manner and create awareness of where opportunities can be found.

REFERENCES

Baghai, M., Coley, S., & White, D. (1999). *The alchemy of growth*. London.

Banbury, C. M., & Mitchell, W. (1995). The effect of introducing important incremental innovations on market share and business survival. *Strategic Management Journal (1986–1998)*, *16*(Special Issue), 161–182.

Barney, J. B. (2002). *Gaining and sustaining competitive advantage* (2nd ed.). Upper Saddle River.

Baron, R. A. (1998). Cognitive mechanisms in entrepreneurship: Why and when entrepreneur think differently than other people. *Journal of Business Venturing*, *13*, 257–294.

Barringer, B. R., & Bluedorn, A. C. (1999). The relationship between corporate entrepreneurship and strategic management. *Strategic Management Journal*, *20*, 421–444.

Batson, R. G. (2002). Getting started in a supplier improvement initiative. Quality congress. ASQ's. *Annual Quality Congress Proceedings*, pp. 397–410.

Bellon, B., & Whittington, G. (1996). *Competing through innovation: Essential strategies for small and medium-sized firms*. Dublin: Oak Tree Press.

Betz, F. (2002). Strategic business models. *Engineering Management Journal*, *14*(1), 21–27.

Bissell, J. (1997). The marketer as 'knowledge broker'. *Brandsweek*, *38*(43), 17.

Boulton, R. E. S., Libert, B. D., & Samek, S. M. (2000). A business model for the new economy. *The Journal of Business Strategy, 21*(4), 29–35.

Bower, J. L., & Christensen, C. C. (1995). Disruptive technologies: Catching the waves. *Harvard Business Review, 73*(1), 43–53.

Byrne, G., & Brandt, W. (1992). The virtual corporation. In: W. A. Davidow & M. S. Malone (Eds), *The virtual corporation.* New York.

Carnall, C. A. (1999). *Managing change in organisations.* London: Prentice-Hall.

Carpinetti, L. C. R., & Martins, R. A. (2001). Continuous improvement strategies and production competitive criteria: Some findings in Brazilian industries. *Total Quality Management, 12*(3), 281–291.

Chapman, R. L., Soosay, C., & Kanampully, J. (2002). Innovation in logistic services and the new business model: A conceptual framework. *Managing Service Quality, 12*(6), 358–371.

Czinkota, M. R., & Ronkainen, I. A. (1990). *International marketing.* (4th ed.). Orlando.

DeSimone, L. D., Hatsopoulos, G. N., O'Brian, W. F., Harris, B., & Holt, C. P. (1995). How can big companies keep the entrepreneurial spirit alive? *Harvard Business Review, 73*(6), 183–189.

Drucker, P. F. (1985). The discipline of innovation. *Harvard Business Review, 63*(3), 67–72.

Drucker, P. F. (1986). *Innovation and entrepreneurship.* Practice and principles. London: Pan.

Dubin, R. (1958). The world of work: Industrial society and human relations. Englewood Cliffs.

Dubin, R. (1974). *Human relations in administration.* Englewood Cliffs.

Eckhardt, J. T., & Shane, S. A. (2003). Opportunities and entrepreneurship. *Journal of Management, 29*(3), 333–349.

Epstein, R. (1995). *Creativity games for trainers.* New York: McGraw-Hill.

Ethan, S. S., Mckeough, D. T., Ayers, A. D., Rinehart, E., & Alexia, B. (2003). How do you best organize for radical innovation? *Research Technology Management, 46*(5), 17.

Flores, F. (1993). Innovation by listening carefully to customers. *Long Range Planning, 26*(3), 95–102.

Franklin, C. (2003). *Why innovations fail.* London.

Goldman, S. (2002). Organic: Beyond the seal. *Beverage World, 121*(1720), 49.

Groat, M. (1997). The informal organisation: Ride the headless monster. *Management Accounting, 75*(4), 40–42.

Hargadon, A. (1998). Firms as knowledge brokers: Lessons in pursuing continuous innovation. *California Management Review, 40*(3), 209–227.

Hargadon, A., & Sutton, R. I. (2000). Building an innovation factory. *Harvard Business Review, 78*(3), 157–168.

Havener, C., & Thorpe, M. (1994). Customers can tell you what they want. *Management Review, 83*(12), 42–46.

Henderson, R. M., & Klark, K. B. (1990). Architectural innovation: The reconfiguration of existing product technologies and the failure of established firms. *Administrative Science Quarterly, 35*, 9–30.

Higgins, J. M. (1994). *101 Creative problem solving techniques: The handbook of new ideas for business.* Winter Park, FL: New Management Publishing Company.

Hills, G. E., & Shrader, R. C. (1998). Successful entrepreneurs' insights into opportunity recognition. *Frontiers of entrepreneurial research.* Retrieved on 28 August 2003 from: www.babson.edu/entrep/fer/papers98/I/I_A/I_A_text.htm.

Jarve, J. W. (1996). Organizing for innovation. *Harvard Business Review, 74*(2), 160–161.

Kaish, S., & Gilad, B. (1991). Characteristics of opportunities search of entrepreneurs versus executives: Sources, interests, general alertness. *Journal of Business Venturing, 6*, 45–61.

Keh, H. T., Foo, M. D., & Lim, B. C. (2002). Opportunity evaluation under risky conditions: The cognitive processes of entrepreneurs. *Entrepreneurship: Theory and Practice, 27*(2), 125–148.

Kloot, L. (1996). Looping the loop: New directions for the learning organisation. *Australian Accountant, 66*(6), 26–27.

Kuratko, D. F., & Hodgetts, R. M. (2001). *Entrepreneurship: A contemporary approach* (5th ed). Fort Worth: Harcourt.

Larkins, E. R., & Jacobs, F. A. (1996). Tax incentives for small businesses with export potential: A capital budgeting decision analysis. *Accounting Horizons, 10*(2), 32–50.

Leverett, E. (2003). Water works. *Foodchain Magazine.* Retrieved on 9 March 2004 from: http://www.foodchain-magazine.com/0308/03.html.

Linder, J. C., & Cantrell, S. (2001). Five business-model myths that hold companies back. *Strategy and Leadership, 29*(6), 13–18.

Lumpkin, G. T., & Dess, G. G. (1996). Clarifying the entrepreneurial orientation construct and linking it to performance. *Academy of Management Review, 21*(1), 135–172.

Markides, C. (1997). Strategic innovation. *Sloan Management Review, 38*(3), 9–23.

Masaaki, I. (1986). *Kaizen, the key to Japan's competitive success.* New York: McGraw-Hill.

McCosh, A. M., Smart, A. U., Barrar, P., & Lloyd, A. D. (1998). Proven methods for innovation management: An executive wish list. *Creativity and Innovation Management, 7*(4), 175–192.

McDonald, W. W. (1995). The great depression reconsidered: Implications for today. *Contemporary Economic Policy, 13*(2), 1–14.

McGahan, A. M., & Silverman, B. S. (2001). How does innovative activity change as industries mature? *International Journal of Industrial Organization, 19*(7), 1141.

Michalko, M. (1991). *Thinkertoys: A handbook of business creativity for the 90's.* Berkeley, CA: Ten Speed Press.

Miller, D. (1983). The correlates of entrepreneurship in three types of firms. *Management Science, 29*(7), 770–791.

Miller, R. E. (1971). *Innovation, organization and environment.* Monograph, Universite de Sherbrooke, Sherbrooke, Quebec.

Monczka, R. M., Trent, R. J., & Callahan, T. J. (1993). Supply base strategies to maximize supplier performance. *International Journal of Physical Distribution and Logistics Management, 23*(4), 42–55.

Monem, T. A., & Collins, R. J. (2000). Incongruities in the fresh produce supply chain: Australia's challenge in meeting Malaysian consumers' needs. Retrieved on 15 October 2003 from:http://agecon.tamu.edu/iama/2000Congress/Forum%2020Final%20PAPERS/Area%20II/Monem_Tamanna.PDF.

Morand, D. A. (1995). The role of behavioural formality and informality in the enactment of bureaucratic versus organic organizations. *The Academy of Management Review, 20*(4), 831–871.

Porter, M. (1980). *Competitive strategy.* New York.

Porter, M. (1985). *Competitive advantage: Creating and sustaining superior performance.* New York.

Robinson, A. G., & Schroeder, D. M. (2003). *Ideas are free.* San Francisco: Brett-Koehler.

Robinson, A. G., & Stern, S. (1997). *Corporate creativity: How innovation and improvement actually happen*. San Francisco: Brett-Koehler.

Root-Bernstein, R. S., & Root-Bernstein, M. M. (1991). *Sparks of genius: The thirteen thinking tools of the world's most creative people*. Boston: Harvard Business Press.

Saloner, G., Shepard, A., & Podolny, J. (2001). *Strategic management*. New York: Wiley.

Schibbye, T., & Verreynne, M. (2004). In search of competitive advantage: How do SMEs find business opportunities. Paper presented at the International Council of Small Business 49th World Conference, Sandton, South Africa.

Schumpeter, J. A. (1934). *The theory of economic development*. Cambridge.

Searle, R. H., & Ball, K. S. (2003). Supporting innovation through HR policy: Evidence from the UK. *Creativity and Innovation Management, 12*(1), 50–62.

Shah, J. B., & Serant, C. (2002, 26 August). Is supply chain prowess enough? Dell confident time is right to enter white-box market. *Manhasset, EBN* (p. 3).

Shane, S. (2000). Prior knowledge and the discovery of entrepreneurial opportunities. *Organisation Science, 11*(4), 448–469.

Shrivastava, P. (1994). Strategic management. Concepts & practices. Ohio.

Stevenson, H. H. (1983). *A perspective on entrepreneurship*. Harvard Working Paper, 9-384-131.

Stevenson, H. H., & Gumpert, D. E. (1985). The heart of entrepreneurship. *Harvard Business Review, 63*(2), 85–94.

Sweet, P. (2001). Strategic value configuration logic and the 'new' economy: A service economy revolution. *International Journal of Service Industry Management, 12*(1), 70–83.

Tanner, D. (1992). Applying creative thinking techniques to everyday problems. *The Journal of Consumer Marketing, 9*(4), 23–28.

Thiagarajan, K. (2003, 10 October). Telecom industry to remain volatile. *The Hindu Business Line*. Internet edition. Retrieved on 24 October 2003 from: http://www.thehindubusinessline.com/2003/10/20/stories/2003102000630300.htm.

Thomke, S., & von Hippel, E. (2002). Customers as innovators: A new way to create value. *Harvard Business Review, 80*(4), 74–81.

Timmons, J. A. (2002). *New venture creation. Entrepreneurship for the 21st century* (5th ed.). Boston.

Tompkins, J. A. (2001). *Future capable company: What manufacturing leaders need to do today to succeed tomorrow*. Raleigh, NC: Tompkins Press.

Utterback, J. M. (1994). Mastering the dynamics of innovation. Boston.

Vickery, G. (1999). Business and industry policies for knowledge-based economies. Organisation for Economic Cooperation and Development. *The OECD Observer, 215*, 9–11.

Webber, A. M. (1993). What's so new about the new economy? *Harvard Business Review, 71*(1), 24–42.

Wickisier, E. L. (1997). The paradox of empowerment – a case study. *Empowerment in Organizations, 5*(4), 213.

Wright, J. N. (1999). *The management of service operations*. London: Caswell.

Zahra, S. A. (1993). Environment, corporate entrepreneurship, and financial performance: A taxonomic approach. *Journal of Business Venturing, 8*, 319–340.

Internet references: www.bottledwaterweb.com

FLEXIBLE INSTITUTIONALIZATION: ON THE ROLE OF MANAGERIAL VARIABLES IN TECHNOLOGY START-UPS

Orly Yeheskel and Miri Lerner

INTRODUCTION

Despite the continuous rise in the establishment of technology-based start-ups (TSUs), the reported statistics indicate high failure rates for these ventures. This has led to a large body of research literature dealing with the identification and assessment of factors affecting TSU performance. Most studies have focused on various business variables or other business areas, including financial aspects, marketing issues, strategic planning, the technological development process, operational and quality management issues, timing of entry, lack of individual knowledge and ability during the founding process (Gartner, Starr, & Bhat, 1999), difficulties in managing the legal aspects, failure to establish and develop the relevant networks with key customers and suppliers (Roure & Maidique, 1986; Roure & Keeley, 1990; Littunen, 2000) and the failure to invest in learning (Schilling, 1998).

The Emergence of Entrepreneurial Economics
Research on Technological Innovation, Management and Policy, Volume 9, 165–187
Copyright © 2005 by Elsevier Ltd.
All rights of reproduction in any form reserved
ISSN: 0737-1071/doi:10.1016/S0737-1071(05)09010-4

Very few studies have related TSU performance to the management process during the different stages of development (Vesper, 1980; Van de Ven, Hudson, & Schroeder, 1984; Cooper & Bruno, 1977; McMillan, Zemann, & Narasimha, 1987). Many salient managerial processes, such as institutionalization; formalization of work procedures, timetables or budgets; task differentiation creating formal communication networks; structuring reward and compensation systems; or creating an organizational culture that fits the needs of the growing business organization have been neglected in the existing literature. The purpose of this study is to examine managerial factors affecting the performance of TSUs in Israel, with potentially wide generalizability to TSUs in other contexts.

Israeli High-Tech Start-ups: The Research Context

Israel has witnessed a swift and impressive increase in TSU activity, as well as in the scope of equity financing activity. Developments in international high-tech markets and the success of Israeli high-tech firms have driven developments in the local venture capital market and in angel activity. Despite a decline in scope due to the recent downturn in the global markets and the grave political situation, the Israeli high-tech sector is still a very vital one.

Measuring TSU Performance

The literature suggests different criteria for defining and measuring start-up performance (Schutjens & Wever, 2000). Performance is often measured by profit, return on investment, or substantial income generation for the entrepreneurs. Other indicators used include added value, growth of turnover, or growth in the number of employees (Schutjens & Wever, 2000), although not all start-ups place expansion among their goals. Frequently, a young venture's performance is operationalized merely in terms of survival (Van Praag, 1999). Subjective measures of new venture performance have also been frequently used, as financial performance measures can be misleading for young businesses, and because of the need for a measure flexible enough to compare performance across numerous industries (Kunkel & Hofer, 1993, p. 8). Moreover, previous findings (Dess & Robinson, 1984) have identified high correlations between objective and subjective performance measures. Hence, in this study performance is measured using subjective perceptions of CEOs regarding various aspects of the performance of their TSUs (survival, financial, technological and marketing performance).

THEORETICAL FRAMEWORK AND HYPOTHESES

In this study we apply the conceptual frameworks of institutional and neo-institutional theories of organizations and the dynamic concept of the institutionalization process to TSUs.

Institutional and Neo-Institutional Theories

Institutionalization is a social process by which structures, policies and programs acquire "rule-like status" as legitimate elements of the organization (Meyer & Rowan, 1977). Scott (1995, p. 33) claims that "institutions consist of cognitive, normative and regulative structures and activities that provide stability and meaning to social behavior". Moreover, in a later book, Scott (1998, p. 117) mentions that organizations are open systems, strongly influenced by their environments and much controlled by socially constructed belief systems and normative rules. According to institutional theories, institutionalization occurs through basic regulative, normative and cognitive processes. Neo-institutional theories place special emphasis on the cognitive elements of institutionalization, i.e. "rules that constitute the nature of reality and the frames through which meaning is made" (Scott, 1995, p. 40), whereby a collection of internalized symbolic representations mediates between the external world of stimuli and the organism's response (D'Andrade, 1984; Scott, 1995).

In this chapter, we follow the institutionalization processes in TSUs and examine their effects on performance. We focus on four managerial variables – formalization, centralization, leadership style and esprit de corps – which represent the unique institutionalization processes of a TSU's establishment. The following sections describe the literature relevant to each of these variables.

Formalization

Formalization refers to programmed coordination or the degree to which divisions of labor and procedures are explicit (e.g. written or otherwise manifested in the form of guidelines), rather than implicit (Price, 1972; Rondeau, Vondrembse, & Ragu-Nathan, 2000). Many researchers have indicated the positive effects of formalization on productivity and efficiency as clarity of rules, policies and guidelines minimize decisional uncertainty (Hage, 1965). More formalized companies received more resources from other organizations in their environment than the less formalized ones

(Molnar & Rogers, 1976), and had higher output levels (Whetten, 1978; Moenaert, Souder, Meyer, & Deschoolmeester, 1994).

A broad body of literature has pointed to the contribution of mechanistic procedures, such as formalization and standardization in response to external threats (Schendel, Patton, & Riggs, 1976; Bozeman & Slusher, 1979; Staw, Sandelands, & Dutton, 1981). Pfeffer and Leblebici (1973) also claim that a stressful environment with a high degree of market competition, coupled with a high degree of environmental change, is associated with higher formalization and control. On the other, various theories (e.g. Burns & Stalker, 1961; Lawrence & Dyer, 1983), addressing the managerial dilemma between mechanistic (highly formalized) and organic (less formalized) organizations, mention that complex and organic forms of organizations are more innovative than the formalized mechanistic ones (Aiken, Bacharach, & French, 1980). One view of the relation between formalization and innovation suggests that while nonformalized organic structures increase the number and quality of proposals for change and innovation, adoption of change occurs only when sufficient integration mechanisms are available to foster some degree of collaboration (Zaltman, Duncan, & Holbek, 1973; Aiken et al., 1980).

Clearly, these environmental characteristics are inherent conditions for TSUs, and thus some level of standardization and control must characterize them. Considering the unique contradictory needs facing the TSU – namely the need to maintain a continuous innovation process while stabilizing its systems and operating according to satisfactory business models – we argue that a basic level of formalization is critical to enable the creation of a managerial infrastructure and prevent chaos. Nevertheless, overly high levels of formalization might impede innovation.

Hypothesis 1. The relationship between the level of formalization and TSU performance is curvilinear, with highest performance at intermediate levels of formalization.

Centralization

Centralization refers to the degree to which authority and decision-making power are concentrated versus dispersed in the organization. Cameron, Whetten, and Kim (1987) examined centralization as one of 12 attributes associated with organizational decline. Although centralization was predicted to be associated with decline, their findings showed it was a characteristic of both stable and declining organizations. Its dysfunctional effects were avoided only in organizations with growing revenues. Whetten (1978) found a strong association between a centralized decision-making structure and productivity, arguing that centralization acts to reduce uncertainty and decisional leeway. Glisson and Martin (1980) note that in highly centralized organizations where workers have minimal say in the decision-making process, workers are free from strategic issues, and thus have more time for the mission at hand. As a result, their performance and productivity are higher than in less centralized organizations.

Conversely, other researchers note that high centralization has negative effects in organizations. Holland (1973) and Pondy (1977) argue that workers in highly centralized organizations are likely to resent the lack of opportunity for decisional participation and tend to be dissatisfied. These consequences might be harmful for organizations, such as TSUs, where employee satisfaction is necessary for performance. Argyres (1995), comparing the effects of centralization on implementation of technology strategies at GM and IBM, concludes that more centralized decisions enhance implementation of technology strategies that require interdivisional coordination, but diminish the link between division-level managers' rewards and their performance. Moenaert et al. (1994), in their research on innovation projects in Belgian companies, found no effect of centralization on project success. Masuch (1985) and Meyer, Stevenson, and Webster (1985) claim that centralization actions may inhibit effective adaptation because bureaucracies become more rigid as a result of attempts to improve productivity through increased supervision. Following this literature, and understanding the TSUs critical need for adaptation to the changing environment, we hypothesized that:

Hypothesis 2. The greater the centralization, the lower the TSU performance.

Management/Leadership Style

The term "leadership style" has been defined as "the relatively consistent pattern of behavior that characterizes a leader" (DuBrin, 1995). The most famous typology of leadership styles is of authoritarian, democratic and laissez faire leadership. A comparison of democratic and authoritarian leadership with laissez faire leadership (White & Lippitt, 1960) showed that laissez faire leadership resulted in less concentration on work and a poorer quality of work than in the other styles. There was less general satisfaction than from the democratic style, but still somewhat more satisfaction than

from the autocratic style. Some literature refers to the relationship between
a laissez faire style and subordinates' preference for autonomy, pointing out
an inherent tension: although it grants freedom to those who need it, it may
lead to anarchy, absence of control and organizational sanctions, individual
concentration on maximizing self-interests, and thus to organizational in-
effectiveness (Tannenbaum, 1968; Miner, 1973).

Although the use of the typology relating to transactional versus transformational leadership (Bass, 1990) is very popular in modern leadership
literature, for methodological reasons we prefer the traditional distinction
between democratic, autocratic and laissez faire leadership. Thus, we make
the following hypothesis concerning leadership style.

Hypothesis 3. TSUs in which the main leadership style is democratic and
participative perform better than TSUs with autocratic or laissez faire
leadership styles.

Team Solidarity: Esprit De Corps

High-performance new firms are rarely started by individuals. Four-fifths of
them are established by teams (Reynolds, 1993). Friendship and solidarity
among entrepreneurial teams of new ventures have been recognized as important for improving early performance (Francis & Sandberg, 2000). It has
been claimed that the close contact, peer status and high interdependence
typical of many entrepreneurial teams characteristically lead to friendships
and stability among team members (Kamm & Nurik, 1993; Francis &
Sandberg, 2000, p. 9), which are conducive to decision-making processes
that enhance the team's effectiveness in solving problems and ultimately
improve venture performance (Watson, Ponthiel, & Critelli, 1995; Francis &
Sandberg, 2000). Several characteristics in particular have been claimed to
relate to high team performance: openness, sensitivity, flexibility, cooperation, commitment and shared responsibility (Buchholz & Roth, 1987). The
linkages between team completeness and prior joint experience have been
strongly associated with firm performance (Roure & Maidique, 1986; Roure
& Keeley, 1990; Chandler & Hanks, 1998).

On the other hand, Hambrick (1994) found that deficiencies in the top
management team could gravely impair a firm's performance and vitality.
The most critical problem exists when the team is not a team at all, but
rather a constellation of senior executives pursuing their own agendas,
with a minimum of collaboration or exchanges. In the face of major

environmental shifts, such teams are slow and generally maladaptive (Chandler & Hanks, 1998, p. 320).

Team solidarity and friendship are similar to the feeling of esprit de corps that is present among officers as a result of the demands for expertise, responsibility and cohesion in the military profession (Huntington, 1964; Sorensen, 1994; Stevens, Rosa & Gardner, 1994). When linking team solidarity/esprit de corps with firm performance, one has to remember that the relationship between them is bilateral. Research shows that members of successful groups perceive their groups to be more attractive. Team members are likely to be more willing to stay and work out problems if it appears that the vision that originally bound them together may be realized (Cooper & Daily, 1997, p. 143). In other words, team solidarity may contribute to firm performance and vice versa. Based on the stream of research mentioned above, we make the following hypothesis.

Hypothesis 4. The more the entrepreneurial team of the TSU is characterized by elements of esprit de corps (solidarity and friendship), the higher the firm's performance.

Control Variables: The Firm's Size, Age and Industry Type

The existing literature indicates the salience of three variables relating to firm performance and survival: industry type, firm size and age (Kirchhoff & Acs, 1997). Hence, we controlled for these three variables in our examination of the linkages between managerial variables and performance.

Firm Size

Many researchers have empirically found a positive relationship between the size and success of new firms (Storey, 1985; Keasey & Watson, 1991; Audretsch, 1994). Some researchers point to scale economies in large firms that may enhance success. Following the transaction cost theory, others claim that the relationship between size and production costs follows a U-shaped pattern because of increasing coordination costs in larger firms, whereby costs increase with firm size up to an "optimal size" and then start to decrease (Schutjens & Wever, 2000). A similar argument holds for the "minimum efficient size" theory, which assumes the existence of a minimum size for profitable production (Scherer & Ross, 1990; Audretsch, 1994). Almus and Nerlinger (1999, p. 150) found that among new technology-based firms, large and mature firms have smaller growth rates than small and young firms, both innovative and noninnovative.

Firm Age

An important determinant of firm performance is age. Firm survival is positively related to firm size and firm age (Kirchhoff & Acs, 1997). The learning model (Jovanovic, 1982) provides an explanation for why young firms have lower rates of survival than older firms (Kirchhoff & Acs, 1997). The explanation is based on the time-consuming accumulation of information and experience by the entrepreneurs, as well as the modification over time of the behavior of financial institutions, such as banks toward young firms. However, many studies show nonlinear effects of age (Evans, 1987; Almus & Nerlinger, 1999), indicating that young firms grow faster than mature firms.

Industry Type

Industry type is another crucial variable that is highly related to the performance of new firms. Kunkel and Hofer (1993, p. 12) argue that the most important industry structural variables affecting new venture performance are different from those that influence the performance of established firms. They also raise the possibility that the impact of industry structure is strongly mitigated by other factors, such as the venture's entry strategy.

The more favorable the industry conditions (e.g. the type of business activities and its market structure), the greater the chance of success (Schutjens & Wever, 2000). Sandberg and Hofer (1987) examine the relations between several market characteristics and firm success. They mention dynamism, entrance thresholds, competitive structure, product heterogeneity and the growth of the market as industry factors having an impact upon firm success. The attractiveness of the industry with respect to business opportunities affects the profit potential of the industry and therefore the expected returns of a venture (Chrisman, Bauerschmidt, & Hofer, 1998).

Research Model

The model developed in this study poses that the four managerial structural variables have a direct relationship with TSU performance (Fig. 1). Given the profound influence of industry type, size and age of firm on TSU performance, they serve as control variables. This means that we expected the

Research Model

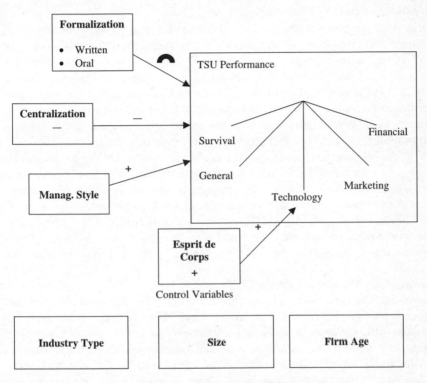

Fig. 1. Research Model.

managerial structural variables included in this model to impact TSU performance, regardless of industry type, size and age of the TSU.

METHOD

Data were collected by questionnaires in 2001 from an updated list of TSUs prepared by the Israeli Ministry of Industry and Trade. The questionnaires were sent to the CEOs of 250 firms at different stages of the business life cycles by either postal or electronic mail. CEOs of 101 firms completed and returned questionnaires, for a response rate of 40%, enabling us to examine our hypotheses in a large sample of Israeli TSUs.

Study Variables

Dependent Variable: Firm Performance

Firm performance was measured by 18 items relating to different aspects of performance. Respondents were asked "To what extent has the firm achieved each of the following organizational goals so far?" and were requested to rate each of the 18 performance variables on a Likert scale, ranging from 1 (not at all) to 5 (to a very high extent). A factor analysis elicited three major performance factors as follows: (1) Financial performance included three variables: firm profitability, growth in sales and income, and satisfied shareholders ($\alpha = 0.75$). (2) Marketing performance included five items: entry to the relevant market in Israel and abroad, growth of the firm's market segment in Israel and abroad, customer satisfaction, the firm's reputation among its customers, and finding strategic partners ($\alpha = 0.84$). (3) Technological performance included two items: technological leadership in Israel and abroad ($r = 0.71$). In addition, employee satisfaction was examined as the fourth performance measure based on one item. A general index of performance including all of these 17 items yielded a high reliability of $\alpha = 0.89$.

Independent Managerial Variables

Formalization was measured by the question: "To what extent do rules, procedures and documents exist in the firm?" Eleven Likert-scale items related to different areas in the firm, each ranging from 1 (to a very low extent) to 5 (to a very high extent). A principal component factor analysis with varimax rotation revealed two factors: written formalization to which seven items related (precisely defined written rules known to the employees, etc.) ($\alpha = 0.78$) and oral formalization, to which three items related ($\alpha = 0.68$). In addition, a general formalization index was constructed based on 10 out of the 11 items ($\alpha = 0.79$).

Centralization was measured by the question, "To what extent are the decisions in your firm made by the highest managerial levels (CEO, Deputy CEO)?" Respondents were asked to relate to 11 items, each ranging from 1 (to a very low extent) to 5 (to a very high extent). A factor analysis elicited two factors: strategic centralization, on which six of the 11 items loaded significantly ($\alpha = 0.90$), and operational centralization, on which five items loaded significantly ($\alpha = 0.89$). In addition, a general index of centralization was created as a simple mean of the 11 items ($\alpha = 0.89$).

Team solidarity (esprit de corps), relating to the level of solidarity among the founding entrepreneurs, was measured by three items: the level of friendship, cooperation and cohesiveness/solidarity among them. Each item ranged from 1 (a low level) to 5 (a high level). An index was built based on these three items ($\alpha = 0.83$).

Management style was measured by seven Likert-scale items relating to the following managerial style of the responding CEOs: centralist, participative, charismatic, empowering/delegatory, directive, controlling and laissez faire. Each item ranged from 1 (to a very small extent) to 5 (to a very great extent).

Control Variables

Firm age was measured by year of establishment. Firm size was measured by two open questions regarding the number of employees in Israel and abroad (if relevant). Industry type was measured by a question relating to the industrial sector in which the firm operates.

Sample Characteristics

All study respondents were CEOs, with 93% of them men and 97% holding advanced academic degrees. About half had previous managerial experience, as well as experience in industry (54% and 47%, respectively), but only about one-third had previous experience in establishing a venture (37%). The mean number of founders was three. A quarter of the firms employed 10 or less employees, 34% employed 10–30 employees, 15% of the firms had 31–50 employees and 26% had 51–300 employees. This distribution reflects the size heterogeneity of the TSUs. The mean number of employees was 44 (SD = 54), most of them employed in Israel, although some firms also had employees in other countries. The TSUs were also heterogeneous in terms of their age: while about one-third of them were recently established (10.5% were less than 1 year old and 24% were 2 years old), about one-third of them were 3–4 years old. The remaining one-third were at least 5 years old.

The TSUs in our sample operated in many technological areas, mainly in software and Internet applications (41.7%), communications, robotics, medical equipment, chemicals and electronics.

RESULTS

Table 1 reports the mean values, SD values and correlation coefficients of variables used in the analysis.

The hypothesis tests used five multiple regression analyses, each having a different performance measure as a dependent variable. Control variables, and the managerial variables, were included in each regression (Table 2).

Table 1. Descriptive Statistics and Intercorrelations of the Research Variables[a].

	Mean	SD	1	2	3	4	5	6	7	8	9	10	11	12	13	14	15	16	17	18	19
1. Written formalization	3.15	0.80	—																		
2. Oral formalization	3.11	0.84	0.38***	—																	
3. Strategic centralization	4.54	0.70	0.05	-0.03	—																
4. Operational centralization	3.58	0.86	0.10	0.19†	0.35***	—															
5. Team solidarity	3.72	0.94	0.29**	0.11	0.08	0.04	—														
6. Centralist	2.81	1.04	-0.04	0.02	-0.16	0.19	0.01	—													
7. Participative	4.01	0.89	-0.15	-0.11	-0.09	-0.14	-0.11	-0.19†	—												
8. Charismatic	3.75	0.96	0.10	-0.08	0.04	-0.07	-0.04	0.20†	0.18	—											
9. Empowering	4.01	0.80	0.13	0.03	0.07	-0.15	-0.04	-0.25*	0.50***	0.41***	—										
10. Directive	3.94	0.65	0.11	0.13	-0.06	-0.03	-0.18	0.02	0.26*	0.21*	0.16	—									
11. Control	3.32	0.86	0.01	-0.05	-0.11	0.13	-0.09	0.38***	-0.03	0.18	0.05	0.35***	—								
12. Laissez faire	2.23	1.02	0.12	0.12	-0.01	-0.03	0.02	-0.08	-0.09	0.02	0.02	0.00	-0.01	—							
13. General performance	3.37	0.60	0.29**	-0.12	0.05	-0.04	0.33**	-0.04	0.00	-0.01	0.00	0.02	-0.02	0.29*	—						
14. Financial performance	2.89	0.91	0.33***	-0.04	0.06	0.04	0.25†	0.02	-0.13	0.06	-0.10	-0.10	-0.03	0.13	0.76***	—					
15. Technological performance	3.20	1.19	0.19	-0.11	0.09	-0.12	0.22†	0.02	0.05	0.01	0.04	0.06	0.08	0.14	0.72***	0.36**	—				
16. Marketing performance	3.27	0.86	0.21†	-0.16	0.03	-0.05	0.40**	-0.01	0.02	0.02	0.01	-0.03	-0.03	0.32*	0.89***	0.67***	0.67***	—			
17. Satisfied employees	3.93	0.71	0.10	-0.03	0.16	-0.10	0.41***	-0.16	0.26*	0.18	0.19†	0.05	-0.09	0.00	0.42***	0.18	0.30**	0.39***	—		
18. Industry	1.41	0.49	-0.28**	-0.20†	0.16	-0.04	-0.06	-0.09	0.19	0.12	0.05	0.08	0.04	-0.11	-0.05	-0.06	-0.13	0.01	0.18	—	
19. TSU age	3.95	2.56	0.26**	-0.01	0.00	0.05	0.08	-0.02	-0.05	-0.15	-0.05	0.01	0.02	0.14	0.07	0.04	0.12	0.06	-0.07	-0.21*	—
20. Employees (n)	44.3	54.2	0.18†	0.04	0.13	-0.30**	0.17	-0.15	-0.02	0.01	0.11	0.15	-0.03	0.12	0.35**	0.32**	0.32**	0.21†	0.11	-0.06	0.43***

†P < 0.06.
[a]n = 101.
*P < 0.05.
**P < 0.01.
***P < 0.001.

Table 2. Regression of the Performance Variables on Managerial Characteristics and Firm Profile.

	General Performance		Financial Performance		Marketing Performance		Technological Performance		Satisfied Employees	
	B	β	B	β	B	β	B	β	B	β
Written formalization	0.18	0.26*	0.30	0.31**	0.18	0.22*	0.20	0.15	0.07	0.09
Written formalization²	—	—	-0.27	-0.24*	—	—	—	—	—	—
Oral formalization	-0.19	-0.28**	-0.18	-0.19†	-0.23	-0.29**	-0.26	-0.19	-0.02	-0.03
Strategic centralization	-0.07	-0.08	-0.16	-0.14	-0.04	-0.04	0.01	0.07	0.16	0.16
Operational centralization	-0.10	0.15	0.19	0.20†	0.07	0.10	-0.02	-0.02	-0.09	-0.11
Team solidarity	0.13	0.21	0.07	0.07	0.24	0.31**	0.19	0.15	0.29	0.36***
Laissez faire	0.12	0.21*	0.06	0.07	0.20	0.29**	0.12	0.10	0.00	0.03
Participative	0.04	0.07	-0.06	-0.06	0.09	0.12	0.14	0.11	0.21	0.27**
Industry	-0.02	-0.02	0.04	0.03	-0.02	-0.01	-0.33	-0.15	0.19	0.14
TSU age	-0.05	-0.22*	-0.07	-0.22*	-0.03	-0.10	-0.02	-0.09	-0.02	-0.08
Employees (n)	0.04	0.38***	0.01	0.40**	0.00	0.20†	0.01	0.26*	0.00	0.04
Constant	2.46		2.47		1.92		2.12		1.10	
r²	0.285		0.272		0.273		0.295		0.216	
Adj r²	0.237		0.177		0.232		0.185		0.199	

† P<0.10.
* P<0.05.
** P<0.01
*** P<0.001.

In the first regression for general performance (Table 2), firm size was the first and strongest variable entering the regression ($\beta = 0.38$, $P<0.001$). Formalization measures that entered strongly were oral formalization, with a negative contribution ($\beta = -0.28$, $P<0.01$) and written formalization, with a positive contribution ($\beta = 0.26$, $P<0.01$). TSU age entered with a negative coefficient and then team solidarity (esprit de corps) and the laissez faire style of management, each with a positive effect on performance. Industry type did not show any contribution. The overall variance explained by these six variables was $r^2 = 28\%$.

The regression analysis of the financial performance included the original written formalization variable, as well as a formalization^2 variable created to enable the examination of our curvilinear interaction hypothesis (H1). This procedure was performed because of the curvilinear interaction between financial performance and written formalization. Contrary to previous results, only formalization measures entered significantly into the regression of financial performance (written formalization positively and oral negatively), beyond the two control variables of firm size (with a strong positive effect) and firm age (with a significant and negative effect). Operational centralization also had a positive effect on financial performance (although it was significant only at $P<0.06$). Together, these variables explained 18% of the variance.

The curvilinear relationship between formalization and financial performance is graphically demonstrated in Fig. 2 by a one-way analysis of variance (ANOVA), which shows significantly higher levels of financial performance at intermediate levels of written and general formalization. This result was not found for oral formalization. Thus, H1 is confirmed with regard to written formalization.

In the third regression, relating to marketing performance, team solidarity and laissez faire style of management had the strongest positive contribution, while the two formalization variables followed them (written formalization with a positive contribution and oral formalization with a negative one). Together, these four variables explained 27% of the variance. The strong impact of managerial variables on the marketing performance of the TSUs is particularly interesting, as the control variables of age of business, size and industry did not add anything to the explanation of the variance in marketing performance.

As for technological performance, firm size was the only significant variable in the regression. No other managerial variable entered significantly, and thus the explanatory power of the regression was very low ($r^2 = 9.5\%$).

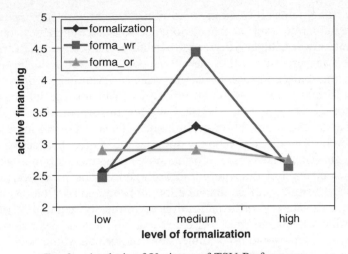

Fig. 2. Analysis of Variance of TSU Performance.
(General formalization, $F(2, 68) = 5.75$ ($P < 0.01$); written formalization, $F(2, 68) = 12.51$ ($P < 0.001$); oral formalization, $F(2, 68) = 0.17$.)

Team solidarity and the participative style of management were the only significant variables in the regression of employees' satisfaction, regardless of size, age or industry.

These results corroborate H1, H3 and H4 except for the technological performance, while they disconfirm H2 with regard to all the performance measures. Formalization, team solidarity and laissez faire style of management were found to be correlated to TSU performance beyond the impact of the classical variables of firm size or age and industry that are known to have a significant impact on performance.

DISCUSSION

The results indicate that the managerial variables examined made an important contribution to the explanation of TSU performance even when size, age and industry type were controlled. Level of formalization was found to have a nonlinear relationship with TSU performance, with a slope negative at low and high levels of formalization. When distinguishing between oral and written formalization, an interesting effect appears. For written formalization, performance rises until formalization is moderate and subsequently declines with increased formalization. For oral formalization, however, the findings do not show an improvement with increasing levels until the moderate level, at which point performance increases, but from that point onward, higher degrees are related to decreased performance. This result suggests that within the unique context of the TSU, an inherent never-ending dialectic process exists between innovation and order. While too rigid formalization may inhibit innovation, which is the core capability needed for a successful TSU, the total absence of formalization might lead the system to chaos and harm performance. Thus, a critical mass of formalization (at a moderate level) may optimize the conflict between these two needs. In this context, free and informal flow of communication might serve as a major channel of innovation; accordingly, written processes promote order while formal oral communication impedes innovation. Moreover, while some dimensions of formalization are critically required in order to preserve the evolving knowledge of the young TSU and to make it accessible to all its members, some other dimensions of formalization, such as dogmatic routines and rigid procedures or norms, might cause fixation and limit flexibility and innovation. In this sense, our findings generally suggest that a moderate level of formalization is critically needed in order to support the TSU in its inherent conflict between order and innovation.

Another structural variable – centralization – which was expected to have a negative relationship with performance, had almost no significant relationship. This finding is probably also related to the unique characteristics of the young TSU early in its life cycle, when it is actually a lean organization, basically composed of professionals and networks of knowledge. Decision making and management are based on knowledge and not on traditional hierarchies, and thus centralization is probably simply irrelevant in predicting performance. Moreover, as one major characteristic of TSUs is the dominant position of the founder or the founding team, the issue of excessive centralization might be problematic. Based upon the assumption that generally the founders have a technological rather than managerial background, the findings suggest that centralizing managerial decisions among entrepreneurs who lack professional managerial capabilities will not affect performance.

Our findings further reveal that, contrary to our hypothesis and the existing literature, the laissez faire style of management showed a positive relationship with performance. This finding corroborates our previous findings regarding formalization and centralization. It might be suggested that once a TSU has achieved a sufficient formalization level, this in itself serves as a basic instrument for leading and controlling the system. Thus, with the backing of a clear enough formalization system, the laissez faire style may be effective, serving the basic needs for innovation and autonomy of the TSU. Moreover, our finding regarding the participative style reinforces this conclusion that within this unique context, participative or democratic styles might lead to employee satisfaction, but they do not actually relate to performance. Regarding this finding, it might be important to note that the laissez faire style was specifically positively related to marketing performance and not to financial performance. We suggest that further examination of other management styles, such as transformational leadership, is still needed and might lead to more explicit results.

Our results also show that esprit de corps is positively correlated with marketing and financial performance, employee satisfaction and general performance of the TSU. The finding that team solidarity and the participative style of management were the only significant variables in the regression of employee satisfaction may indicate that these two managerial variables probably form an organizational climate that is attractive for high-tech employees and promotes their satisfaction. On the other, having esprit de corps is not a guarantee of technological achievements. We suggest that, while the findings of the positive relationships of team solidarity with performance do corroborate existing literature (Francis & Sandberg, 2000), our findings regarding technological performance might specify those general findings and demonstrate that technological performance is dependent on direct technological competences rather than on managerial variables.

Applying institutional theory to the context of TSU performance, the concepts of regulative, normative and cognitive processes can be linked together to give an explanation of the special dynamics in the process of institutionalization of these young organizations. During the course of developing their technological idea, we find all three processes of institutionalization. While formalization processes, centralization and laissez faire styles of management reflect the regulative process, team solidarity and participative style reflect normative and cognitive processes.

The Positive Effects of Institutionalization

At the theoretical level it seems that the findings of this study indicate mainly the positive effects of institutionalization in the special context of the TSUs. For these organizations, which are inherently notable for the back side of the organization, that is, their outstanding technological development capabilities, institutionalization processes are extremely critical in creating a basic infrastructure for crystallizing a cultural identity – communal values, a synergy of knowledge and definition of a joint direction for the various divisions that come into existence in these stages of the organization's life cycle. Specifically, the entire front side of the organization, that which faces the customer, the market and the industry, is usually constructed around the R&D upon which the organization is founded. Therefore, success in creating institutionalization processes will enable better integration between the technological back and the emergent marketing front, and thus, effect the transformation from firms offering technological products to client-oriented high-tech firms offering solutions. Thus, we see the managerial variables examined in this study as processes that lead the young organization toward the level of institutionalization it requires to meet the challenges ahead. The findings that indicate average levels of formalization and centralization best express the inherent duality of these entities: on the one, their *raison d'etre* is innovation and disorder, and, on the other, the condition for realizing this innovation and translating it into accepted dimensions of success is the ability to create a certain measure of order. As the findings show, this appropriate level of order is apparently achieved through an average level of institutionalization that in fact enables flexible institutionalization. The manifestations of flexible institutionalization are moderate formalization, which creates a semi-structured environment, alongside a laissez faire management style based on empowering and delegation, and is therefore not supported by centralization. Moreover, in the special setting of the TSU, the team solidarity is a managerial substitute for a single centralist figure, and it too creates the flexibility of decision-making based on synergy of the knowledge of the founding members, and not on the personal knowledge of a single individual. This synergy is one of the conditions that also enable the translation of the various capabilities of the organizational back into a better capability of the front to engage with the market, which is clearly expressed in the strong relations between team solidarity and marketing performance measures.

Thus, understanding the critical role of this flexible institutionalization process for the young TSU has significant implications for its top managers and the challenges they face in leading it along the road from the technological garage to the family of firms.

Implications

We found that three managerial variables – formalization, team solidarity and management style, whether laissez faire or participative – are important in explaining certain performance measures. Second, it is clear that technological performance must be looked at separately from other performance measures, as none of the managerial variables was found to distinctly impact technological performance.

Insights from this research should help to develop a conceptual framework linking managerial variables and performance in technological ventures. The recent collapse of many TSUs, mainly in Internet-related industries, makes such a study particularly timely. It may also help define managerial procedures that could help emerging start-ups better handle the obstacles they encounter.

Two clear patterns emerge from the research results. On the one hand, there is a need for a managerial disposition that gives rein to creativity and entrepreneurship, and, on the other, procedures have to be in place to ensure an appropriate measure of order. According to our results, formalization is the main order ensurer, but future research will no doubt expand this particular tool box. It can therefore be said that the managerial level has to be able to maintain a delicate balance between two opposing forces. It needs the leadership qualities that allow personnel to make the best possible use of their technological capabilities, granting the appropriate measure of autonomy to specialists while clearly maintaining control over the direction the organization is taking. Not to be forgotten in this array are the intangible managerial assets that need to be accumulated, such as esprit de corps, vision (which is not examined in this study) and organizational culture, and the infrastructure-creating managerial assets, such as documentation routines, knowledge transfer procedures through frontal meetings, incentives to motivate personnel to transfer knowledge and others.

Limitations

A basic methodological constraint of the study was the difficulty in obtaining objective performance data, which meant that we were forced to make do with subjective measures. This limitation is related to the well-known problem of measuring the performance of young TSUs by financial performance variables. It is therefore necessary to use subjective measures if we are to give full meaning to the performance of these organizations.

Moreover, leadership style was measured by means of a battery of questions, each of which related to a different style of leadership. We could have extended or improved the measure to more than just one item per leadership style.

Future Research

The research results clearly indicate a relationship between optimal levels of managerial variables and the performance of TSUs. This finding certainly needs to be specified and elaborated in further research. It is important to extend the range of types of managerial variables investigated, and perhaps even to group them into order-ensuring, integration-supporting, leadership and other variables. In particular, we suggest that further examination of management styles, such as transformational leadership, might lead to more explicit results. Yet another research direction is to conduct a longitudinal follow-up study on the various performance measures of TSUs that examines the relationships with managerial variables over the time dimension.

REFERENCES

Aiken, M., Bacharach, S. B., & French, J. L. (1980). Organizational structure, work process, and proposal making in administrative bureaucracies. *Academy of Management Journal*, *23*(4), 631–652.

Almus, M., & Nerlinger, E. A. (1999). Growth of new technology-based firms: Which factors matter? *Small Business Economics*, *13*, 141–154.

Argyres, N. S. (1995). Technology strategy, governance structure and interdivisional coordination. *Journal of Economic Behavior and Organization*, *28*, 337–358.

Audretsch, D. B. (1994). Business survival and the decision to exit. *Journal of Business Economics*, *1*, 125–138.

Bass, B. M. (1990). From transactional to transformational leadership: Learning to share the vision. *Organization Dynamics*, *18*, 19–31.

Bozeman, B., & Slusher, E. A. (1979). Scarcity and environmental stress in public organizations: A conjectural essay. *Administration and Society*, *2*, 335–355.

Buchholz, S., & Roth, T. (1987). *Creating the high-performance team*. New York: John Wiley & Sons.

Burns, T., & Stalker, G. M. (1961). *The management of innovation*. London: Tavistock.

Cameron, K. S., Whetten, D. A., & Kim, M. U. (1987). Organizational dysfunctions of decline. *Academy of Management Journal*, *30*(1), 126–138.

Chandler, G. N., & Hanks, S. H. (1998). An investigation of new venture teams in emerging businesses. In: P. D. Reynolds & W. D. Bygrave et al. (Eds), *Frontiers of entrepreneurship research* (pp. 318–330), Wellesley.

Chrisman, J. J., Bauerschmidt, A., & Hofer, C. W. (1998). The determinants of new venture performance: An extended model. *Entrepreneurship Theory and Practice*, *23*(1), 5–22.

Cooper, A. C., & Bruno, A. (1977). Success among high technology firms. *Business Horizons*, *20*, 16–22.

Cooper, A. C., & Daily, C. M. (1997). Entrepreneurial teams. In: D. L. Sexton & R. W. Smilor (Eds), *Entrepreneurship 2000*. Chicago: Upstate.

D'Andrade, R. G. (1984). Towards a model of organizations as interpretation systems. *Academy of Management Review, 9*, 284–295.

Dess, G. G., & Robinson, R. B. (1984). Measuring organizational performance in the absence objective measures: The case of private-held firm and conglomerate business unit. *Strategic Management Journal, 5*(3), 265–273.

DuBrin, A. J. (1995). *Leadership: Research findings, practices, skills.* Boston, MA: Houghton Mifflin.

Evans, D. S. (1987). The relationship between firm growth, size, and age: Estimates for 100 manufacturing industries. *The Journal of Industrial Economics, 35*(4), 567–592.

Francis, D. H., & Sandberg, W. R. (2000). Friendship within entrepreneurial teams and its association with team and venture performance. *Entrepreneurship Theory and Practice, 24*(winter issue), 5–25.

Gartner, W. B., Starr, J. A., & Bhat, S. (1999). Predicting new venture survival: An analysis of anatomy of a start-up. Cases from INC magazine. *Journal of Business Venturing, 14*, 215–232.

Glisson, C. A., & Martin, P. Y. (1980). Productivity and efficiency in human service organizations as related to structure, size and age. *Academy of Management Journal, 23*(1), 21–37.

Hage, J. (1965). An axiomatic theory of organizations. *Administrative Science Quarterly, 10*, 289–320.

Hambrick, D. C. (1994). Top management groups: A conceptual integration and reconsideration of the 'team' label. *Research in Organizational Behavior, 16*, 171–213.

Holland, T. P. (1973). Organizational structure and institutional care. *Journal of Health and Social Behavior, 14*, 241–251.

Huntington, S. P. (1964). *The soldier and the state.* New York: Vintage Books.

Jovanovic, B. (1982). Selection and the evolution of industry. *Econometrica, 50*, 49–670.

Kamm, J. B., & Nurik, A. J. (1993). The stages of team venture formation: A decision-making model. *Entrepreneurship Theory and Practice, 17*(2), 17–28.

Keasey, K., & Watson, R. (1991). The state of the art of small firm failure prediction: Achievements and prognosis. *International Small Business Journal, 9*(4), 11–29.

Kirchhoff, B. A., & Acs, Z. J. (1997). Births and deaths of new firms. In: D. L. Sexton & R. W. Smilor (Eds), *Entrepreneurship 2000.* Chicago: Upstate (Chapter 8).

Kunkel, S. C., & Hofer, C. W. (1993). The impact of industry structure on new venture performance: Some new findings. In: N. C. Churchill, S. Birley, J. Doutriaux, E. J. Gatewood, F. S. Hoy & W. E. Wetzel, Jr. (Eds), *Frontiers of entrepreneurship research* (pp. 1–15). Wellesley: Babson College.

Lawrence, P. R., & Dyer, D. (1983). *Renewing American industry.* New York.

Littunen, H. (2000). Networks and local environmental characteristics in the survival of new firms. *Small Business Economics, 15*, 59–71.

Masuch, M. (1985). Vicious circles in organizations. *Administrative Science Quarterly, 30*, 14–33.

McMillan, I. C., Zemann, L., & Narasimha, P. N. S. (1987). Criteria distinguishing successful from unsuccessful ventures in the venture screening process. *Journal of Business Venturing, 2*(2), 123–137.

Meyer, J. W., & Rowan, B. (1977). Institutional organizations: Formal structure as myth and ceremony. *American Journal of Sociology, 83*, 340–363.

Meyer, M. W., Stevenson, W., & Webster, S. (1985). *Limits to bureaucratic growth.* Berlin: Walter de Gruyter.

Miner, J. B. (1973). *The management process: Theory, research, and practice.* New York: Macmillan.

Moenaert, R. K., Souder, W. E., Meyer, A. D., & Deschoolmeester, D. (1994). R&D-marketing integration mechanisms, communications flows, and innovation success. *Journal of Product Innovation Management, 11,* 31–45.

Molnar, J. J., & Rogers, D. L. (1976). Organizational effectiveness: An empirical comparison of the goal and system resource approaches. *The Sociological Quarterly, 17,* 401–413.

Pfeffer, J., & Leblebici, H. (1973). Executive recruitment and the development of interfirm organizations. *Administrative Science Quarterly, 18,* 449–461.

Pondy, L. R. (1977). Effectiveness: A thick description. In: P. S. Goodman & J. M. Penning (Eds), *New perspectives on organizational effectiveness* (pp. 226–234). San-Fransisco.

Price, J. (1972). *Organizational effectiveness: An inventory of propositions.* Homewood.

Reynolds, P. (1993). High performance entrepreneurship What makes it different? In: N. C. Churchill, S. Birley, J. Doutriaux, E. J. Gatewood, F. S. Hoy & W. E. Wetzel, Jr. (Eds), *Frontiers of entrepreneurship research* (pp. 88–101). Wellesley: Babson College.

Rondeau, P. J., Vondrembse, M. A., & Ragu-Nathan, T. S. (2000). Exploring work system practices for time-based manufacturers: Their impact on competitive capabilities. *Journal of Operations Management, 18,* 509–529.

Roure, J. B., & Keeley, R. H. (1990). Predictors of success in new technology-based ventures. *Journal of Business Venturing, 5,* 201–220.

Roure, J. B., & Maidique, M. A. (1986). Linking prefunding factors and high-technology venture success: An exploratory study. *Journal of Business Venturing, 1*(3), 295–306.

Sandberg, W. R., & Hofer, C. W. (1987). Improving new venture performance: The role of strategy, industry structure and the entrepreneur. *Journal of Business Venturing, 2*(1), 5–27.

Schendel, D., Patton, G. R., & Riggs, J. (1976). Corporate turnaround strategies: A study of profit decline and recovery. *Journal of General Management, 3,* 3–11.

Scherer, F. M., & Ross, D. (1990). *Industrial market structure and economic performance.* Boston: Houghton Mifflin Company.

Schilling, M. A. (1998). Technological lockout: An integrative model of the economic and strategic factors driving technology success and failure. *Academy of Management Review, 23*(2), 267–284.

Schutjens, V. A. J. M., & Wever, E. (2000). Determinants of new firm success. *Papers in Regional Science, 79*(2), 135–159.

Scott, W. R. (1995). *Institutions and organizations.* Thousands Oaks, CA: Sage Publications.

Scott, W. R. (1998). *Organizations* (4th ed.). NJ: Upper Saddle River, Prentice-Hall.

Sorensen, H. (1994). New perspectives on the military profession: The I/O model and esprit de corps reevaluated. *Armed Forces and Society, 20*(4), 599–617.

Staw, B. M., Sandelands, L. E., & Dutton, J. E. (1981). Threat-rigidity effects in organizational behavior: A multilevel analysis. *Administrative Science Quarterly, 26,* 501–524.

Stevens, G., Rosa, F. M., & Gardner, S. (1994). Military academies as instruments of value change. *Armed Forces and Society, 20*(3), 473–484.

Storey, D. J. (1985). The problems facing new firms. *Journal of Management Studies, 22,* 327–345.

Tannenbaum, A. (1968). *Control in organizations.* New York: McGraw-Hill.

Van de Ven, A. H., Hudson, R., & Schroeder, D. M. (1984). Designing new business startups: Entrepreneurial organizational and ecological considerations. *Journal of Management, 10,* 87–107.

Van Praag, C. M. (1999). Some classic views on entrepreneurship. *The Economist, 147*(3), 311–335.

Vesper, K. H. (1980). *New venture strategies.* Englewood Cliffs, NJ: Prentice-Hall.

Watson, W. E., Ponthiel, L. D., & Critelli, J. W. (1995). Team interpersonal process effectiveness in venture partnership and its connection to perceived success. *Journal of Business Venturing, 10*, 393–411.

Whetten, D. A. (1978). Coping with incompatible expectations: An integrated view of role conflict. *Administrative Science Quarterly, 23*(2), 254–271.

White, R. K., & Lippitt, R. (1960). *Autocracy and democracy: An experimental inquiry.* New York: Harper and Row.

Zaltman, G., Duncan, R., & Holbek, J. (1973). *Innovations and organizations.* New York: Wiley.

QUANTIFYING CREATIVE DESTRUCTION: ENTREPRENEURSHIP AND PRODUCTIVITY IN NEW ZEALAND

John McMillan[1]

1. INTRODUCTION

Creative destruction "revolutionises the economic structure *from within*", Joseph Schumpeter famously said, "incessantly destroying the old one, incessantly creating a new one". Innovation in business – bringing new goods, new markets, new methods of production, new ways of organising firms – is the "fundamental impulse that sets and keeps the capitalist engine in motion" (Schumpeter, 1975, p. 83). Does the economy have enough flexibility? Are there barriers in the way of entrepreneurship? This paper develops a framework for quantifying creative destruction.

Applying the framework to New Zealand, I conclude that the sluggish productivity growth of the past 15 years cannot be blamed on economic rigidities. Contrary to the perception of an economy held back by obstacles to doing business, the data show that enterprise is flourishing. There is ample creative destruction. Ascribing New Zealand's slow growth to a business-unfriendly culture is a misdiagnosis.

The Emergence of Entrepreneurial Economics
Research on Technological Innovation, Management and Policy, Volume 9, 189–210
Copyright © 2005 by Elsevier Ltd.
ISSN: 0737-1071/doi:10.1016/S0737-1071(05)09011-6

2. THE MICROECONOMICS OF PRODUCTIVITY GROWTH

Productivity in New Zealand grew slowly during the 1990s. Low investment was the source of the problem, according to the NZ Treasury (2004), as the capital–labor ratio grew less than in comparable countries. Productivity growth appears to have picked up in the late 1990s and early 2000s, with Buckle, Hall, and McLellan (2004) estimating output per hour of work estimated to be growing at 1.7% per year compared with the previous decade's 1% (see also Black, Guy, & McLellan, 2003; Razzak, 2003). Nevertheless, concerns continue to be aired about New Zealand's slippage in the world per capita income ranks – from third highest in the world in 1953 to 22nd in 1978 to 40th in 2003 – and about the prospects for future growth.[2]

One of the "key areas for action", Prime Minister Helen Clark says, is "creating an environment in which small and medium-sized companies can more easily become large companies" (Clark & Christie, 2002). Inadequacies in the institutional environment could bring slow productivity growth. The government might impede markets either by doing things it should not do or by failing to do things it should do. For example, it might obstruct entrepreneurship by setting onerous licensing rules for new firms. On the other hand, an undersupply of financial-market regulation could make it hard for firms to grow.

Historically, obtrusive government was the big issue in New Zealand. Controls hamstrung the economy (Blyth, 1964; Tower, 1979; Evans, Grimes, Wilkinson, & Teece, 1996). Adjectives like "inflexible" and "sclerotic" were commonly used to describe it. "New Zealand was a more distorted and inflexible economy than most other countries that we compared ourselves with", notes Geoff Lewis (2002, p. 5). Overregulation having been addressed by the reforms of the 1980s, however, we should consider the possibility that today the government is neglecting to do some of what it should be doing. Informational asymmetries – lemons-market problems and the like – mean that markets, in order to work as they are supposed to, need structural underpinnings, some of which only the government can provide (McMillan, 2002).

Why does the flexibility of the economy matter for productivity growth? There are two ways to make an industry more productive: raising the productivity of all of the firms in it or holding each firm's productivity constant but increasing the market share of the more productive firms (or creating new, more productive firms) while decreasing the share of the less productive.

If best practice readily diffused across firms, market shares would not need to change. To a surprising extent, however, such diffusion fails to occur.

Empirical studies in the U.S.A. and elsewhere find interfirm productivity gaps to be wide and persistent (Bartelsman & Doms, 2000). In any given industry, output per worker can be twice as high or more in the better-performing firms than in the lesser ones. The skills of a firm's workforce, the size and age of its capital stock and the talents of its managers affect its productivity (though the existing econometric studies leave a large unexplained residual, so we do not have much understanding of why the productivity differences are so persistent). The productivity laggards often continue as laggards for years. It is because of these interfirm productivity gaps that the turnover of firms measurably contributes to industry productivity. In the U.S.A., about an half of a typical industry's productivity growth is attributable to firm turnover (Caves, 1998, pp. 1971–1975; Haltiwanger, 2002).

In an economy in which firm turnover is blocked, then, unblocking it could potentially double overall productivity growth. The reallocation of resources from less productive activities to more productive ones via the rise and fall of firms is one of the main sources of any economy's dynamism.

3. QUANTIFYING CREATIVE DESTRUCTION

In the town of Bunnythorpe in the Manawatu in 1873, Joseph Nathan, an immigrant seeking escape from the poverty he had been born in, set up a general trading company selling anything from tools to clocks to patent medicines (Millen, 2003). Innovative from the start, the company broke through in 1904 with an improved process for dried milk, which it exported under the brand name Glaxo. It started manufacturing a vitamin D preparation in 1924, marking a move into pharmaceuticals. Shifting its headquarters to England in 1947, it listed on the London Stock Exchange as Glaxo Laboratories Ltd. Several mergers later, it was GlaxoSmithKline, with more than 100,000 employees worldwide and a market capitalization of USD 135 billion. Nathan's creation grew from a Manawatu shop to the world's largest pharmaceutical company.

Could such a story be repeated today? Are New Zealand's entrepreneurs freely able to create firms and see them grow to large scale? A quick gauge of the economy's flexibility is the number of small firms. New Zealand has more than 240,000 firms with five or fewer employees (NZ MED, 2003,

p. 5). Entrepreneurship is abundant. One of nine adult New Zealanders runs one of these tiny businesses.

Twelve further criteria will be used in what follows to measure the economy's flexibility:

- turnover of wealth
- the accessibility of the business sector
- firms' receptiveness to new technologies
- regulatory impediments to doing business
- the amount of job creation and job destruction
- gaps in the size distribution of firms
- the likelihood of growing from small to medium-sized
- the likelihood of downsizing
- the likelihood of becoming large
- competitive discipline on large firms
- hindrances to converting to share ownership
- changes in the list of the top 10 corporations

3.1. Turnover of Wealth

A measure of an economy's receptiveness to enterprising individuals is the source of rich people's wealth, inherited or self-earned. How the rich got to be rich affects economic growth, according to Morck, Stangeland, and Yeung (2000). Adding up the wealth of various countries' USD billionaires, self-made and inherited, and correlating the totals with economic growth, they find that in countries where self-made billionnaire wealth is a larger fraction of GDP, economic growth is faster. This is unsurprising, being consistent with the notion of wealth as an incentive for productive effort. More striking, they further find that in countries where inherited billionnaire wealth is a larger fraction of GDP, economic growth is *slower*. (They call this the "Canadian disease".) A preponderance of inherited wealth might result from education being unattainable for the poor, or from financial markets malfunctioning so as to exclude those who are not already established, or from firms staying family run because the managerial labor market cannot cope with a transition from founder to professional manager. Whatever the reason, entrenching the rich and their offspring is bad for growth.

Is the New Zealand business sector accessible to enterprising people regardless of their upbringing? If we take the source of rich people's wealth, inherited versus self earned, as a measure of accessibility, New Zealand looks to be in good shape. Using as the cut-off a net wealth of at least NZD10 million, Hazledine and Siegfried (1997) calculate that 74% of New Zealand's rich did not get their start in life from inherited wealth. This is a larger fraction of self-made rich people than in Australia, with 66%, Britain, with 61% or the U.S.A., with 59%. (A caveat: a higher wealth cut-off is used for these other countries than for New Zealand, which could make such comparisons questionable).

New Zealand's rich tend to be self-made. The belief that those from modest backgrounds can succeed by their own hard work, the creed of "strive and succeed" associated with the writer Horatio Alger, is central to the American self-image. It seems to be more a reality in New Zealand than in the U.S.A.

3.2. Accessibility of the Business Sector

A caveat on the business sector's openness to those not already established is that members of the various groups in society are not all equally likely to be entrepreneurs. There are discrepancies by gender: 9.3% of males are classified as "employers" in the 2001 census, compared with 4.4% of females. There are discrepancies by race: 8.4% of Europeans are employers, compared with 7.4% of Asians, 3.1% of Māori and 1.6% of Pacific Islanders (NZ MED, 2003, pp. 25–26). In other words, males are twice as likely to be employers as females, while Europeans are three times as likely to be employers as Māori and six times as likely as Pacific Islanders.

These discrepancies could arise from any of a number of possible sources (Chapple, 2000; Te Puni Kōkiri, 2000; Gibson & Scobie, 2004). Some are amenable to policy, such as disparities in education or in access to information networks. Others are innocuous, such as differences in the number of people of working age relative to children and the elderly. While equality of opportunity is usually discussed in terms of equity, it also has an efficiency aspect, for it can affect productivity; equity and efficiency are linked (Loury, 1981; Bénabou, 1996). Given the assumption that innate talent is equally distributed across gender and across race, differences in the propensity of being an employer implies that females, Māori and Pacific Islander entrepreneurs are less far down the talent distribution than white male entrepreneurs, and so the marginal female or Māori or Pacific Islander entrepreneur is more talented than the marginal white male entrepreneur. If so, the nation's potential stock of entrepreneurial talent may not be fully utilized, perhaps at some cost to overall productivity growth.

However, the discrepancies in the stock of entrepreneurs are a holdover from the past and, in the case of Maori, may already be on the way to being eliminated, according to a recent survey. In the early 2000s, Fredericks (2004, pp. 36–37) reports, more Maori than non-Maori, as a percentage of their working-age population, started new businesses. Maori were creating firms at a faster rate than the overall firm-creation rate in Australia, the U.K. and the U.S.A. The male–female discrepancy persists, with fewer females than males starting new businesses in the early 2000s (Fredericks, 2004, pp. 32–33). Nevertheless, females in New Zealand were creating firms at a faster rate than females in Australia, the U.K. and the U.S.A. While discrepancies exist, the business sector in New Zealand seems to be more accessible than in comparable countries to females and nonwhites.

3.3. Firms' Receptiveness to New Technologies

Are New Zealand firms taking advantage of the opportunities offered by new technologies? According to Paul Romer's (1986) growth model, the key to sustainable economic growth is that firms are motivated to invest in new technologies. Innovation raises productivity in any country, but it is especially important when the country is remote from its export markets and the technologies in question improve information processing and communication.

Australia's relatively fast 1990s growth is attributed by some to its ready adoption of the new information and communications technologies (Parham & Roberts, 2004). As an explanation of the growth differential between Australia and New Zealand, however, this founders on the fact that New Zealand adopted those technologies just as rapidly. Internet penetration is higher in New Zealand than Australia, with 46% of New Zealanders being internet users versus 37% of Australians (Chinn & Fairlie, 2004, p. 8 and Table 1). The prices charged by internet server providers are lower in New Zealand, as are domain-name registration fees. More web sites and domain names are registered in New Zealand, per capita, than in Australia (Boles de Boer, Evans, & Howell, 2000; Howell & Marriott, 2001).

Online business-to-business exchanges were set up in the 1990s, early in the e-commerce revolution, to run services such as banking, procurement and transportation, as well as for matching buyers and sellers in export industries such as timber. New Zealand has been, according to Boles de Boer et al. (2000, p. 9), "among the world leaders in uptake of electronic commerce".

Table 1. The Firm-Size Distribution. Employment by Firm Size, as a Percentage of Total Private-Sector Employment.

	Firm Size (Number of Employees)		
	0–19	20–99	≥ 100
New Zealand	42%	19%	39%
Australia	47%	19%	34%
U.K.	30%	12%	58%
U.S.A.	28%	16%	56%

Source: NZ MED (2003, p. 27).

3.4. Regulatory Obstacles

In the view of the New Zealand Business Roundtable, business has continued to be obstructed, even since the reforms, by big government. Wolfgang Kasper (2002a, p. 15; 2002b, p. 18) opines that New Zealanders are not "daring to be self-reliant and free" because "benevolent state paternalism" has created "unjustified barriers to entrepreneurial activity", resulting in "poor growth and a stifling, though comforting serfdom". Bryce Wilkinson (2001a, p. 5) argues, "New Zealand suffers from avoidable and undesirable regulatory excesses". Roger Kerr (2000) says the "quagmire of regulation" is a "massive deterrent to investment and economic growth". In some countries, to be sure, regulation has been shown to be very harmful. Where the regulatory environment is hostile to business, enterprise is held back and productivity is low (Johnson, McMillan, & Woodruff, 2002; Klapper, Laeven, & Rajan, 2004). For New Zealand, is there any evidence that regulation is a "massive" deterrent to investment?

The vast number of firms with 5 or fewer employees, already noted, suggests that the red tape for setting up a firm is inconsequential. New Zealand's regulatory costs of starting a business are among the world's lowest, according to Djankov, La Porta, Lopez-de-Silanes, and Shleifer, (2002), who describe the procedures for registering a firm as "streamlined". It takes 3 days to begin operating legally in New Zealand, compared with 2 days in Australia, 4 days in the U.S.A. and the U.K., 42 days in Germany and 53 days in France. The data offer no reason for concern about regulatory barriers to entry in New Zealand.

Ongoing businesses face costs of complying with regulations on taxation, worker relations, health and safety, labelling and certification, natural-resource management and so on. In a quarterly survey of small businesses run by the National Bank, regulation is usually the respondents' most cited or second-most cited complaint, with about 20% saying it is their biggest problem (National Bank, various dates). Managers everywhere grumble about red tape, however, just as farmers grumble about the weather. Some firms do suffer from high compliance costs. From time to time, a newspaper publishes an article describing a manager being hounded by bureaucrats. (Several such news reports are collected in Wilkinson (2001a); the Resource Management Act in particular gives rise to complaints.) Anecdotal evidence is of limited use, though. The firms that get written up in newspaper articles do not constitute a random sample. It is extreme cases that are newsworthy. To judge whether the anecdotes of regulatory interference are typical or not, we need data.

How big are regulatory compliance costs in New Zealand? They are small, according to one survey of small firms (Alexander et al., 2004), averaging 1 h per week of the manager's time. They are larger, according to another survey (KPMG, 2003), averaging 5 h of managers' time per week for firms with 5 or fewer employees, 13 h for firms with 6–9 employees, and 20 h for firms with 20–49 employees. Which survey is more accurate is an open question, as neither is definitive. (The Alexander, Bell, & Knowles, survey was more thorough but had a small sample. The KPMG survey relied questionably on the respondents' memories, asking them retrospectively to estimate the total number of hours spent on regulatory issues within the firm over the preceding 12 months.) Compliance costs differ markedly from firm to firm in the data of Alexander et al. (2004), showing the unreliability of extrapolating from anecdotes about a few selected firms. Complying with regulations in the smallest firms, the two surveys suggest, typically takes up between 2% and 10% of the manager's time: not an insignificant burden, but not massive.

Red tape seems to be less burdensome in New Zealand than elsewhere. A survey by the OECD finds compliance costs per employee to be 40% lower in New Zealand than Australia (OECD, 2001, p. 22), and a survey by the Auckland and New South Wales Chambers of Commerce finds them to be 16% lower (Read, 2004). A survey by the World Bank (2004), quantifying the regulatory costs worldwide of starting a business, hiring and firing workers, registering property, getting credit, protecting investors, enforcing contracts and closing a business, finds New Zealand's business rules and regulations to be the least intrusive in the world.

While some firms suffer higher compliance costs than others, the data indicate that regulation is not a heavy burden for the typical New Zealand firm. Current or future policy changes could place new impediments in the way of entrepreneurs. In 2004, Roderick Deane warned about a plethora of re-regulation, which he said will bring "reduced flexibility and reduced adaptability for private sector firms" (O'Sullivan, 2004). Fears of a reversion to overregulation should not be assessed by anecdotes, however. The way to assess whether regulation is excessive is by systematically tracking the data.

3.5. Job Creation and Destruction

In the U.S.A., about 10% of all jobs are destroyed each year. Meanwhile, roughly as many are created anew (Davis, Haltiwanger, & Schuh, 1996; Haltiwanger, 2002). Job creation slightly exceeds job destruction in some years, and the reverse in other years, with job destruction showing more cyclical variation than job creation. When you think about it, 10% of all jobs is an astonishingly big number. In the European Union, turnover is high but not as high in the U.S.A., with 6% of jobs being created and destroyed each year. The rate varies from country to country: for example, in Germany it is 4%, in France, 5%, in the U.K., 7% and in Spain, 9% (Gómez–Salvador, Messina, & Vallanti, 2004). More volatility is seen in small firms than in large and more in services than in manufacturing.

In New Zealand, jobs were created at a rate of 18% each year between 1995 and 2001 and jobs were destroyed at a rate of 15%, according to Carroll, Hyslop, Mare, Timmins, and Wood (2002). Another estimate, using data definitions more consistent with the overseas studies, found the rate of job creation and destruction to be just under 12% (Mills & Timmins, 2004). New Zealand's job creation and destruction is somewhat more rapid than in the U.S.A. and considerably more rapid than in Europe.

While the chief effect of job creation and destruction is to increase the economy's productivity by reallocating labor and capital to more productive uses, there are some caveats. More turnover is not necessarily better.

An efficiency concern is that market frictions could cause job destruction to be excessive. Because information does not flow perfectly freely in the labor market, job seekers and job vacancies coexist. While the laid-off workers search for jobs, output and wages are lost. Firms have no incentive to take these social costs into account when they make their lay-off decisions, and so too many workers might be laid off (Howitt & McAfee, 1987). Also, if a firm is capital constrained, as small firms often are, it may be unable to wait out a temporary drop in demand for its product, and so it lays off workers whom it would have kept had it been able to obtain a bank loan.

A distributional concern is that the burden of adjustment is borne by the workers who, through no fault of their own, are thrown out of work when their firms shrink. The severity of this burden is an empirical issue, depending on the duration of laid-off workers' unemployment and the level of unemployment benefits. Even those not laid off suffer uncertainty about whether they will keep their job. However, the costs borne by the workers bear no simple relationship to the amount of job destruction, for across the economy job destruction is approximately equal to job creation.

Firm turnover, then, is simultaneously beneficial, in increasing productivity by shifting resources into their best uses, and harmful, in putting the burden of adjustment on the workers who lose their jobs. The data do not allow us assess whether New Zealand is at the right point in this trade-off: that is, whether the current amount of firm turnover is optimal. They do, however, allow us to examine the claim that, as a result of business-unfriendly policies, there is too little. By comparison with other countries, New Zealand's high job turnover suggests that the labor market is not over constrained. In its job creation and destruction, the New Zealand economy exhibits a lot of flexibility.

3.6. Gaps in the Size Distribution of Firms

The firm-size distribution in many countries, especially developing economies, shows a missing middle. There is a lot of employment in tiny firms and quite a lot in large firms but not much in mid-sized firms (Snodgrass & Biggs, 1996). The missing middle is a symptom of weak legal and regulatory institutions. Small firms can survive in an institution-free environment, by using personal networks and ongoing relationships to substitute for missing laws of contract and retained earnings and personal savings to make up for a lack of access to financial markets (McMillan & Woodruff, 2002). Large firms can also prosper without institutions, getting by instead by cultivating political favors. They got to be big in the first place, usually, through knowing the right people. Where the lack of institutions shows up is for small firms wishing to grow. Needing to make discrete investments, they can no longer rely on retained earnings, and may be unable to grow if the financial market is underdeveloped. A symptom of inadequate institutions, therefore, is relatively few mid-sized firms.

Even in industrialized countries, small firms get much of their finance from retained earnings and trade credit. There is a "pecking order", in which a firm exhausts its internal funds before it seeks external funds. An informational asymmetry – the entrepreneur knows the firm's prospects better than a bank does – puts a wedge between the value of internal funds and the cost of external funds (Petersen & Rajan, 1997). If information sources are lacking and investment uncertainties are prevalent, banks may be reluctant to lend to small firms, preventing them from growing to medium size.

Is there a missing middle in the size distribution of New Zealand firms? The data say there is not. Table 1 shows the percentage of total private-sector employment by firm size (measuring firm size by number of employees). New Zealand has proportionately as much employment in firms with 20–99 employees as Australia and more than the U.K. and the U.S.A. To judge by the distribution of firm sizes, New Zealand's firms do not seem to be hampered in growing from small- to mid-sized.

3.7. Barriers to Growing from Small- to Medium-Sized

Another way of asking whether firms that show initial success face undue barriers to growth is to compute the likelihood of transitioning from small to larger (using data in NZ MED, 2003, pp. 5, 17–18). Among firms that had five or fewer employees in 1995, 6% had grown by 2002 to have 6–9 employees and another 2% to have 10–19, and another 0.5% to have more than 20. By a back-of-the-envelope calculation, the firms that in grew, in the 7 years, from less than 6 employees to 6 or more created more than 150,000 new jobs. Among firms that had 6–9 employees in 1995, 21% had grown by 2002 to have more than nine employees and another 3% to have more than 20. Among firms with 10–19 employees in 1995, 19% had grown by 2002 to have 20–49 employees and another 2% to have 50 or more. Among firms with 20–49 employees in 1995, 12% had grown by 2002 to have 50 or more employees. On the face of it these numbers do not look low.

The average New Zealand firm still in business 4 years after its birth has 22% more employees than when it started, according to Mills and Timmins (2004). In the U.S.A., firms show much faster growth, with the average surviving new firm doubling its employment in 4 years. However, new firms grow unusually quickly in the U.S.A., and the New Zealand growth rates are similar to those in the U.K. and other OECD countries.

New Zealand has a relatively high-rate of self-employment (Mills & Timmins, 2004). In some countries, a large number of single-person firms is a bad sign, for it is a symptom of impediments to firm growth (Snodgrass & Biggs, 1996). However, in the case of New Zealand, given the evidence that firms are able to grow, the prevalence of self-employment need not be a concern.

Promising small firms, it would appear, are able to attract the capital and other resources they need in order to grow to medium-sized.

3.8. Barriers to Downsizing

The flip side of the ability of successful firms to expand is the ability of unsuccessful firms to shrink, freeing their labor and capital for other uses. The data on firm transitions (NZ MED, 2003, pp. 17–18) show downward as well as upward flexibility. Among firms with 10–19 employees in 1995, 30% had shrunk to less than 10 employees by 2002. Among firms with 20–49 employees in 1995, 28% had shrunk to less than 20 employees by 2002. Among firms with 50–99 employees in 1995, 29% had shrunk to less than 50 employees by 2002. Among firms with more than 100 employees in 1995, 14% had shrunk to 20–99 employees, and another 9% to less than 20 employees.

The market winnows out the weaker firms ruthlessly. In New Zealand, by 2 years after founding, 23% of new firms have exited; after 4 years, 52% have exited (Mills & Timmins, 2004, p. 19). In other words, a start-up firm has a mere 50–50 chance of surviving beyond 4 years. Fast as this attrition may appear, it is comparable to, and actually somewhat slower than, in the USA and in the OECD overall.

These data do not allow us to judge whether the current amount of downsizing is optimal, but they do at least suggest that there is no major barrier to downsizing.

3.9. Barriers to Becoming Large

Are there impediments to medium-sized firms becoming large? More than simply getting bigger, turning into a large firm entails metamorphosis. The organization becomes inherently more complex. A large firm is qualitatively different from a small- or medium-sized firm. Instead of being owned by an individual or a partnership, it (usually) has share ownership. Instead of all decisions being made by the owner-manager, decision-making is delegated down a managerial hierarchy. Trust becomes needed. The owners must trust the top manager to pursue their interests, and the top manager must trust middle managers to make the right decisions. Finding good managers requires an effective managerial labor market. Sustaining an efficient level of trade in stocks requires financial markets to have attained a degree of sophistication.

The data on firm transitions suggest New Zealand firms face no blockage to getting beyond 100 employees. Among firms with 20–49 employees in 1995, 2% had grown by 2002 to more than 100, and among firms with 50–99 employees, 22% had grown to more than 100 (NZ MED, 2003, p. 18). Each year about 70 firms, employing about 1% of the total workforce, grew from less than 100 employees to more than 100.

While there seems to be no barrier to passing the 100-employee mark, conceivably there is a glass ceiling to firm growth at some higher number of employees. (A 100 employees is a low cut-off for "large".) Small- and medium-sized firms have been the focus of much of the policy analysis up to now. (For example, the NZ Treasury report (2004, p. 71) discusses the financial market only as it affects small firms.) The evidence on firm transitions cited above suggests, however, that the small-and-medium sector is in fact in good shape. Perhaps it is time to focus the policy analysis on New Zealand's largest firms. Most of the data collection up to now has examined small and medium firms (for example, NZ MED, 2003), so collecting more data on large firms could be useful. Whether large firms face institutional or policy impediments to efficient operation and growth is a question that warrants further empirical research.

3.10. Competitive Discipline on Large Firms

"The best of all monopoly profits", John Hicks quipped, "is a quiet life". Large firms, facing weaker market disciplines than smaller firms, may lack the incentive to seek out new, more efficient ways of running themselves. How productive are New Zealand's large firms? After reviewing the available evidence on the largest firms, Simmons (2004) concludes that they have been performing poorly, measured by value added or return on assets; he calls this poor performance a "mystery".[3] In their ability to create shareholder value, according to Healy (2000), the largest firms have been "hugely disappointing", which he attributes to agency costs and "a lack of focus on managing shareholder wealth on the part of management".

One possible reason for large-firm underperformance is a shortage of managerial talent: though this might be just a temporary shortage. The skills asked of a top manager in the pre-1984 protectionist economy were distinct from those needed in a competitive global marketplace. In the old economy, success came from negotiating favors from the government. Understanding how to compete was not the issue, for the government sheltered its chosen firms from the inconveniences of competition. As described, with a little hyperbole, by Alan Gibbs, who ran companies during that era, "Every area of our economy was licensed and if you had a license you were protected and no one could break into your market" (Russell, 1996, p.12). Nowadays, managers must know how to plot competitive strategies. It could take a decade or two for the new breed of manager to develop expertise and rise to the top, and this could perhaps explain a slow reform response of large firms.

A second possible reason for large-firm underperformance is geography. "The death of distance", remark Anderson and van Wincoop (2004), "is exaggerated". Despite the internet, the transaction costs of trading internationally remain sizeable. Firms might be unable to attain scale economies because New Zealand's market is limited and foreign markets are far away (Skilling, 2001).

A firm may be condemned to producing below minimum efficient scale unless it exports to some larger markets, and there may be barriers to moving into exporting. The direct costs of exporting – transport costs and tariff and nontariff barriers – are roughly proportional to the quantities traded, but there is a fixed-cost component to other trade costs, like language barriers, different currencies, contracting insecurities and learning about foreign demands and how to do business overseas. The internet may have reduced trade costs but it has not eliminated them. Trade costs are especially high for differentiated goods with scale economies (Anderson & van Wincoop, 2004). Most New Zealand firms do not export. Among firms with an annual turnover of at least $30,000, just 4% are exporters, and just 10% of those exporters account for 95% of exports (Simmons, 2004). The transaction costs of selling overseas could inhibit firms from exporting and thus from growing to an efficient scale.

Within the domestic market, conversely, in an industry with substantial trade costs the local firms may face little competition from overseas producers. If the industry has scale economies, there may be room for only a few local producers. Lacking competitive discipline, the firms in such an industry may have little incentive to improve their productivity. (Even if the relevant market is Australia plus New Zealand, the same point applies. A market of 24 million people is not large relative to the minimum efficient scale of some industries.)

Beyond managerial shortcomings and trade costs, a third possible reason for large firms' poor performance, to be considered next, is frictions in the financial market.

3.11. Financial-Market Frictions

For the shareholders of a large company, it is hard to evaluate the managers' decisions, for they lack information about the firm's affairs. Informational asymmetries can cause lemons-market problems to arise (McMillan, 2002, Ch. 13). In some countries, lax financial-market oversights allow insiders to expropriate minority shareholders (Johnson, La Porta, Lopez-de-Silanes, & Shleifer, 2000). If the rules governing the financial markets are inadequate, shareholders' property rights go unprotected. Investment is deterred and firms are hindered from getting the finance they need to grow.

Countries that have effective financial markets rely on the oversight not only of the courts but also of a regulator. Even Alan Greenspan, by the way, now concedes this. In 1966, as a disciple of Ayn Rand, he believed regulation was uncalled for because "it is in the self-interest of every businessman to have a reputation for honest dealings". Thus "the only protection required is that of criminal law" (Greenspan, 1966). In 2002, after the scandals of Enron, WorldCom and the rest, he changed his mind, saying, "Our most recent experiences clearly indicate…that adjustments to the existing structure of regulation…are needed". A regulatory agency supplements the courts because it offers "rule-making flexibility" (Greenspan, 2002).

In New Zealand, according to Minister of Commerce Paul Swain, "securities laws do not work as effectively as they should. Our insider trading laws are lax and the institutions regulating the market do not have adequate power to ensure the laws are effectively implemented" (Swain, 2002). Are there gaps in New Zealand's financial market regulation? The evidence is mixed.

In a comparison of investor protections across the industrialized countries, La Porta, Lopez-de-Silanes, Shleifer, and Vishny (2002) calculate, as a rough proxy for investor protections, an "index of antidirector rights", reflecting the ease with which shareholders can vote for directors as well as the existence of grievance mechanisms for shareholders. This index (with a higher number representing stronger protections) scores the U.S.A. and the U.K. 5, Australia 4, France 3 and Germany 1. New Zealand's score is 4. An OECD study of financial systems (Leahy, Schich, Wehinger, Pelgrin, & Thorgiersson, 2001) compiles a summary measure of investor protections, reflecting the effectiveness of disclosure rules and enforcement as well as shareholder and creditor rights. With a higher number meaning stronger protections, the U.K. scores 0.86, Australia 0.60, the U.S.A. 0.42,

Germany 0.23 and France −0.61. New Zealand's score is 0.66. By these measures, in the 1990s New Zealand was protecting its investors as stringently as other industrialized countries.

On the other hand, some measures suggest that all is not well in the financial market. One is the ownership of large firms. New Zealand's companies tend not to be widely held. Looking at the 20 largest publicly traded firms in industrialized countries, and defining "widely held" to mean no single shareholder has more than 20% of the voting rights, La Porta, Lopez-de-Silanes, Shleifer, and Vishny (1999, p. 492) calculate that in the U.K. 100% of the largest companies are widely held, in the U.S.A. 80%, in Australia 65%, in France 60% and in Germany 50%. In New Zealand, by contrast, just 30% of the largest companies are widely held. Examining family ownership, again using the 20% cut-off for control, they find that in the U.K. none of the 20 largest companies is family controlled, in Australia 5%, in Germany 10%, in France 20% and in the U.S.A. 20%. In New Zealand, 25% of the 20 largest companies are family controlled.

A further indication that the market for firm ownership is not as active as it might be is the size of the stock market. The total capitalization of the New Zealand Exchange is about USD 45 billion, less than that of many individual corporations overseas. (For comparison, the 10th-largest company on the New York Stock Exchange, Procter and Gamble, with a market capitalization of USD 130 billion, is three times the size of the entire New Zealand corporate sector.) In 2002, according to the World Federation of Exchanges, market capitalization in New Zealand was 32% of GDP. While this is similar to Germany and France, it is far lower than in Australia, 92%, the U.S.A., 105%, or the U.K., 111%.[4] Relative to the economy, the U.K., U.S. and Australian stock markets are about three times as large as New Zealand's. Further research is warranted on firms' propensity not to convert themselves to share ownership and, among those that do convert, to have concentrated ownership.

3.12. Changes in the Top 10 Corporations

Turnover in the list of a country's largest corporations is related to economic performance, according to data in He et al. (2003). With initial per capita GDP, education level and capital stock held constant, economic growth is faster in countries with more turnover on the top 10 list. Greater instability among the largest corporations is associated with faster productivity growth and more investment. The economy performs well where new firms are able to rise to the top; it performs badly where established firms are entrenched. The causality could go either way. Fast-growing firms could drive economic growth; or the inability of new firms to rise to challenge the established corporations might be a symptom of deeper market rigidities. Turnover matters for growth, then, at the level of not only the smallest firms but also of the largest.

Are there barriers to reaching the top of the New Zealand corporate sector? One piece of evidence suggests not. In New Zealand, just three of the 10 largest companies (by employment) in 1975 were still in the top 10 in 1996. For comparison, two companies stayed in the top 10 from 1975 to 1996 in the U.K., four in France, five in the U.S.A. and Australia and seven in Germany (He, Morck, & Yeung, 2003). A caveat: this period includes the deep deregulation and privatization of the 1980s, so these data may overstate the current amount of fluidity. Nevertheless, New Zealand has seen considerable turnover at the heights of the corporate world.

4. WHY HAS PRODUCTIVITY GROWN SLOWLY?

The data indicate, then, that barriers to doing business in New Zealand for the most part are inconsequential. Left unexplained by this conclusion is the low aggregate investment of the 1990s and the continuing income gap between New Zealand and Australia (and other OECD countries). If the culprit is not an inflexible economy, what else could it be?

Perhaps it is geography, as argued by Skilling (2001). New Zealand's remoteness and the small size of the domestic market might cause growth to be slow by impeding technology diffusion and trade flows. Large firms in concentrated sectors might lack competitive pressure to seek out ways of improving their productivity. Distance and smallness clearly are disadvantages. However, geography would not seem to be destiny, for Australia, with GDP a quarter of California's, is a small economy too.

Another possibility is lags in adjustment. The disappointing productivity growth before the 1980s was doubtless caused, at least in part, by the over-regulation which, starting in the 1930s, reached its peak in the 1970s. The slow growth of the 1990s might perhaps have been nothing worse than a delayed response to the reforms of the mid-1980s to early 1990s. Why was the reform response so slow?

Major adjustments were called for, the economy-wide distortions being extreme: broader and deeper than in most other industrialized nations. It is not possible to turn an economy around instantaneously. It took time for the government to implement the new policies, and additional time for firms and workers to retune their behavior.

Systemic effects may have further slowed the reform response. Reforms complement each other, in that any one is more effective if others are already in place (McMillan, 1998, 2004). For example, trade opening is complemented by labor-market reforms. Taking advantage of trade reform entails shrinking some industries and expanding others, which requires that the labor markets – including the managerial labor market – be flexible. Each separate reform may be useless until its complementary reforms have had time to take hold. The interactions among the reforms could mean that gains would take a decade or so to show. Given the diagnosis that the malady is transitory, no major change in policy is prescribed.

There is evidence of a productivity upturn during the late 1990s and early 2000s (Black et al., 2003; Razzak, 2003; Buckle et al., 2004). The period is only a few years long, so it is too early to conclude anything for sure, but perhaps the improved productivity is sustainable over the longer term. Sluggish productivity growth has persisted in New Zealand for decades (Hall, 1996; Kehoe & Ruhl, 2003). It may finally be a thing of the past.

5. MARKETS ARE DOING THEIR JOB

New Zealand has plenty of creative destruction. The data show that enterprise is flourishing. One in nine adult New Zealanders runs a firm with five or fewer employees. Barriers to entry being low, new firms start up at a rapid clip. Entrepreneurs are able to succeed by their own efforts, without having to rely on inherited wealth. In each year, many firms disappear and many grow. There seem to be no major barriers to growth or shrinkage, so those firms that are revealed to have poor prospects shrink or shut down, while those that have a marketable product and are well managed expand. For large firms the evidence is less clear-cut, and further empirical research is needed on their apparently limp performance. (Is it the financial market? The managerial labor market? A product market too small for efficient production?) The list of the largest firms does, at least, show flux. The ebb and flow of firms – one of the most fundamental of all market processes – seems to be unrestrained.

New Zealand's labor and financial markets are by and large doing their job. Although for the largest firms there is a question mark, for small- and medium-sized firms the current evidence on firm turnover, to my reading, calls for neither more government action nor less. Harm could be done if policy was changed to address a nonexistent problem. As the saying goes, "If it aint broke, don't fix it".

NOTES

1. I thank Robert Buckle, Tim Hazledine, Robert Joss, David Skilling, Bryce Wilkinson and Mark Wright for comments. I acknowledge support from the Center for Global Business and the Economy at the Stanford Graduate School of Business. An earlier version was presented at the workshop on "Productivity: Performance, Prospects and Policies", sponsored by the Treasury, the Reserve Bank and the Ministry of Economic Development, Wellington, July 28–29, 2004. This chapter was published in *Zealand Economic Papers* 38, December 2004, pp. 153–173.

2. The per capita income rank data are from Gould (1982, p. 21) and World Bank (2003). For analyses of New Zealand's long-term growth performance, see Hall (1996) and Kehoe and Ruhl (2003).

3. The view that these firms are underperforming is, however, questioned on methodological grounds by Wilkinson (2001b).

4. http://www.world-exchanges.org/publications/INDICATOR503.pdf

REFERENCES

Alexander, W. R. J., Bell, J. D., & Knowles, S. (2004). *Quantifying compliance costs of small businesses in New Zealand.* Discussion paper. University of Otago. http://www.business.otago.ac.nz/econ/research/discussionpapers/DP0406.pdf.

Anderson, J., & van Wincoop, E. (2004). Trade costs. *Journal of Economic Literature, 42,* 691–751.

Bartelsman, E. J., & Doms, M. (2000). Understanding productivity: Lessons from longitudinal microdata. *Journal of Economic Literature, 38,* 569–594.

Bénabou, R. (1996). Heterogeneity, stratification, and growth: Macroeconomic implications of community structure and growth. *American Economic Review, 86,* 584–609.

Black, M., Guy, M., & McLellan, N. (2003). Productivity in New Zealand: 1988 to 2002. *New Zealand Economic Papers, 37*(1), 119–150.

Blyth, C. A. (1964). Introduction. In: C. A. Blyth (Ed.), *The future of manufacturing in New Zealand.* London: Oxford University Press.

Boles de Boer, D., Evans, L., & Howell, B. (2000). *The state of e-New Zealand. Institute for the study of competition and regulation.* http://www.iscr.org.nz/documents/e-new_zealand.pdf.

Buckle, R. A., Hall, J., & McLellan, N. (2004). *Accounting for New Zealand's economic growth.* Wellington: NZ Treasury.

Carroll, N., Hyslop, D., Mare, D., Timmins, J., & Wood, J. (2002). The turbulent labour market. *NZ Association of Economists conference.* http://www.nzae.org.nz/conferences/2002/2002-Conference-Paper-16(2)-CARROLL-TEXT.PDF.

Caves, R. E. (1998). Industrial organization and new findings on the turnover and mobility of firms. *Journal of Economic Literature, 36,* 1947–1982.

Chapple, S. (2000). Māori socio-economic disparity. *Political Science, 52*, 101–115. Also available at: http://www.act.org.nz/content/20887/maorisocioeconomicdisparity.pdf.

Chinn, M. D., & Fairlie, R. W. (2004). *The determinants of the global digital divide. Economic growth center paper 881.* Yale University. http://www.econ.yale.edu/growth_pdf/cdp881.pdf.

Clark, H., & Christie, R. (2002). *Moving on with the growth and innovation agenda.* Media statement D.D. 11 October. http://www.giab.govt.nz/uploadedfiles/Documents/Reports/press_growth.pdf.

Davis, S., Haltiwanger, J., & Schuh, S. (1996). *Job creation and job destruction.* Cambridge: MIT Press.

Djankov, S., La Porta, R., Lopez-de-Silanes, F., & Shleifer, A. (2002). The regulation of entry. *Quarterly Journal of Economics, 117*, 1–37.

Evans, L., Grimes, A., Wilkinson, B., & Teece, D. (1996). Economic reform in New Zealand 1984–95: The pursuit of efficiency. *Journal of Economic Literature, 34*, 1856–1902.

Fredericks, H. H. (2004). *The global entrepreneurship monitor.* Unitec. http://www.gemconsortium.org/document.asp?id = 350.

Gibson, J. K., & Scobie, G. M. (2004). *Wealth and ethnicity: Evidence from the household savings survey.* NZ Treasury. http://yoda.eco.auckland.ac.nz/lew2004/Gibson_Scobie_2004%20LEW.pdf.

Gómez-Salvador, R., Messina, J., & Vallanti, G. (2004). *Gross job flows and institutions in Europe.* Working Paper No. 318. European Central Bank. http://www.ecb.int/pub/pdf/scpwps/ecbwp318.pdf.

Gould, J. (1982). *The rake's progress? The New Zealand economy since 1945.* Auckland: Hodder and Stoughton.

Greenspan, A. (1966). The assault on integrity. In: A. Rand (Ed.), *Capitalism: The unknown ideal.* New York: New American Library.

Greenspan, A. (2002). *Testimony before the US senate committee on banking, housing, and urban affairs.* http://www.federalreserve.gov/boarddocs/hh/2002/july/testimony.htm.

Hall, V. (1996). Economic growth. In: B. Silverstone, A. Bollard & R. Lattimore (Eds), *A study of economic reform: the case of New Zealand.* Amsterdam: North Holland.

Haltiwanger, J. (2002). Understanding economic growth: The need for micro evidence. *New Zealand Economic Papers, 36*(1), 33–58.

Hazledine, T., & Siegfried, J. (1997). How did the wealthiest New Zealanders get so rich? *New Zealand Economic Papers, 31*(1), 35–47.

He, K. S., Morck, R., & Yeung, B. (2003). *Corporate stability and economic growth.* William Davidson, Working Paper No. 553. http://eres.bus.umich.edu/docs/workpapdav/wp553.pdf.

Healy, J. (2000). Corporate governance and shareholder value. Presentation to the NZ Treasury, March.

Howell, B., & Marriott, L. (2001). *The state of e-New Zealand, 12 months on.* Institute for the Study of Competition and Regulation. http://www.iscr.org.nz/navigation/research.html.

Howitt, P., & McAfee, R. P. (1987). Costly search and recruiting. *International Economic Review, 28*(1), 89–107.

Johnson, S., La Porta, R., Lopez-de-Silanes, F., & Shleifer, A. (2000). Tunneling. *American Economic Review Papers and Proceedings, 90*, 22–27.

Johnson, S., McMillan, J., & Woodruff, C. (2002). Property rights and finance. *American Economic Review, 92*, 1335–1356.

Kasper, W. (2002a). *Losing sight of the lodestar of economic freedom: A report card on New Zealand's economic reforms.* NZ Business Roundtable. http://www.nzbr.org.nz/documents/ publications/publications-2002/losing_sight.pdf.

Kasper, W. (2002b). *New Zealand economic growth: On the road to Helsinki or Buenos Aires? Keynote address.* Wellington: NZ Association of Economists conference.

Kehoe, T. J., & Ruhl, K. J. (2003). Recent great depressions: aggregate growth in New Zealand and Switzerland. *New Zealand Economic Papers, 37,* 5–40.

Kerr, R. (2000). *The quagmire of regulation.* NZ Business Roundtable. http://www.nzbr.org.nz/ documents/speeches/speeches-2000/the_quagmire_of_regulation.pdf.

Klapper, L., Laeven, L., & Rajan, R. (2004). *Business environment and firm entry.* NBER paper 10380.

KPMG (2003). *The business New Zealand-KPMG compliance cost survey.* http://www. businessnz.org.nz/file/556/BusinessNZ_KPMG_ComplianceCostSurveyReport.pdf.

La Porta, R., Lopez-de-Silanes, F., Shleifer, A., & Vishny, R. (1999). Corporate ownership around the world. *Journal of Finance, 54*(2), 471–517.

La Porta, R., Lopez-de-Silanes, F., Shleifer, A., & Vishny, R. (2002). Investor protection and corporate valuation. *Journal of Finance, 62,* 1147–1170.

Leahy, M., Schich, S., Wehinger, G., Pelgrin, F., & Thorgiersson, T. (2001). *Contributions of financial systems to growth in OECD countries.* OECD Economics Department Working Paper No. 280. http://www.oecd.org/dataoecd/38/43/1888670.pdf.

Lewis, G. (2002). *The economic transformation debate: Where have we got to?* NZ Association of Economists conference. http://www.nzae.org.nz/conferences/2002/2002-Conference-Paper-61-LEWIS.PDF.

Loury, G. (1981). Intergenerational transfers and the distribution of earnings. *Econometrica, 49,* 843–867.

McMillan, J. (1998). Managing economic change: Lessons from New Zealand. *The World Economy, 21,* 827–843.

McMillan, J. (2002). *Reinventing the bazaar: A natural history of markets.* New York: Norton.

McMillan, J. (2004). Avoid hubris. *Finance and Development, 41*(3), 34–37. http://www.imf.org/ external/pubs/ft/fandd/2004/09/pdf/counterp.pdf.

McMillan, J., & Woodruff, C. (2002). The central role of entrepreneurs in transition economies. *Journal of Economic Perspectives, 16,* 153–170.

Millen, J. (2003). Nathan, Joseph Edward, 1835–1912. *Dictionary of New Zealand biography.* http://www.dnzb.govt.nz/.

Mills, D., & Timmins, J. (2004). *Firm dynamics in New Zealand.* NZ Association of Economists conference. http://www.nzae.org.nz/conferences/88-Mills-Timmins.pdf.

Morck, R., Stangeland, D., & Yeung, B. (2000). Inherited wealth, corporate control, and economic growth: The Canadian disease. In: R. Morck (Ed.), *Concentrated corporate ownership, Chicago.*

National Bank, various dates *Small business monitor.* http://www.nationalbank.co.nz/business/ banking/information/publications/monitor/.

NZ Ministry of Economic Development (2003). *SMEs in New Zealand: Structure and development.* http://www.med.govt.nz/irdev/ind_dev/smes/2003/index.html.

NZ Treasury (2004). *New Zealand economic growth: An analysis of performance and policy.* http://www.treasury.govt.nz/release/economicgrowth/.

Organisation for Economic Cooperation and Development. (2001). *Businesses' views on red tape.* Paris: OECD. http://www1.oecd.org/publications/e-book/4201101E.PDF.

O'Sullivan, F. (2004). Deane hits at burden of red tape. New Zealand Herald d.d. 25 March 2004.

Parham, D., & Roberts, P. (2004). Productivity growth and its sources: How do NZ and Australia compare? *Productivity: performance, prospects and policies workshop*. Wellington.   http://www.treasury.govt.nz/productivity/workshoppapers2004/pw-parham. pdf.

Petersen, M. A., & Rajan, R. G. (1997). Trade credit: Theories and evidence. *Review of Financial Studies, 10*, 661–692.

Razzak, W. A. (2003). *Toward building a new consensus about New Zealand's productivity*. Wellington: Labour Market Policy Group.

Read, E. (2004). Winning the paper war. New Zealand Herald d.d. 15 March.

Romer, P. M. (1986). Increasing returns and long-run growth. *Journal of Political Economy, 9*, 1002–1037.

Russell, M. (1996). *Revolution: New Zealand from fortress to free market*. Auckland: Hodder Moa Beckett.

Schumpeter, J. A. (1975) (1942). *Capitalism, socialism and democracy*. New York: Harper.

Simmons, G. (2004). The impact of scale and remoteness on New Zealand's industrial structure and firm performance. In: J. Poot (Ed.), *On the edge of the global economy, Cheltenham*.

Skilling, D. (2001). *The importance of being enormous: Towards an understanding of the New Zealand economy*. NZ Treasury. http://www.treasury.govt.nz/et/.

Snodgrass, D. R., & Biggs, T. (1996). *Industrialization and the small firm*. San Francisco: ICS Press.

Swain, P. (2002). On a path of global best practice. New Zealand Herald d.d. 11 June.

Te Pune Kōkiri (2000). *Progress toward closing social and economic gaps between Maori and non-Maori*. Ministry of Maori Affairs. http://www.tpk.govt.nz/publications/docs/gap00.pdf.

Tower, E. (1979). Profit control in New Zealand. *New Zealand Economic Papers, 13*, 1–23.

Wilkinson, B. (2001a). *Constraining government regulation*. NZ Business Roundtable. http:// www.nzbr.org.nz/documents/publications/publications-2001/constraining_govt.pdf.

Wilkinson, B. (2001b). *A management scandal? Interpreting measures of shareholder value*. NZ Business Roundtable. http://www.nzbr.org.nz/topic.asp?Topic = Business.

World Bank (2004). *GNI per capita 2003*. http://www.worldbank.org/data/databytopic/ GNIPC.pdf.

World Bank (2004). *Doing business in 2005: Removing obstacles to growth*. http://rru. worldbank.org/Documents/DB-2005-Overview.pdf.

A THEORY OF HOMO ENTREPRENAURUS

Anders Kjellman and Mikael Ehrsten

1. INTRODUCTION

How can we foster entrepreneurship? This was one of the basic questions to ask when we, like many others, started to consider different approaches concerning how to motivate students to become interested in entrepreneurship. We soon became puzzled by the theoretical approaches to entrepreneurship. Something seemed to be lacking, for example, the important question of how should one educate entrepreneurs? However, as noticed by Landström (2000) and Sundnäs, Kjellam and Eriksson (2002), it is through the expansion of the theoretical roots of entrepreneurship, i.e. from the economic, behavioural and business studies to multidisciplinary research, that the picture becomes more understandable, albeit more complex.

The aim of this chapter is to present a model concerning entrepreneurial behaviour and to provide some suggestions with regards to how it can be utilised in an educational context. Although the model is holistic, socio-cultural and constructivistic, it starts from the notion of a 'psychological life space' construct, suggested by Kurt Lewin (1890–1947) in the early 1930s. The concepts will be developed further, thereby expanding the area concerning entrepreneurship and modern theories of human behaviour. The field theory, or as it has also been named, topological psychology, has been

The Emergence of Entrepreneurial Economics
Research on Technological Innovation, Management and Policy, Volume 9, 211–232
Copyright © 2005 by Elsevier Ltd.
ISSN: 0737-1071/doi:10.1016/S0737-1071(05)09012-8

more or less forgotten for a long time, or overshadowed by other theories of human behaviour. However, according to Martin Gold (1999), Lewin has in recent years again become one of the most frequently quoted social researchers. Although Kurt Lewin's work still seems to be fairly unknown among entrepreneurship researchers, it is interesting to ask why Lewin's ideas have regained new actuality in social psychology? There is no simple answer to this question, but it is most certainly related to the ongoing societal changes in the Western World, and the fact that several other modern theories include central elements similar to Lewin's field theory. Since the 1980s the field has been rediscovered and in some sense reinterpreted and developed by several researchers. The most recent developments of the field theory are often called Cognitive Field Theory (see e.g. Bull, 1999). We argue that Lewin's 'life space' can be further developed and thus help us understand entrepreneurial learning. Furthermore, it can serve as a tool for creating and testing new educational methods for fostering entrepreneurship.

Over the years there has been a quest for a unified theory of human behaviour, and also for a comprehensive theory, or even a clear single definition, of entrepreneurship. Both have eluded researchers. Field theory, and subsequent contemporary theoretical constructions (for example, the various theories of self-regulatory or self-organising behaviour, the theory of autopoiesis and the complexity and chaos theories, respectively) can serve in the search for the secrets of entrepreneurial behaviour and provide some ideas concerning how to rethink education in order to better foster entrepreneurship. Theoretically, the field theory is in line with social learning theory (see Bandura & Walters, 1970), socio-cognitive theories (see Bandura, 1995; Delmar, 2001) and Ajzen's theory of planned behaviour (see Delmar, 2001; Ajzen, 2002). Bandura's notion of perceived self-efficacy can be held as a more sophisticated way of expressing or further developing the mechanism of internal motivation described earlier by Julian Rotter (1966) and in accordance with Kurt Lewin's 'level of aspiration'.

Entrepreneurship can hardly be discussed without recognising the role of culture. Field theory, to some extent also allows an explanation as to how environment and culture can form entrepreneurial behaviour. The basic ideas of our holistic model can be summarised as follows. The individual's choice to become or be forced to become an entrepreneur will be based on the individuals past activities, present situation and future aspirations. This choice will be affected by the surrounding environment and culture, with the process being seen as a specific change in an individual's life space. The choice is conscientiously made by the individual;

however, the factors contributing to or leading to the decision may not all be in the sphere of the individual's conscience awareness. Thus, some of the factors enabling this decision are arguably based on tacit knowledge or intuition.

2. BACKGROUND

2.1. Current Changes in Society

We should broaden our contextual perspective in order to understand the role of field theory, and the roles of other similar theories in the development of entrepreneurial programmes or methods. Human behaviour should be seen not only as a psychological function; the links to sociology, biology, philosophy, modern cognitive science and other scientific disciplines are also important. Last but not least, we should see education as being at the crossroads of all disciplines.

During the second half of the 20th century, and especially in the last two decades, the changes in most western industrial societies have led to serious discussions concerning the role of SMEs and the entrepreneur as an agent for development and prosperity. The term post-modern society was coined by the French sociologist and philosopher Jean-Francois Lyotard to label the ongoing paradigm shift (e.g. Beck, 1998; Uljens, 2001). The implication of this paradigm shift is that modern society, i.e. industrial society, is gradually coming to an end and a new and different type of society is developing. Behind this transition we find several macro-level political, economic, technological and cultural factors. Among the most important factors of this change are; the capitalistic societal model winning by a knock-out over the rival socialistic model, a transition from national economies to a global economy; and a development of new technologies along with the emergence and importance of new types of networks (both digital and human).

The German sociologist Ulrich Beck (1998) calls the post-modern society a 'risk society'. He also states that in the post-modern (risk) society risks are redistributed. What could constitute a risk in the modern or industrial society is not necessarily the same in the post-modern society. Entrepreneurship in the industrial era was connected with risk-taking. In the future the situation may well be the opposite. It can be a greater risk not to be entrepreneurial, i.e. not being able to see self-employment as a personal alternative of action.

2.2. A Brief Overview of Entrepreneurship Theory Building

Richard Cantillon (1680–1734) is considered to have introduced entrepreneurship in an economic context. The entrepreneur could be seen as a risk-taker who transformed investments into profit or loss. Landström (2000) and Sundnäs et al. (2002) provide fairly good overviews of the roots of entrepreneurship (see Table 1). The economic theories of entrepreneurship can be, as suggested by Landström (2000), divided into five main groups based on the role of the entrepreneurs. These entrepreneurial groups are: (1) the risk-taker, (2) the capitalist, (3) the innovator, (4) the opportunity seeker and (5) the co-ordinator of scare resources. However, let us go forward and look at the broadening of the entrepreneurship theories. It must, however, be stressed that all of these roles of the entrepreneur are important

Table 1. An Overview of the Main Economic Contributions to Entrepreneurship Theories (Based on Landström, 2000, p. 54).

Role of the Entrepreneur	Example of Researchers
Risk-taker	Bernard F. de Belidor (1729) La science des ingenieurs
	Richard Cantillon (1755) Essai sur la nature du commerce en général
	Jean-Baptiste Say (1828) Cours complet d'économie politique pratique
	Frank Knight (1921) Risk, uncertainty and profit
Capitalist	Adam Smith (1776) Inquiry into the nature and causes of the wealth of nations
	David Richardo (1821) On the principles of political economy and taxation
	Alfred Marshall (1920) Principles of economics
Innovator	Nicholas Badeau (1767) Premiere introduction à la philosophie economique
	Johann Heinrich von Thünen (1850) The isolated state with respect to agriculture and political theory
	Joseph Schumpeter (1911) The theory of economic development
	William Baumol (1993) Entrepreneurship, management and the structure of payoffs
Alert opportunity seeker	Friedrich A. Hayek (1945) The use of knowledge in society
	Ludwig von Mises (1949) Human-action: a treatise on economics
	Israel Kirzner (1973) Competition and entrepreneurship
Coordinator of scares resources	Jean-Baptiste Say (1814) Traité d'économie politique
	Mark Casson (1982) The entrepreneur – an economic theory

and still valid. Joseph Schumpeter (1883–1950) brought out the importance of entrepreneurs in transforming our society. Schumpeter (1911) is often characterised as the father of entrepreneurship research and usually lifted into the category of contributors that stress the innovative role of the entrepreneur. The entrepreneur commercialises new ideas and brings society forward. The Harvard tradition can be seen as a continuation of Schumpeter's initial ideas. In brief, it stresses that entrepreneurship is crucial for changes in society, and that entrepreneurs create new organisations and profit and this is an essential driving force. The human action tradition, with Friedrich Hayek and Ludwig von Mises as front-runners, in turn stresses the capabilities of the individual. Only a few individuals have what it takes to become successful entrepreneurs. Elements of these different entrepreneurship schools are still valid, however. In the 1960s, the theories of entrepreneurship were broadened by behavioural issues. The traditional equilibrium economics based on demand and supply had left little room for the entrepreneur and thus there were social needs concerning new explanations.

David McClelland (1961) was one of the first to stress the importance of human behaviour in explaining why some societies were more successful than others. He argues that the individual is formed by both society and the individual's own performance and achievement needs. Julian Rotter (1966) expands these theories of the behavioural school with the introduction of the concept 'locus of control'. He stresses the importance of a feeling of control over the actions of the entrepreneur. This behavioural school can be divided into several subgroups. More importantly, beginning in the 1970s, research into entrepreneurship gained increasing interest among business researchers. This has led to a situation where today most of the influential business schools include entrepreneurship in their curriculum. The broadening of entrepreneurship research into business studies has led to openings concerning organisation building, management, networks and the marketing of small enterprises. As noticed by Swedberg (2001) and Sundnäs et al. (2002), the entrepreneurship models have been further expanded (in particular in the 1990s) into multi-disciplinary approaches (see Fig. 1). Lee and Peterson (2000) utilise the concept of entrepreneurial orientation while stressing the role of culture. However, they argue that: "There is a need for an entrepreneurship model that acknowledges the individual person without discounting the portion of the external environment that is beyond the individual or the firm's control ... The study of entrepreneurship under a cultural umbrella seems appropriate" (Lee & Peterson, 2000, p. 403).

In the research field of human behaviour, during the first part of the 20th century, two traditions became dominant – the behaviourist and the

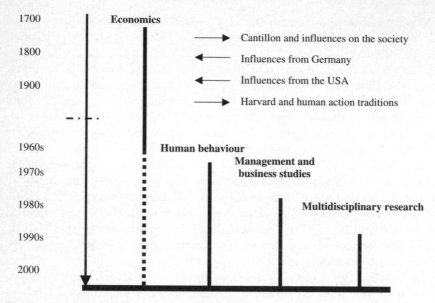

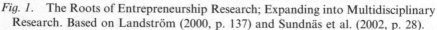

Fig. 1. The Roots of Entrepreneurship Research; Expanding into Multidisciplinary Research. Based on Landström (2000, p. 137) and Sundnäs et al. (2002, p. 28).

psychodynamic. The former, apparently due to its (simplistic) methodological approaches, corresponded well with the more or less reductionist tradition of analytical rationalism or logical positivism. Consequently, this was the tradition largely adopted by the natural sciences from the late 18th century onwards. These traditions then also influenced entrepreneurship research after this field began to broaden from economic research into other disciplines.

The early psychological theories of entrepreneurship were more or less based on a 'trait chasing' approach, i.e. a search for the optimal combination of relatively stable personality factors that together could form or explain entrepreneurial behaviour. These theories were profoundly influenced by behaviourist thinking, and research was supported by new tools in the form of mathematical methods such as factor analysis. A good example of such an approach is McClelland's research and The Big Five-theory. An example representing the psychodynamic tradition is in the entrepreneurship research and theory of Kets de Vries (see e.g. Leskinen, 1999). Kets de Vries and other psychoanalytic researchers often see the entrepreneur as an 'innovative rebel' or a misfit. Seen through the lens of industrial society this is not surprising. 'Homo Entreprenaurus' is certainly different from 'Homo Industrialis'. In society he may have been tolerated, but within the schools of the industrial era, 'Homo Entreprenaurus' was a problem.

2.3. Aspects Concerning Learning and Knowledge

Learning is not only a matter of the memorising and the retention of facts or learning to master practical (vocational) skills. It is widely agreed today that learning is connected with the formation of individual cognitive, social and behavioural patterns. Furthermore, we must acknowledge that education is both a formative and a transformative process, regardless of the age of the student. The environment influences learning both at home and at school.

Learning is a highly individualised process and modern research has formed a variety of different theories and typologies of individual learning styles. On the one hand, in most western countries, these new elements are gradually finding their way into everyday educational practice. On the other, we need to accept that education is a conservative business and that education still retains much of the thinking of the modern industrial society. The origin of this thinking is old. Most of it stems from the 17th and 18th century era of Enlightenment and is basically equivalent to the ideas of René Descartes, his contemporaries and followers.

The Russian psychologist, Lev S. Vygotsky (1896–1934), was among the first to challenge the behaviouristic thoughts of human action and his ideas have often been classified as cultural psychology. Today, Vygotsky, usually together with Jean Piaget, is referred to as one of the first constructivists. Vygotsky, who focused on children's cognitive development and the mediating function of language in human behaviour, concluded that human language is a double-functioning process. In small children it allows communication to take place with their immediate environment, thus making socialisation possible. Later on, language develops into a central element in human thought, consciousness and cognitive functions, see e.g. Consciousness as a problem in the psychology of behaviour (Vygotsky, 1925). Vygotsky's texts have only been widely discussed in the Western Hemisphere long after his death and there have been some discussions concerning the accuracy of the translations of his texts from Russian.[1] Alfred Lang (1994) has compared the ideas of Kurt Lewin and Lev Vygotsky and found some similarities and classifies them both as meta-theorists. Lang has suggested that their ideas would deserve a closer comparison and that this should be done through a semiotic analysis in order to avoid misinterpretations regarding their use of words and terminology. Vygotsky's ZPD[2] ('zone of proximal development') construct is especially

Articulated knowledge (Easily recognisable and measurable)	Theoretical knowledge (factual)	Practical knowledge (vocational skills)
Unarticulated knowledge ('hidden', hard to measure)	Tacit knowledge (social and emotional skills)	Intuitive knowledge (paranoesis)

Fig. 2. Types of Knowledge.

interesting for educators (Wells, 1999), since it is easy to link to and compare with Lewin's 'life space' construct.

In the industrial era, education has focused on two types of knowledge: (a) technical and theoretical knowledge and (b) practical (vocational) skills (see Fig. 2). Coincidentally, these types of knowledge are those easiest to articulate, transfer and evaluate. They also correspond well with the behaviourist (or positivistic–analytic), ontological and epistemological traditions that have prevailed in most western societies, especially in vocational education (see Doolittle & Camp, 1999). In the post-modern society this may not be enough. Equipped only with these types of knowledge a person may not be able to be entrepreneurial and self-sustaining. We therefore suggest that education, in order to support the development of more entrepreneurial behaviour, will have to add more tacit knowledge, i.e. social and emotional skills to the curricula. Innovation and intuition are also often mentioned when speaking of entrepreneurship, which leads us to believe that schools should start preparing for how they can deal with intuition (sometimes called 'hidden intelligence').

In modern (industrial) society, the educational system has focused on the easily recognisable and measurable types of skills, i.e. theoretical and practical knowledge. However, the hidden types of skills will also have to be considered in order to support an entrepreneurial orientation and creative individual. Both tacit and intuitive knowledge should be recognised in the educational system. Bringing in new types of knowledge into the curricula should not be allowed to weaken the already established educational structures that function well. Much of the knowledge needed in industrial society will still be needed in post-modern society. This may be the biggest dilemma for education: how can new types of skills and knowledge be added without destroying or weakening those parts that already function well? Brown (1997) and Brown, Collins, and Duguid (1989) stresses the role of intuitive thinking – paranoesis – in this process.

Lewin was also among the first of modern behavioural scientists to recognise the importance of concrete experience in the learning process, an idea later taken on by John Dewey and many other philosophers and educators. In fact the principle of experiential learning, today widely known as the Kolb Learning Circle, is yet another of the many ideas of Kurt Lewin. David Kolb and his associates only have brought this principle onto a larger audience (Egidius, 2000, pp. 117–119). This principle describes how experience in real-life situations through a process of observation and reflection is formed or transformed into new knowledge, which thereafter can be used in a new context.

Many efforts to foster entrepreneurship in educational settings are tied to some kind of courses (usually elective), practice enterprises, entrepreneurial projects or business incubators. These approaches, however, have at least one serious problem. They seem to require a pre-selection of the student, and thus, exclude a majority of them. Ultimately, this can constitute a problem of equality. The current changes in society indicate the need for all students to receive some type of entrepreneurship education in order to prepare them for self-employment. The ecological validity of elective courses and business incubators as a mean of fostering entrepreneurship in larger student populations can likewise be doubted or at least discussed. Ecological validity refers to the discussion whether results from laboratory experiments can be generalised to explain natural behaviour (Schmuckler, 2001). Our view is that entrepreneurship should be integrated into the regular curricula, which will raise a need for both new instructional methods and a new epistemology.

In business education, some small-scale experiments mixing entrepreneurship elements into the standard educational programmes have been conducted in selected student groups during the years 1992–2000 (Ehrstén, 2001). The results of these experiments indicate that, when allowed or requested to work with virtual or 'real' practice enterprises during a learning period, student's behaviour gradually changes and become more goal-oriented, self-regulated and self-organised. This could be seen as an emerging entrepreneurial behaviour. The entrepreneurial elements in these groups have been 15–25% of the total time spent and the length of the projects has varied from 2.5 to 7 months. Unfortunately, these types of experiments have often been too short-termed to observe and conclude if the observed behavioural changes become generalised and more permanent. In four groups, students' perception or understanding of the word entrepreneur and some other occupational categories were tested with a semantic differential. The results from the testing with the (proto-type) semantic differential gave almost identical profiles on the 15 variable bipolar scales, regardless of whether the students tested were engaged or interested in entrepreneurial activities nor not. The results indicate that, although there is no single or definite definition of entrepreneur/entrepreneurship, students perceive the word and the phenomenon quite similarly.

3. LINEARITY AND CAUSALITY VERSUS NON-LINEARITY AND DYNAMICS

The traditional Cartesian view of man and knowledge, which has influenced education for several hundred years, is based on a notion of linearity and causality. In this view every action and behaviour is explainable and has a specific cause. In this tradition it has more or less been a standard procedure that, if something is not explainable along this empirical logic–rationalist line, it does not exist, or it belongs to the domain of 'unscientific phenomenon'.

When seen from the perspective of field theory (Lang, 1979, 1981), system theory (Flint, 1997), complexity theory (Ferdig, 2000; Markowsky, 1999), second-order cybernetics (Heylighen & Joslyn, 2001), the autopoiesis theory, (sometimes called 'theory of observing systems') or synergetics (Coulter, 2002), Open systems are seen as being non-linear and changes are often said to happen 'on the edge of chaos' and follow the principle of equifinality.[3] If we consider humans as open living systems, we will have to rethink both the linearity and the simple causality and will need a totally new equation of human behaviour. The old formula from Kurt Lewin's field theory: $B = f(P, E)$, where human behaviour (B) is a function of the person (P) and the environment (E) may be valid for this purpose. However, we would argue strongly that one should expand this formula to also include the impact of culture (C) and other factors.

Yet another interesting concept related to system or complexity theories, which leads us even closer to the world of business and entrepreneurship, is Economy Nobel Laureate Friedrich von Hayek's concept of Connectionism. v. Hayek derived his idea partly from biologist D.O. Hebb's theory of neural feedback. Cognitive Scientist Barry Smith (1997) writes: "the central idea behind the connectionist paradigm is at home not only in psychology and neurology but also in the sphere of economics". This indicates that human behaviour and the market process, to a certain extent, are similar or analogous processes.

Lewin's view on the life space can be found in his article on Field Theory and learning, which can be found in Cartwright (1951, pp. 62–63) "The properties of the 'life space' of the individual depend partly upon the state of that individual as a product of his history, partly upon the nonpsychologic – physical and social – surroundings. The latter have a relation to life space similar to that which "boundary conditions" have to a dynamic system ... field theory finds it advantageous, as a rule, to start with a characterization of the situation as a whole".

Field theory, complexity theory and autopoiesis theory have long been connected with social systems in general (Markowsky, 1999; Coleman Jr., 1999). One of the scientists applying these thoughts is sociologist Niklas Luhmann (Whitaker, 1995; Manuel-Navarrete, 2000). From here it is a short step to organisational and management theories and theories of organisational learning and learning organisations. In this context we also find Chris Argyris' (1993) theory of 'single-loop' and 'double-loop' learning (Argyris & Schön, 1996). When considering human learning we can conclude that both kinds of learning exist. Simpler learning schemes, such as conditioning and social modelling, can be seen as single-loop learning, while more complex or higher-level cognitive behaviour most certainly must follow the principle of double-loop learning. Perhaps this is the ultimate difference also between 'Homo Industrialis' and 'Homo Entreprenaurus'?

The schools of the industrial society have no doubt contributed to the creation of 'Homo Industrialis' and they have effectively produced the skilled and semi-skilled workers for industrial society. Can education be transformed to create 'Homo Entreprenaurus'? To express this in other words: Can the 'Enigma of Entrepreneurship' (see Carland, Carland, & Stewart, 1996) be solved by studying human behaviour and how could we alter educational practice to be more effective in fostering entrepreneurship? Our conclusion is that the post-modern society will need a new ontology and a new epistemology. Both these are particularly important in order to understand entrepreneurship and entrepreneurship education.

4. TOWARDS A NEW ENTREPRENEURIAL MODEL BASED ON FIELD THEORY

To the best of our knowledge, Lewin's view of human behaviour, a view that was influenced by gestalt psychologists, has not been largely utilised by entrepreneurship researchers. In general, as stated by Swedberg (2001), social psychology also has still much to contribute to the field of entrepreneurship research. Lewin's untimely death in 1947, a fate that he shared with Lev Vygotsky who died even earlier (Wells, 1999), may have contributed to the fact that his field theory has been more or less forgotten since the 1960s. Psychological theories of entrepreneurship only started to develop after his death. Lewin influenced many years after his death a great number of other behavioural scientists (Marrow, 1969), both in his native Germany and in America. Over the years, ontological and epistemological elements of a similar nature to those in the field theory have found their way into many theory constructions of human behaviour. Similar elements can also be found in various other disciplines, not only in psychology.

The field theory covers – or touches on – several different scientific disciplines. The Swiss scholar Alfred Lang (1979, 1981), for instance, suggests that the field theory could be considered as being a for-runner of the general system theory, created by Ludwig von Bertalanffy in the late 1950s. Lang also comments that similarities can be found comparing the theory with Bronfenbrenner's theory of ecological psychology.

It is important to broaden our perspective considerably if we are to understand the field theory itself and its implications for entrepreneurship research. It will be necessary to bring in to the discussion both elements of modern and post-modern Sociology and Philosophy. Without these elements our approach to using the field theory to help the understanding of entrepreneurship formation (i.e. how an individual becomes, chooses or develops into being an entrepreneur) and how to use education to influence this process, cannot be understood. It is also essential to clearly point out that Lewin's field theory is only the starting-point, and serves as an instrument and a method of analysing and understanding causal relations. The field theory is, as Kurt Lewin (Cartwright, 1951, pp. 43–45) himself pointed out, not a theory in the usual sense of the term:

> methods like field theory can really be understood and mastered only in the same way as methods in a handicraft, by learning them through practice. ... Field theory, therefore, can hardly be called correct or incorrect in the same way as a theory in the usual sense of the term. Field theory is probably best characterized as a method: namely, a method of analysing causal relations and of building scientific constructs. This method of analysing causal relations can be expressed in the form of general statements about the "nature" of the conditions of change.

The central concept in Lewin's field theory was his construct concerning the psychological life space. Lewin defined the 'psychological life space' as "the totality of coexisting facts, which are conceived of as mutually interdependent" (Cartwright, 1951, p. 240). For Lewin, learning was synonymous with the expansion of the life space. Egon Brunswik, a contemporary of Lewin, criticised Lewin's notion of the life space for not considering the significance of the outside environment enough and its impact on the

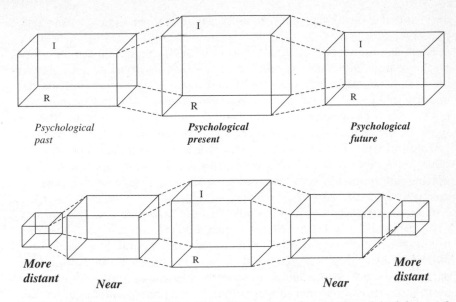

Fig. 3. The life space in Lewin's field theory. According to the original figure of Lewin's "the development of the life space". R, the reality level; I, the irrational level. The first illustration in the figure represents a more basic division, while the second divides the psychological past and future into near and more distant. Hence, a more extended version of the life space concept. *Source*: Sandström (1981, p. 85).

psychological life space. Their ideas of human psychology were otherwise astonishingly similar, but in their dialogue the border zone between an individual's life space and the environment seems to have been a detail they could not agree on (Wolf, 1986). Other contemporary scientists criticised Lewin for not developing the formula $B = f(P, E)$ further. This, however, has to be seen in the context of the mathematical science of that time (1930s). Kurt Lewin did not have the powerful instruments of today. The Finnish scholar Kullervo Rainio (1986) showed later, in the 1980s, through his stochastic field theory of human behaviour that human behaviour can be mathematically explained.

Fig. 3 illustrates Lewin's life space concept according to the original figure by Lewin. According to Lewin, the life space is a power field, where the individual is the focal point surrounded by closer and more distant areas as well as barriers and boundaries that affect the individual's behaviour. Depending on the situation at hand, the individual's movements vary and the life space never stays constant (e.g. Sundnäs et al., 2002, pp. 34–42).

Kjellman, Sundnäs, Ramström, and Elo (2004) argues that the life space of the central individuals is one factor that affects decisions and actions made by the management of a firm. Hence, together with other firm internal and external factors, the life space concept may assist our understanding of how and why choices are made in a firm. Specifically, we argue that the life space of the central figure also affects the chosen degree of international orientation (IO). For example, if a small firm manager has a positive in- ternational experience from his past or future ambitions for the firm in- volving international activities, then the chosen degree of IO may be positively affected.

We have expanded Lewin's psychological life space (see Fig. 4) by adding two peripheral fields, i.e. the environmental and cultural aspects. The centre of our model still contains what Lewin called the temporal dimension of the individual life space. The temporal dimension can be divided into three parts: i.e. the past (experience), the present (real-time) and the future (as- pirations). All actions and changes happen in the present, although they are affected by the past and the aspirations for the future. Thus, these three parts will continually affect the individual's decision-making. In other words

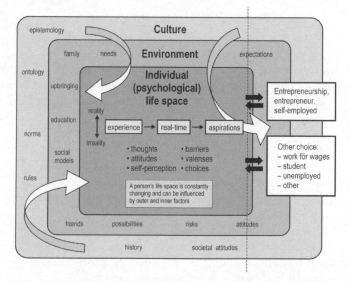

Fig. 4.   Lewin's 'Life Space' Redrawn.

the life space is never static, but constantly changing over time. By influencing this dynamic process, we argue that education can affect the choice of the individual. Obviously this process also varies from individual to individual. Thereby, several supportive strategies or methods concerning entrepreneurial learning will most likely be needed.

The model (see Fig. 4) suggests that the individual choice of becoming an entrepreneur or making other choices will be affected by situational factors, the 'here and now'. In other words there may be a number of emerging behaviours. Some individuals may never come into a situation where entrepreneurship or self-employment is a logical option. This model does not contradict previous theoretical contributions such as seeing the entrepreneur as a risk-taker (e.g. Cantillon, 1755) capitalist (e.g. Richardo, 1821) innovator (Schumpeter, 1911), opportunity seeker (e.g. von Hayek, 1945; Kirzner, 1973) and co-ordinator of scare resources (e.g. Say, 1814). In fact it supports these theoretical contributions by applying a more holistic view of entrepreneurship. Furthermore, our model is an attempt to expand the entrepreneurship theory by including behavioural, management, cultural and social impacts as being factors that effect individual choices. This leads us back to Kurt Lewin's formula that of behaviour being a function of person and environment.

$$B = f(P, E)$$

where human behaviour (B) is a function of the person (P) and the environment (E). However, we argue that one should expand this formula to also include culture (C) and possibly other factors in order to capture the complexity of entrepreneurship formation. In the basic form we see entrepreneurship behaviour (EB) as a complex function of person (P) in his social environment (E) and prevailing culture (C). However, in addition to this we have found that in some cases it is also necessary have to take into account factors such as contextual chances (ε). From a theoretical perspective the impact of personal factors (P) are of utter importance in order to understand the emergence of entrepreneurial behaviour. In addition to traditional opportunity and necessity entrepreneurship, as described by Global Entrepreneurship Monitor (2001), and also specific events may create the entrepreneurial opportunity for an individual e.g. marriage, occasional social contacts and subjective urge for a career change.

$$EB = f(P, E) + g(C) + \varepsilon$$

We do not argue that a formula such as this has a profound impact on our understanding of entrepreneurial behaviour. We argue that human behaviour is too complex in order to be fully captured in a basic formula, because the function of personal factors $f(P,E)$ is so complex and individual. In essence though, we argue that individual life spaces can be explored and analysed in order to capture entrepreneurial behaviour. Therefore, we also argue that factors contributing to entrepreneurial behaviour can be influenced by education, and a multitude of other measures. Entrepreneurship can, as we see it, be characterised as an emerging behaviour in a complex social context and this fact will place entrepreneurship in the research field of complexity theories (see e.g. Whitaker, 1995; Ferdig, 2000). In a complex world the individual's life space can be expanded by acquiring new knowledge. This new knowledge can be unarticulated (i.e. intuitive, tacit) or articulated (i.e. theoretical, practical). It can be an insight of how to expand the life space into new innovative thinking. However, it may as well be an insight of how to utilise already existing products or services.

The model can also be extended to apply to a situation when an individual or a group of individuals have already chosen to act as entrepreneurs. Another implication of this model is that it gives us a tool in order to understand how individuals can be either stimulated or not to become entrepreneurs. The educational task is to also mentally prepare individuals to recognise and manage potential entrepreneurial opportunities, not only to prepare them to technically run a business. We need to prepare the individuals so that they can see potential opportunities, and act upon them. The role of innovations in this model will thus be tacitly stressed. The innovative role of the entrepreneurs as described by Schumpeter (1911) is naturally important. However, we have chosen to include the aspects of innovations as only one of the many factors that affect the individual's choice to become an entrepreneur or not. It is in this process that the individuals will need different types of knowledge, i.e. theoretical, practical, tacit and intuitive knowledge. If the individual only has factual and practical knowledge, he will probably ignore an upcoming opportunity, while a potential entrepreneur will be better mentally prepared to identify and act upon given opportunities or to create opportunities by being innovative.

Other scientists and philosophers have also used concepts or terms similar to Lewin's life space. One example is Bauman (1999). Bauman uses terms such as 'social field' or 'social room'. It is important to clearly point out the differences. Our perception is that Lewin's 'life space' is directly connected to the Self, while Bauman's concept is more connected to the social environment and the social roles individuals adopt in their environment. Kjellman et al. (2004) have further developed the concepts to also include the issue of entrepreneurial orientation when it comes to explaining internationalisation of small firms. Thus, by expanding this basic model so that it is not seen as an individual choice but rather as a choice of a firm or an organisation, the performance of the firm will then be a function of its – and its members – past activities, present situation and future ambitions, and strategies.

Given this theoretical framework it is possible to look at their implications for future educational needs. How to foster entrepreneurship in education has been a popular topic since the mid-1980s and a challenge education has taken up. Vesper and Gartner (1999) reported that different kinds of entrepreneurial programmes in universities have rapidly increased worldwide during the last decades. Marilyn Kourilsky (1995) noted that 'Generation-X' in the USA had already adopted an attitude of 'creating-a-job' rather than 'taking-a-job'. In almost every western country business incubators and science parks have been created to support new entrepreneurs and help them develop their firms. However, little has been done to create a pedagogy for fostering entrepreneurship in larger student populations.

Drawing from the fact that entrepreneurship seems to evolve more effectively in an environment where entrepreneurship already exist (Uusitalo, 1999), we propose an educational model where students are directly exposed to entrepreneurship during their whole time in education. Petri Uusitalo's longitudinal research shows that in Finland young males have a 3–4 times greater chance of becoming entrepreneurs if they grow up in a family with at least one of the parents being an entrepreneur. The unanswered question is why? We assume entrepreneurial behaviour can be acquired through – and may be only through – an active experiential learning process in a social context. Similar ideas are presented in David Rae's conceptual model of how entrepreneurial capability develops (Rae, 1999; Rae & Carswell, 2001).

We suggest that the educational system is redesigned in such a way that it supports the formation of entrepreneurial knowledge and skills accumulatively under long periods of time. For those raised in an entrepreneur family, entrepreneurship already becomes a natural part of their life in the family. However, for those without natural entrepreneurial influences education with a focus on entrepreneurship could be a good option simply because education is an integral part of every person's 'psychological life space' for long periods of their lives. We argue that Kurt Lewin's construct, and contemporary developments of his theory (i.e. the cognitive field theory), gives us a workable instrument or a tool to help us focus on the individual dimensions of learning. Thereby, these instruments could be used to rethink education in order to foster entrepreneurship.

5. CONCLUSIONS

Entrepreneurship can, as we see it, be characterised as an emerging behaviour in a complex social system, primarily established through an experiential learning process. This will place entrepreneurship research in a grey zone between the field of complexity theories and social and cognitive learning theories. Bandura's theory of social learning, and later his theory of self-efficacy are now classified as social constructivist theories, although they stem from a neo-behaviouristic tradition. The theory of autopoiesis is usually considered to belong in the category of radical constructivism. We also find some interesting elements regarding entrepreneurship in Lev Vygotsky's socio-cultural theory, especially in his construct ZPD. All these theories have much in common and can be utilised to develop effective entrepreneurship programmes.

We assume that the process of becoming an entrepreneur is not a simple or linear process and many separate theories substantiate this. Each individual's perception of himself (perceived self-efficacy) and motivational structure are central elements in the process of becoming an entrepreneur. The way they develop may not be the same in each person; it may be that entrepreneurs develop because of equifinality (a term adopted from system theory), self-observation and self-organising (terms adopted from auto-poiesis theory) and the results of non-linear dynamic development (a term adopted from synergetics). The fact is that there may be infinite sets of behavioural complexity, which need to be shaped or supported. This gives us different possibilities with regard to educational planning and pedagogy, rather than simply assuming that there is one single mode for entrepreneurs. Perhaps, there is an entrepreneur in all of us, and it is up to educational researchers, planners and educators to develop schools, methods and curricula to support this development in a multitude of ways. In the light we find that of this the field theory is most practical and fruitful to work with. As Kurt Lewin put it: "there is nothing as practical as a good theory".

With this reasoning we arrive at a point where constructivist theories fit better into the picture than the traditional content and skills based view of vocational education. Constructivism[4] is, however, not always easy to communicate to educators. Constructivist thinking and theories are based on a different philosophical perspective than the familiar instructivism. Constructivist ideas easily become fuzzy and can be misunderstood. It is therefore crucial that we can also coach (vocational) teachers, who are perhaps more focused on and familiar with their own field of expertise than with educational philosophy and constructivist thinking.

In designing educational programmes fostering entrepreneurship we may run into problems, not only with ontology and epistemology, but also with problems of terminology and allocating sufficient resources. In order to do this it will be necessary to relax the boundaries between schools and the outside world. Educational entrepreneurship research has traditionally concentrated on content and curricula, not on the philosophical questions of human behaviour (Kyrö, 2001). Therefore, we should be prepared to partly break with the old thinking traditions of knowledge, learning and instructional education. We will have to prepare and coach students to learn and to use other kinds of knowledge than the traditional and familiar types, i.e. social, emotional and intuitive knowledge. We also see this as a path to new entrepreneurial innovations. We believe that such courses will increase the self-confidence and self-efficacy of students. In the long run this will prepare them for self-employment and entrepreneurship, but we will probably experience problems with evaluating the outcome of the courses since we do not anticipate that students will start up firms immediately. This long-term exposure could well be more effective than the present type of short-course courses (5–10 credits) often offered in educational settings today.

In essence, brutally simplified, what this model suggests is that reality is personal and subjective and that creating an active individual is part of a learning process. Thus, we suggest that entrepreneurship should be infused into the 'life space' of the students during their entire time of education. Entrepreneurship elements should be integrated in the curricula in such a way that it allows long-term formative learning. It should be done by using a variety of experimental learning methods to match different learning styles, but it should not be allowed to disturb the content-based education. Students should be coached to use self-monitoring and self-evaluative techniques and reflective thinking. In order to create 'ZPD' for every student, real entrepreneurs functioning as mentors, will support entrepreneurial learning. Hence, students can learn about issues that are not possible to teach using traditional methods. With this approach, which is largely based on the theoretical view of a cognitive field theory, we believe that students will leave school with a better 'perceived self-efficacy' and that they will be better mentally prepared later in life to become entrepreneurs or self-employed. If, however, they choose not to be entrepreneurs or self-employed, we think that their future employers will also benefit from the self-observing and self-organising way of working and learning they have developed.

Finally, we believe that future entrepreneurship research, in order to create a better understanding of the development of the complex behavioural patterns and factors behind entrepreneurship formation, could focus on designing methods to explore and analyse individual life spaces. We believe the key to find these methods may be found through narrative research. Having such methods we might be able to see how and why individuals' behaviour becomes entrepreneurial, thereby giving use effective ways and new instruments to support this by educational means.

NOTES

1. Nikolai Veresov in 1999 retranslated Vygotsky's article "Conciousness as a problem in the psychology of behaviour", see Veresov's appendix article (http://www.marxist.org/archives/).
2. Vygotsky's construct 'zone of proximal development' (ZPD) can be described with the following: "children's ability to learn and achieve at a higher level, when learning happens in the company of or assisted by an adult".
3. Equifinality is a term used in system theories to describe an outcome of similar nature preceded by totally different development processes.
4. An easy-to-read document on constructivism is Dougiamas (1998).

ACKNOWLEDGEMENT

The authors would like to thank Bengt Johannisson, Jerome Katz, David Rae, Paul Wilkinson, Elizabeth Nyman and the 2005 IECER participants for constructive comments.

REFERENCES

Ajzen, I. (2002). Perceived behavioral control, self-efficacy, locus of control, and the theory of planned behavior. *Journal of Applied Social Psychology, 32*, 1–20.
Argyris, C. (1993). *Knowledge for action: A guide to overcoming barriers to organizational change*. San Francisco, CA: Jossey-Bass.
Argyris, C., & Schön, D. A. (1996). *Organizational learning II: Theory, method, and practice*. Reading, MA: Addison-Wesley.
Bandura, A. (1995). *Self-efficacy in changing societies*. Cambridge: Cambridge University Press.
Bandura, A., & Walters, R. H. (1970). *Social learning and personality development* (3rd ed). London: Holt, Reinhard & Winston.
Bauman, Z. (1999). *Postmodern etik*. Gothenburg: Daidalos.
Beck, U. (1998). *Risksamhället*. Gothenburg: Daidalos.
Brown, J. S. (Ed.) (1997). *Seeing differently: Insights on innovation*. Boston: Harvard Business School Press.
Brown, J. S., Collins, A., & Duguid, P. (1989). Situated cognition and the culture of learning. *Columbia University in Educational Researcher, 18* (February).

Bull, K. S. (1999). *Psychology of learning.* Internet textbook http://home.okstate.edu/homepages.nsf/toc/EPSY5463chapterindex (accessed 20.11.2002).

Carland, J. C., Carland, J. W., & Stewart, W. H. (1996). Seeing what's not there: The enigma of entrepreneurship. *Journal of Small Business Strategy, 7,* 1–20.

Cartwright, D. (Ed.) (1951). *Field theory in social sciences – selected theoretical papers.* New York: Harper & Brothers Publishers.

Coleman, Jr., H. J. (1999). *What enables self-organizing behavior in business?* Emergence, 01/01/99.

Coulter, A. N. (2002). *Human synergetics revisited* (Internet Edition originally published in 1976) www.synearth.net/coulter/synergetics.pdf (accessed on 2.4.2002).

Delmar, F. (2001). *The psychology of the entrepreneur.* Stockholm: ESBRI Reprint Series 2001/4.

Doolittle, P. E., & Camp, W. G. (1999). Constructivism: The career and technical education perspective. *Journal of Vocational and Technical Education, 16,* 23–46.

Dougiamas, M. (1998). *A journey into constructivism.* http://dougiamas.com/writing/constructivism.html (accessed 28.6.2002).

Egidius, H. (2000). *Pedagogik för 2000-talet.* Stockholm: Bokförlaget Natur och Kultur.

Ehrstén, M. (2001). Entreprenörskap i Handelsutbildningen. In: A. Kjellman & H. Eriksson (Eds), *Aroina Business Papers, 1*(Special Issue), 119–131.

Ferdig, M. A. (2000). *Complexity theories: Perspectives for the social construction of organizational transformation.* http://www.sba.muohio.edu/management/mwAcademy/2000/21d.pdf (accessed 26.6.2002).

Flint, L. (1997). *System theory.* http://www.bsu.edu/classes/flint/system.html (accessed 28.5.2000).

Global Entrepreneurship Monitor (2001). In: P. Arenius, E. Autio, A. Kovalainen & P. D. Reynolds (Eds), GEM 2001 Finnish executive report. Espoo: Helsinki University of Technology.

Gold, M. (Ed.) (1999). *The complete social scientist – a Kurt Lewin Reader.* Washington, DC: American Psychological Association.

Heylighen, F., & Joslyn, C. (2001). Cybernetics and second-order cybernetics. In: R. A. Meyers (Ed.), *Encyclopedia of physical science and technology* (3rd ed.). New York: Academic Press.

Kjellman, A., Sundnäs, A.-C., Ramström, J., & Elo, M. (2004). *Internationalisation of small firms.* Vaasa: Anders Kjellman Consulting.

Kourilsky, M. (1995). Entrepreneurship education: Opportunity in search of curriculum in business education. *Forum* 10/95.

Kyrö, P. (2001). Yrittäjäkasvatuksen Pedagogisia Lähtökohtia Pohtimassa. *Aikuiskasvatus, 2,* 92–101.

Landström, H. (2000). *Entreprenörskapets rötter* (2nd ed.). Lund: Studentlitteratur.

Lang, A. (1979). Die Feldttheorie von Kurt Lewin. In: A. Hegl-Evers (Ed.), *Lewin und die folgen.* Kindlers enzyklopädie: Die psychologie des 20. Jahrhunderts, Zurich, Kindler, 51–57.

Lang, A. (1981). Vom nachteil und nutzen der gestaltpsychologie für eine theorie psychischen entwicklung. In: K. Foppa & R. Groner (Eds), *Kognitive strukturen und ihre entwicklung* (pp. 154–173). Bern: Huber.

Lang, A. (1994). *Lewin and Wygotsky – the radical and promising metatheorists.* University of Bern. http://www.cx.unibe.ch/psyk/ukp/langgpapers/pap1994-99/1994_lewin_vygotsky.htm (accessed 28.6.2002).

Lee, S., & Peterson, S. (2000). Culture, entrepreneurial orientation, and global competitiveness. *Journal of World Business, 35,* 401–416.

Leskinen, P.-L. (1999). *Yrittäjällä on koko elämä kiinni yrityksessä*. ActaWasaensis, *71*. Vaasa: University of Vaasa.

Manuel-Navarrete, D. (2000). *Approaches and implications of using complexity theory for dealing with social systems.* http://research.yale.edu/CCR/environment/papers/manuel_complexity. pdf (accessed 28.6.2002).

Markowsky, B. (1999). *Social network and complexity theory.* Presentation transcript 11/1/98 at the International Conference on Social Networks and Social Capital, Duke University, USA.

Marrow, A. (1969). *The practical theorist: The life and work of Kurt Lewin.* New York: Basic Books Inc.

Rae, D. (1999). *The entrepreneurial spirit.* Dublin: Blackhall Publishing.

Rae, D., & Carswell, M. (2001). Towards a conceptual model of understanding entrepreneurial learning. *Journal of Business and Enterprise Development, 8,* 150–158.

Rainio, K. (1986). *Stochastic field theory of behaviour.* Helsinki: Commentationes Scientarium Sociallium, 34/1986.

Rotter, J. B. (1966). Generalized expectancies for internal versus external control of reinforcement. *Psychological Monographs, 80,* 1–28.

Schmuckler, M. A. (2001). *What is ecological validity? A dimensional analysis division of life sciences.* University of Toronto at Scarborough. http://www.utsc.toronto.ca/~marksch/ Schmuckler%202001.pdf (accessed 25.6.2002).

Schumpeter, J. (1911). In: R. Opie (Trans.), The theory of economic development: An inquiry into profits, capital, credit, interest, and the business cycle. New York: Oxford University Press (Translated in 1962).

Smith, B. (1997). *The connectionist mind: A study of Hayekian psychology.* Department of Philosophy and Center for Cognitive Sciences, University of Buffalo. http://ontology. buffalo.edu/smith/articles/hayek.htm (accessed 26.6.2002).

Sundnäs, A.-C., Kjellman, A., & Eriksson, H. (2002). *Entreprenörskap och utveckling.* Espoo: Schildts Förlag.

Swedberg, R. (2001). *The social science view of entrepreneurship: Introduction and practical applications.* Stockholm: ESBRI Reprint Series 2001/2.

Uljens, M. (2001). Pedagogik och (Sen) modernitet - utgångspunkter för ett forskningsprojekt. Unpublished Working Paper, Helsinki: University of Helsinki.

Uusitalo, R. (1999). *Homo entreprenaurus?* Discussion Paper No. 205. Helsinki: VATT.

Vesper, K. H., & Gartner, W. B. (1999). *University entrepreneurship programs.* Lloyd Greif Center for Entrepreneurship Studies, University of Southern California.

Vygotsky, L. S. (1925, 1999). *Conciousness as a problem in the psychology of behavior.* Translation from Russian to English by Nikolai Veresov. http://www.marxists.org/archive/ vygotsky/works/1925/consciousness.htm (accessed 8.6.2001).

Wells, G. (1999). *The zone of proximal development and its implications for learning and teaching in dialogic inquiry: Towards a sociocultural practice and theory of education.* New York: Cambridge University Press (Chapter 10). http://oise.utoronto.ca/~gwells/resources/ ZPD.html (accessed 10.11.2002).

Whitaker, R. (1995). Overview of autopoetic theory. http://www.acm.org/sigois/auto/ ATReview.html (accessed 25.6.2002).

Wolf, B. (1986). Theoretical positions of Kurt Lewin and Egon Brunswik – controversial or complementary points of view. In: E. Stivers & S. Wheelan (Eds), *The Lewin legacy – field theory in current practice.* Heidelberg: Springer.